BORDERLANDS

BORDERLANDS

LIVING IN TWO WORLDS

The Story of Hispanics in the American Southwest

ANGEL VIGIL

IM Education *and* Fulcrum Publishing
Lakewood, Colorado

Library of Congress Cataloging-in-Publication Data
On file with the Library of Congress

Printed in the United States of America
0 9 8 7 6 5 4 3 2 1

IM Education and Fulcrum Publishing
7333 W. Jefferson Ave., Suite 225
Lakewood, CO 80235
(800) 992-2908 • (303) 277-1623
www.fulcrumbooks.com

CONTENTS

Chapter 6: Great Reads

Chapter 7: Great Movies

Dedication

I dedicate this book to my five grandchildren.

Arlo, Remi, Zora, Gigi, and Gabo

I wish them a life filled with love and happiness
as they go forward into their future.

FOREWORD

by Federico Peña

As our nation approaches its 250th birthday and Colorado celebrates 150 years of statehood, we have a rare opportunity to look back and reflect on what—and who—has shaped our history. *Borderlands*, by Angel Vigil, invites us to rediscover a powerful and often overlooked part of history, the extraordinary contributions of the Hispanic community, stretching from Spain's earliest explorations of the Americas to Mexico's settlement of the northern frontier that became today's American Southwest.

This history could not be more relevant or timely. In this moment when harmful anti-Latino rhetoric dominates our national conversation, it is critical to remember the truth of how deeply Hispanic and Latino people have influenced and strengthened our country. *Borderlands* reminds us that our roots run wide and deep—woven into the very foundation of the United States.

Few people know that Spanish admirals Bernardo de Gálvez and Luis de Córdova y Córdova played a pivotal role in America's fight for independence by blocking the British Navy in the Gulf of Mexico in 1781, ensuring George Washington's victory at Yorktown. Or that Spanish families contributed the equivalent of nearly $50 million to fund Washington's troops and supplies. These acts of courage, generosity, and support by the Spanish military and Spanish families for the American Revolution are early examples of the centuries-long contributions Hispanos have made to America.

Borderlands also reveals how incomplete our national history has often been. While textbooks tend to focus on the thirteen colonies, they rarely acknowledge that Spanish explorers and settlers had already established vibrant communities across what is now the American South and Southwest. St. Augustine, Florida—founded in 1565—predates Jamestown by more than forty years. Santa Fe, New Mexico, was established in 1598, long before the Pilgrims arrived in Massachusetts. These facts demonstrate how Hispanics were an integral part of building this nation.

Vigil's work takes readers through centuries of exploration, faith, and perseverance. From the Spanish missionaries who built the Camino Real linking twenty-one missions from San Diego to San Francisco, to the families who made their lives in what was once northern Mexico, this story captures both the spirit and the struggle of a people whose history is essential in defining the American landscape.

When the United States took over 50 percent of Mexico's lands following the Mexican-American War of 1846–1848, generations of Mexican families faced a choice: remain or leave, stay Mexican or become American. My own ancestors, who founded Laredo in 1755, chose to become American by paying a fee. As Vigil quotes, many felt, "I didn't cross the border—the border crossed me." Their courage and resilience shaped what would become one of the fastest-growing and most influential communities in our nation.

Through vivid storytelling, *Borderlands* traces the evolution of Mexican American life—from the Mexican Revolution through the Bracero labor program to the rise of the United Farm Workers and the Chicano Movement. It celebrates our deep traditions in art, music, food, and language and the unbreakable value placed on family. It honors the patriotism of Latinos who have served our nation in every war and contributed leadership across every field. Vigil showcases the lives of Hispanic leaders in Colorado who, through perseverance and hardship, contribute to Colorado's success.

Ultimately, Borderlands is more than a history—it's a reminder of who we are. It invites every reader to see the Hispanic community not as a separate thread but as an integral part of the American fabric. By understanding this shared past, we can better appreciate the promise of our shared future.

As we celebrate these milestone anniversaries, *Borderlands* offers a powerful perspective: that the story of America is, and always has been, a story of many peoples, united by courage, faith, and hope. Latinos in particular have and will continue to prosper and propel our nation in increasingly dramatic ways toward our next anniversaries.

Federico Peña is a former mayor of Denver, Colorado, and served in the Clinton Administration as Secretary of Transportation and Secretary of Energy. He is the first and only Latino to serve in two presidential cabinet positions. His own memoir is titled *...Not Bad for a South Texas Boy*.

ACKNOWLEDGMENTS

This book is a testament to the faith many people have put into this project. I am deeply thankful for their support throughout the process. Writing a book is a very humbling experience. So many things have to line up perfectly, and it is an impossibility without the help of many good people.

I must begin with the whole team at Fulcrum Publishing: Bob Baron, Charlotte Baron, Ed Nichols, Patty Maher, Nancy Enriquez, and Kateri Kramer. They have been with the book literally from the very beginning. From the early formative, idea-generating meetings to the extremely helpful feedback they provided during the writing process, they have been supportive and encouraging. They shared my enthusiasm for the ideas in the book. I also wish to thank editor Betty Christiansen for her careful and detailed review of the manuscript. An excellent editor makes a book better, and this book is better because of her work. I am so fortunate that Fulcrum Publishing is the publishing company that took on this book. I am thankful for their commitment to publishing books about Hispanic culture. I am proud to be one of their authors.

This book is the result of the generous contributions of many people. Longtime colleagues Carol Kimball, Alfredo Cárdenas, Daniel Salazar, Judy Miranda, and Emanuel Martinez all shared their artistry to make the book better. Charlene Garcia Simms shared many hours discussing the themes of the book, and her insights helped me shape the narrative. Judy Miranda helped me solve a couple of roadblock moments, and I appreciated so much her immediate positivity and helpful ideas.

I give a special heartfelt acknowledgment to the Hispanic leaders who graciously agreed to share their life stories for the book. I appreciated their personal support and belief in this project. I respect each of them greatly and am honored they gave of their time, knowledge, and friendship. Their stories are the heart of the book, and they give truth to the story of the book. Words cannot express the depth of my thankfulness to Juana Bordas, Ramon Del Castillo, Renee Fajardo, Nita Gonzales, Tony Ortega, Yolanda Ortega, and Lorenzo Trujillo. In addition to their personal stories, they have shared their own great knowledge of Hispanic culture, history, and tradition.

CHAPTER 1

THE AMERICAN DREAM

The Twin Anniversaries: America's 250th and Colorado's 150th

Sesquisemiquincentennial! Wow, what a word to start a book with.

In 2026, when the United States celebrates its 250th anniversary, the semiquincentennial, Colorado marks its 150th anniversary of statehood, the sesquicentennial. The History Colorado Center, the state's premier history museum, has named the historic combined commemorations the Sesquisemiquincentennial.

Figure 1—America's 250th anniversary logo

Figure 2—Colorado's 150th anniversary logo

These two events, twin anniversaries, coincide because Colorado, nicknamed the Centennial State, gained statehood a century after America became a country. Colorado gained entrance to the Union in 1876, exactly one hundred years after America declared its independence in 1776, becoming the thirty-eighth state to enter the Union.

Life is filled with many significant events, and there are just as many ways to celebrate these significant markers of the passages of time. One of the best is birthdays. There are several agreed-upon key years: five and entering kindergarten and beginning your formal years of education; sixteen and getting your driver's license; eighteen and becoming recognized as an adult; twenty-one and all the privileges that accompany that milestone; thirty and the beginning of the "Yikes! I'm getting older" years; fifty, a true milestone; and finally sixty-five, the beginning of the final stages.

It is in this grand tradition of celebrating significant birthdays that America and Colorado share these impressive numbers: 250 and 150. The year 2026 will be a yearlong celebration of the magnificent histories of both America and one of its fifty states, Colorado. No other state will have the honor of sharing this celebration with America.

Birthdays, especially significant ones, offer a time to pause and reflect upon life's journey. They offer the opportunity to examine the past that has been traveled, to embrace and understand the present we live in, and to prepare for the future we will build together. The shared celebrations of America and Colorado give us a unique opportunity and challenge to examine our shared history and to develop the vision of our shared destiny.

This book will have a tight focus as it examines America's and Colorado's histories over the past 250 and 150 years in relation to the Hispanic lives that have flourished in that time period. With an even tighter focus, it will tell the story of Hispanics in the American Southwest.

Colorado is the chosen state for this discussion for two reasons. One is because it shares the birthday with America. As mentioned previously, it is the only state to share this significant event with America, and that has its own merit. The other is because, as one of the original territories ceded to America in the Treaty of Guadalupe Hidalgo in 1848, after the Mexican-American War, it has the honor of being one of the founding states of the American Southwest. Colorado is a member of the Class of 1848.

These states, the Class of 1848—California, Nevada, Utah, Arizona, New Mexico, Texas, and parts of Colorado, Oklahoma, Wyoming, and Kansas—completed America's dream of Manifest Destiny, a country from sea to shining sea. They possess a designation of historic importance equal to the original thirteen founding colonies. The Eastern

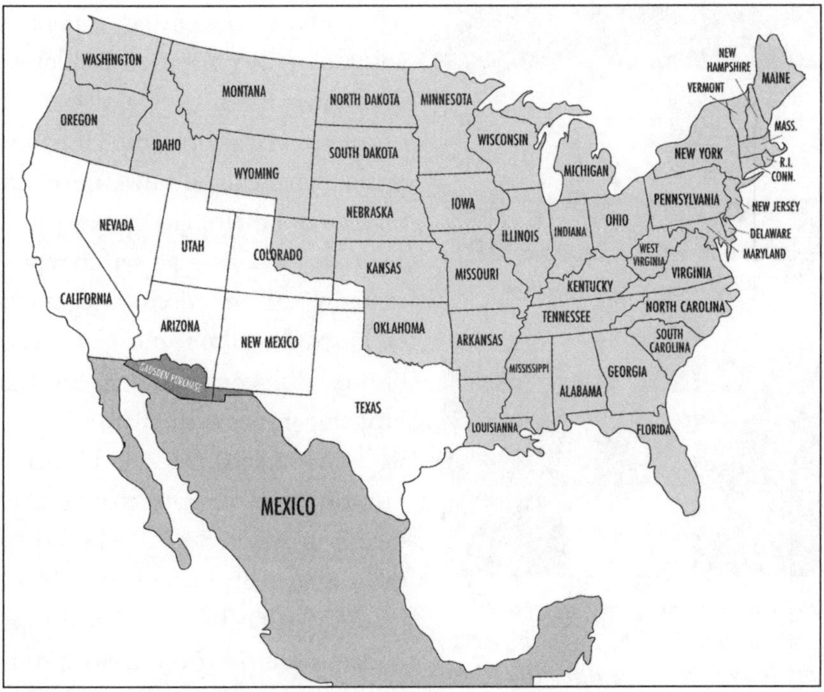

Figure 3—The Class of 1848. Southwestern states formed from the Mexican Cession and the Gadsden Purchase.

colonies began the United States; the Southwest territories fulfilled the impulses of Manifest Destiny.

Adding to Colorado's historical significance is the fact that it was the only state admitted to the Union between Nebraska statehood, 1867, and the Dakotas, Montana, and Washington, all in 1889. This twenty-two year gap in statehood admittance allowed Colorado to become firmly established in the roster of states. It had its stunning vistas and towering mountains as the foundation of its natural beauty. It also had a Native population that had been in Colorado for thousands of years. Early Spanish explorers established the Hispanic presence in Colorado in the sixteenth century.

History is the only guide in telling the story of America and Colorado and its Hispanic people. The history of America and Colorado has been recounted innumerable times by academic historians and popular writers alike. The year 2026 will see a plethora of books and

Firgure 4—Spanish flag

Figure 5—Mexican flag, with a central image depicting the Aztec myth that they should build their capital city, Tenochtitlan, upon a lake with an island in the middle of the lake, with a cactus on the island, with an eagle on the cactus, with a snake in the eagle's mouth.

Figure 6—Thirty-star United States flag of 1848 at the time of the Mexican-American War.

news events presenting America's and Colorado's histories. By closely examining the history and lives of one particular people, the Hispanos of the American Southwest, we can understand their place in history.

Colorado is a powerful representative of the deep integration of Hispanic culture into American history. By concentrating on the Hispanic history of this one state, we can understand the Hispanic histories of all the states that became members of America in 1848. While each state that entered the Union in 1848 at the Treaty of Guadalupe Hidalgo has its own history, this emphasis on Colorado's Hispanic history will provide an illuminating example of what happened in all the states in the Class of 1848.

The Hispanos in the states of the Class of 1848 have lived under three national flags: the Spanish flag, the Mexican flag, and the American flag. The most interesting aspect of their tri-nation experience is that they never moved. A common refrain that is repeated in the telling of their history is that they didn't cross the border; the border crossed them. A variation of this refrain is that they didn't leave their country; their country left them.

An interesting side note to begin this discussion is that Colorado's very name is a Spanish word. *Colorado* is not an English word. It has two meanings in the Spanish language: the color "red" and also "colorful." When the Spanish explorers entered Colorado in search of the three Gs—God, glory, and gold—they encountered the natural beauty of the state—its red landscape, its red sunsets, its red mountains—and they named the place "the red land"—*Colorado* in their language. From Garden of the Gods to Red Rocks Park to Mesa Verde, the stunning red rocks are ever-present. *Colorado* eventually became the name of the state, cementing its connection to Hispanic heritage.

The deep influence of Hispanic culture is omnipresent throughout Colorado. Much of Colorado's Spanish heritage and history resides in its place names. In addition to the early Spanish explorers giving the state its name, numerous mountains, mountain passes, cities, and rivers are christened with Spanish names. Five of the state's fabled 14,000-foot mountains have Spanish names. Five mountain passes have Spanish names. Seven major rivers have Spanish names. One-third of the counties—nineteen out of sixty-three—have Spanish names. Seventy-seven cities and towns have Spanish names. The Spanish names embedded throughout the state represent the vibrant Hispanic cultural richness of the early Spanish explorers and settlers.

Much of Colorado's 150-year history is directly linked to its Hispanic heritage. Colorado's history is an example of the deep penetration and establishment of Spanish culture in the American Southwest, repeated throughout the other states of the Class of 1848.

Other states in this class that have Spanish-derived names are California, Nevada, and New Mexico. The name *California* first appeared in a Spanish-language book written by Garcia Ordóñez de Montalvo around the year 1510. *Nevada* is from the Spanish word meaning "snow-clad," "snowy land," or "snowy"—descriptive of the snow-clad mountains of the area. *New Mexico* is the English translation of *Nuevo Mexico*, the name the Spanish gave to its northern province. By 1561, Spanish explorers had named this region north of the Rio Grande River *Nuevo Mexico*.

El Norte, the southwestern United States, has for centuries been a crossroads of histories, trade routes, languages, communities, families, and cultural traditions. In the American Southwest, these intersecting narratives have created a modern world of a tightly woven tapestry of

Historical Coda #1

In music, the coda is a concluding section that revisits themes previously presented in a musical piece. It can also elaborate on musical themes or motifs in the composition. The coda can either rework the musical theme or create variations. The coda is essentially an additional reflection on the musical themes of the composition.

In this book, I am going to adapt this idea of the musical coda to include occasional historical "codas" to the themes of this book. These historical codas will elaborate on the themes discussed and further expand on the issues with personal memories and reflections. These historical codas are my own personal memories of the history I am writing about.

History is more than the listing of dates, names, places, and events. At its best and most interesting, history is the story of people's lives. At its core, history is deeply personal. The truest understanding of history is the story of how people live it. All the facts of history only make sense within the context of individual lives.

American writer, poet, and philosopher Ralph Waldo Emerson expressed this idea in his famous words that "there is properly no history, only biography." The idea that history is biography is a path to understand how history is best understood through the lives of people living in their own times.

The story of Hispanos in the American Southwest is a personal story, for I have directly experienced many of the events presented in the book. Like others of my generation, I am a primary source reference to many moments of modern American history. Only now in my adult life am I aware that I have experienced events that are now recorded as history.

The poet Gary Snyder wrote a wonderful sentiment about the "present moment that lives on to be some long ago." It so succinctly expresses the idea that our lives, even though we are unaware of it in the present moment, eventually become the facts of history.

I will include personal historical codas occasionally throughout the book as examples that a personal story best illustrates how history presents itself in the life of a family and an individual. These historical codas are also my own answers to the interview questions asked in chapter 5, Giving Witness: Latino/a Voices Speak Their Truth. My own answers will form an eighth interview to accompany the other seven in chapter 5.

This first historical coda involves memories of Fourth of July celebrations. It tells my family story about the patriotic symbolism of the American flag, one of the three flags my family has lived under.

As America celebrates its 250th birthday on July 4, 2026, national celebrations will explode like fireworks throughout the country. The waving and flying of the American flag will be omnipresent as a sign of patriotism, a gesture of celebration of America's 250-year history.

America has its own legendary origin story about the creation of the American flag. The legend tells that George Washington commissioned Betsy Ross to create the iconic stars and stripes design. While historians have found no conclusive evidence as to the truth of the legend, the story of Betsy Ross creating the first flag is a mythic American story. Betsy Ross was a real historical character who did participate in the American Revolution, and she has become an enduring symbol of patriotism and the birth of the nation. There is no story of the origin of the American flag without the story of Betsy Ross.

My father, a World War II vet who fought in the Pacific Theater in the Solomon Islands and Luzon, would proudly fly the flag from our front porch every Fourth of July. It was a ritual for him. It involved getting the flag out, carefully posting it on the porch, and saluting it as a personal gesture of his enduring patriotism. As a child, I never really understood the importance of it for him, but as an adult, I now understand how meaningful his service in World War II was for him. My own father was a member of the Greatest Generation, and his simple, personal, and quiet flag ceremony allowed me to witness a man who had lived history, who had fought for this country. After he died, my brother continued this family tradition.

On July 4, 2026, as America celebrates its 250th, I will wave a personal flag because I know my long-dead father would appreciate that I continued his patriotic tradition of celebrating America.

the lives of Spanish, Mexican, and Indigenous people. Their shared history has given them a rich heritage. This is their story.

It is the story of the enduring presence of Hispanic culture in the American Southwest. It is the story of the lives of generations of Hispanos who have contributed to the grand mosaic of American history.

An Alternative Narrative: Not East to West, but South to North

In the story of America, the dominant narrative is one of America's western expansion and exploration. This narrative is complete with its dramatic tales and mythos-building characters. The tales include the landing of the Pilgrims at Plymouth Rock, the forging of the western frontiers, the building of the transcontinental railroad, the Gold Rush in the West, the Oregon Trail, and the Lewis and Clark expeditions. There are many other examples, but they are all summed up in the phrase often credited to newspaper editor Horace Greeley, attributed to Greeley in the *New York Daily Tribune*, July 13, 1865, concerning America's expansion westward: "Go West, young man, go West and grow up with the country."

Driving this narrative of western expansion is America's belief in its Manifest Destiny. The term *manifest destiny* first appeared in 1845 in an article by journalist John O'Sullivan in an essay praising the annexation of Texas. To advocates of western expansion, it was both inevitable and morally right. It was America's God-given destiny to spread its ideals and civilization.

The key historical events of western expansion were the Louisiana Purchase, the Oregon Treaty, and the Mexican-American War. Each of these events substantially increased American territory. America increased its size by purchasing its land, by negotiating treaties to resolve boundary disputes, or through deliberate imperialist wars of territorial expansion. In addition to its land expansion goals, Manifest Destiny was also an ideology justifying the forced removal of Native Americans from their ancestral lands.

Manifest Destiny also created continuing debates over historical issues of nationalism, expansionism, and the treatment of marginalized groups. As more western states were admitted to the Union, these events increased tensions over slave and non-slave state balances as America was heading toward its Civil War. Manifest Destiny accomplished its goal of creating a country from sea to shining sea, but historians still debate its consequences today.

While Manifest Destiny's east-to-west narrative offers one model for the story of America's development over its 250 years, another equally compelling and dramatic narrative is one of its south-to-north

Figure 7—American Progress, *1872, John Gast. This painting shows Manifest Destiny, the belief in westward expansion of the United States from the Atlantic to the Pacific Ocean. It was widely distributed as an engraving called "Spirit of the Frontier." Columbia, the female figure of America, called Progress, leads Americans, aided by technology like the railroads and the telegraph, from the enlightened East into the darkness of the West. Columbia, dressed in a Roman toga to represent classical republicanism, brings America into the future and Native peoples and bison, seen fleeing the settlers into the darkness, into obscurity.*

development, specifically the story of the American Southwest. The story of America is incomplete without an exploration of this history.

The dominant narrative of east-to-west expansion is a partial and half-told story of America's development. The story of America's south-to-north development is a powerful history that resulted in the American Southwest. It is the story of Spanish exploration, Spanish colonization and settlement, confrontations with the existing Native populations and cultures, Mexican immigration, and the development of the Hispanic presence in the American Southwest.

The American census data between 1970 and 2020 illustrates the expansive growth of the Hispanic population in the Class of 1848 borderland states and other western states. This significant increase in Hispanic population has many reasons, including employment in agriculture, construction, medical services, retail trade, and the service industry. Some of these families and individuals have been in the United States for generations; others are new arrivals. They almost all came north through Mexico and not from the east, from Cuba or Puerto Rico.

The census data reflects individuals who identified as Hispanic/Latino.

State	Hispanic/Latino 1970 population	Hispanic/Latino 2020 population
Arizona	17.3%	30.7%
California	13.7%	39.4%
Colorado	11.6%	21.9%
Idaho	2.6%	13.0%
Kansas	2.1%	13.0%
Nebraska	1.4%	12.0%
Nevada	5.6%	28.7%
New Mexico	37.4%	47.7%
Oklahoma	1.4%	11.9%
Oregon	1.7%	13.9%
Utah	4.1%	15.1%
Texas	17.7%	39.3%
Washington	2.1%	13.7%
Wyoming	5.6%	10.2%

This census data clearly demonstrates the fact that the Hispanic population in the American West and Southwest is dramatically increasing. Each of the states of the Class of 1848 has its own history of Hispanic settlement and development. The story of these border states and the Hispanic people living in them is a critical, essential, and fascinating part of the story of America as it enters its 250th year.

The Promise of America: An Immigrant Nation

As America celebrates its 250th anniversary, the founding words of the American experiment ring as strongly as they did 250 years ago.

The Declaration of Independence, adopted in 1776, declares that "We hold these truths to be self-evident, that all men are created equal, that they are endowed by their Creator with certain unalienable Rights, that among these are Life, Liberty and the pursuit of Happiness."

The opening statement in the preamble of the US Constitution has the phrase "in order to form a more perfect union." While the statement addressed the desires of the Constitution framers to create a stronger, more unified national government than under the Articles of Confederation, modern speakers have adapted the phrase to address the vision of America becoming a more perfect nation for all its peoples.

The famous quote written on the plaque on the Statue of Liberty in New York Harbor is from Emma Lazarus's poem "The New Colossus": "Give me your tired, your poor, / Your huddled masses yearning to breathe free, / The wretched refuse of your teeming shore. / Send these, the homeless, tempest-tost to me, / I lift my lamp beside the golden door!"

The "golden door" is the door of opportunity for all immigrants entering the United States. The poem's themes of freedom, hope, and opportunity gave a signal of welcome to these immigrants.

It is an undeniable truth that America is a nation of immigrants. Successive waves of immigrant populations have crossed oceans and borders to build their futures in America. These immigrant waves follow historical periods and world events that cause people to leave their home country to seek the promise of a better life in America.

Sixteenth and seventeenth centuries:

- Spanish settlement in the American Southwest. The beginnings of the Spanish colonial period.

Seventeenth and eighteenth centuries:

- The early eastern colonial period of immigration primarily from the British Isles, with some from other parts of Europe and Africa.

1840s–1880s:

- A large influx of immigrants, mostly from northern and western Europe, including significant numbers from Germany, Ireland, and the United Kingdom.

Late nineteenth and early twentieth centuries:

- Another wave of immigrants, primarily from southern and eastern Europe, including Italians, Austrians, and Russians.

Post–1965 wave:

- A shift in the origins of immigrants, with a significant increase in arrivals from Latin America and Asia.
- About half of US immigrants since 1965 have come from Latin America, with a quarter from Mexico alone.
- About another quarter have come from Asia, including large numbers from China, India, the Philippines, and other countries.

In spite of this fact of continued immigration to America over centuries, many people feel that because of it, America has yet to reach its more perfect union and its promise of freedom, hope, and opportunity for all its people. Instead of being recognized as a strength of America and its history, each successive wave of immigration has faced rejection. Only the passage of time has eventually seen the integration of diverse people and their cultures into mainstream American life.

The chorus of our times is the conflict over who is an American and what constitutes an American. As each wave of immigrants settles into their American lives, they become self-describing as Americans and rejecting of the following wave of immigrants.

At the heart of the discussion of immigration is the concept of belonging: who belongs in America and who gets to stay in America. While the present day is torn by these ideas, they have always been part of the American dilemma. Essential questions about American identity center around the concept of foreignness. Who is a foreigner? Why are they here? How did they get here? Are foreigners dangerous? How do we get rid of them? Do they contaminate the essence of being American? Who gets to be a citizen?

These are almost rhetorical questions without an answer. The struggle to answer them has always been a part of the conversation about who is an American. Our time now is especially fraught with these questions. The search for answers has again divided America.

Immigration to America has always been a contentious issue. America has experienced waves of hostility to groups entering America. As far back as 1891, Massachusetts Senator Henry Cabot Lodge expressed the concern that immigration "is bringing to the country people whom it is very difficult to assimilate and who do not promise well for the standard of civilization in the United States."

Examples of America's effort to define who is an American and to control immigration are easily described. The Naturalization Act of 1790 restricted naturalization to "free white persons." The Treaty of Guadalupe Hidalgo in 1848 granted citizenship to Mexicans living in the newly annexed territory if they chose citizenship. In 1868, the Fourteenth Amendment stated that anyone born in the United States was automatically a citizen.

The 1917 literacy test, the 1921 Emergency Quota Act, the 1924 National Origins Act, and the 1929 Immigration Act are all examples of America's efforts to legislate limits to immigration. The Chinese Exclusion Act of 1882, the first American law to restrict immigration based on nationality, specifically prohibiting immigration of Chinese laborers for ten years and denying them the right to become citizens, is another direct example of America's concerns over who will be a true American.

The irony is how quickly people forget their immigrant history and how quickly they do not grant that title of American to more recent immigrants. Unless you are a descendant of the Native nations, the first inhabitants of the Americas, you are an immigrant to this country. It could be said that the only true Americans are its first inhabitants.

The first original inhabitants of the Americas were the Native Americans. While it is actively debated in academic circles the time and era in which these original inhabitants first appeared in the Americas, the earliest widely accepted archaeological evidence of human presence in the Americas dates back around fifteen thousand years. The Denver History Colorado Center has on display evidence of Native inhabitants in Colorado from twelve thousand years ago.

It has now become almost *de riguer* for public events to open with a land acknowledgment that the event is happening on land originally inhabited by America's first inhabitants, usually mentioned by tribal name. While some view this practice as useless performative theater by colonizing people, it does give recognition that others were here first. The challenge to this land acknowledgment is to follow it up with action to support the acknowledged communities. It is deeds, not words, that speak the loudest.

Immigrant populations have a historical indebtedness to the First Nations and Indigenous populations. The stories of the conflicts between Native peoples and immigrant populations expanding westward under the flag of America's Manifest Destiny impulse is not the topic of this book. But the presence of Native populations will play a defining and critical part of the story of Spanish, Mexican, and Indigenous people as they create the story of Hispanos in the American Southwest historically and in today's modern world.

It is unavoidable to recognize that the present landscape of discussion over immigration issues has fractured America. Balancing the issues of national security, immigration police, economic policies, cultural assimilation, employment equality and possibilities, the threat of immigrants to national integrity and immigration enforcement policies all return to the original essential questions: Who is an American, and who gets to be an American?

The story of immigration to the United States has to include the many significant contributions immigrant populations have made in American life: in politics, education, arts, business, science, entrepreneurship, and cultural diversity. This history will include the stories of unsung Hispanic heroes who made significant contributions to American life only to be marginalized and written out of history. A concluding aspect of this discussion of immigrant populations will present several notable modern-day Hispanic leaders, who tell their own stories of being a proud Hispanic in America that began with their own family's immigrant origins.

As America celebrates is 250th anniversary, the story of the American experiment begun 250 years ago is still being written. America's promise will always be a beautiful goal each generation recreates, building upon the foundations laid by previous generations.

Historical Coda #2

The issues of belonging and being an American have always been central to my identity. My family has been here for centuries and generations. We go back eleven generations in New Mexico to 1693 and five generations in Colorado to 1917. We have lived under three flags: the Spanish flag, the Mexican flag, and the American flag.

In spite of our long history of living in America, even before there was an America, my family has experienced rejection and racism through its many generations. We have experienced the charge of being foreigners in a land we have lived in for centuries. We do not view ourselves as immigrants even though others consider us as immigrants and foreigners.

My father's generation, many of them World War II veterans, struggled with hidden racism in employment and housing. Two of my uncles anglicized their last name from Martinez to Martin. My mother was questioned by her parish priest as to why we lived in a predominantly Anglo suburb and not in the downtown area, where there were more of our own kind. Whenever I am in a group in which I am the only person of color, I feel a subtle pressure to be a "credit to my race."

These experiences are not unique to me or my family. They are shared by many who do not fit the images of the dominant culture. But we are here and we are not going away. Our history here is long. In fact, I am proud to be an American. My father fought in World War II so I could say those words.

Borderlands

The twin anniversaries of America's 250th and Colorado's 150th provide the opportunity to examine the intense history of the borderland experience that exists in the American Southwest for Hispanics. Of particular interest is the origins of this borderland and the complex identities that formed inside these borderlands. A common refrain that is repeated throughout borderland history is "I didn't cross the border; the border crossed me." This simple statement contains the history of a people.

The idea of borderlands and their significance has long existed in many cultures. The Aztecs had a concept of nepantla. *Napantla* is a Nahuatl (Aztec language) word describing the space between two boundaries, two lived experiences, two levels of awareness. It can be a physical, psychological, spiritual, or personal space. It can also represent "in-between-ness" or "in the middle."

Modern Latino and Chicano writers and artists influenced by Aztec mythology have utilized the concepts of nepantla to describe their own experiences of living in a borderland and being a borderland citizen. They have used the concept to express their ideas on questions of identity between different cultures.

Whether one calls it nepantla or borderlands, the experience is the same—what is it like to live between two different cultures?

Borderlands are traditionally identified as boundaries either political or natural. Political boundaries can identify nations, states, cities, provinces, or any other officially recognized land. Natural boundaries can be as simple as a river or as monumental as a mountain range.

Borderlands are not just geographic or political spaces; they can also be cultural, psychological, or emotional borders. A borderland can be as intimate an individual's "personal space" or as vast as the space where nations and cultures intersect.

These boundaries can serve as markers of individual, community, and national identities. They also can create divisions among people who once felt they had a common bond, only to see that bond separated. A prime example of this is the Upper Rio Grande Valley of southern Colorado and northern New Mexico. This area to this day shares a common Hispanic cultural reference of religion, language, and traditional customs. Extended Hispanic families have lived throughout the Upper Rio Grande Valley for generations.

The creation of a political borderland where one did not exist before resulted in profound changes for the Hispanic people of the Upper Rio Grande Valley. The creation of the New Mexico and Colorado state lines separated this area into two different governmental areas. New Mexico territory originally included the borderlands of southern Colorado, creating the Upper Rio Grande area. The US Congress, wanting to establish the Colorado territory before the Civil War, created the four borders of

Colorado territory. The southern border along the 37th parallel created a separation between New Mexico and Colorado.

What was once one area historically and culturally was now two areas separated by a created boundary, the state line. Now families lived on either one side of the line or the other. A common bond was broken. A borderland was created where one did not exist before. What was once simple was now complicated.

On a larger scale, the history of the borderland between America and Mexico encompassing the southwestern United States is a prime example of the complexities of a borderland between two nations. This borderland is a place where culture blends, assimilates, and co-influences. It is a place in constant transition as people move within the borderland, as well as in and out of it.

Living within a borderland creates a new awareness, a new identity: the borderland citizen. Blending Indigenous, Mexican, and American cultures, the borderland citizen crosses boundaries and creates a unique world. Their lives really do exist across both sides of the border. Their lives are a blend of cultures, traditions, and identities. They live in two worlds, and essentially they live in a land with no borders. Just as the mestizo is a blended mix of identities that create a new people, the border citizens are a new people living in a land *sin fronteras*, without borders.

This borderland between Mexico and America is an example of the complexities created in borderland lives. It has been the site of both war and conflict. It has been the site of unequal power dynamics and inequality. It has been the site of a people losing one identity and gaining another without any choice.

This borderland has been the site of competition for resources, territory, and ownership. It continues to this day to be the site of national conversation and conflict. A famous quote by nineteenth-century Mexican President Porfirio Diaz expressed the complexity of the borderland relationship between Mexico and the United States: "Poor Mexico. So far from God, so close to the United States."

People living in the borderlands of the American Southwest live in two worlds, influenced by both sides of the border. Their lives are places where different cultures, languages, and traditions meet, blend, and adapt. People living in borderlands juggle a complex set of emotions and history with attachments on both sides of the border. They develop unique identities combining their multicultural experiences formed by both sides of the border. They form cultural connections unique to their experiences. Their lives are a convergence of cultural and ethnic forces.

The fact of a political boundary evaporates in the fact of a people living in two worlds and embracing both sides of the borderland. The political boundary cannot stop the constant state of transition, flux, and influence across the borderlands. People's lives are complex, and they will always embrace their common culture, traditions, and history, even when separated by an artificial boundary.

The 250 years of American history and the 150 years of Colorado history in the Southwest is the history of a borderland experience. It is a fascinating history, and it is the story of a fascinating people, the Southwestern Hispanics successfully living in two worlds.

Whose Story Gets Told and Who Tells It

As America celebrates its 250th and enters a time of historical reflection, and before telling the story of Hispanos in the American Southwest, one must confront the truism that history is written by the victors. The challenge of this situation is that history is complicated. It is dense with conflicting narratives. To tell only one side of historic events, while shining a positive light on only one aspect of the events, is a great disservice to the truth of history. It also does not allow for the complete understanding of past events that led to greater outcomes in the future. Without learning, there is no growth.

Many great writers and leaders have reflected on history's role in the lives of countries and individuals. Martin Luther King Jr. famously said, "We are not makers of history. We are made by history." The American writer William Faulkner in his novel *Requiem for a Nun* stated, "The past is never dead. It is not even past." The writer-philosopher George Santayana wrote, "Those who cannot remember the past are condemned to repeat it."

These powerful reflections on the role of history in people's lives reveal the truth that our lives are shaped by the events of the past. History is not a simple listing of names, dates, and events to be studied for the test and then forgotten. It is the foundation of our current lives and experiences.

For this reason, it is imperative to search for the truths of history. Too often, since history is written by the victors, the stories of history are one-sided to reflect a projected heroism, a desired nobility, and an admirable moral certitude. These stories always devalue, ignore, and erase the complete narrative of all others involved in the historical events remembered and shared. The tragic fault in this self-serving telling of history is that it reduces and limits the possibility for greater learning from the events of history. To hear only one side of the story is to learn only half of the story. It is necessary to know the complete truths of history in order to understand the events of today and how they were shaped by and connected to the events of the past.

One of the wonderful developments in recent museum practices is the recognition that there are many American stories that have never been heard. The challenge, of course, is to ask whose story gets told and who gets to tell it. The long tradition of historical narrative in museums and history books has been that museum and academic scholars tell the stories of peoples with little input from those whose stories they are actually presenting.

For example, in the telling of the histories of Indigenous and Hispanic people, the original inhabitants of the American Southwest, the authentic voices of Indigenous and Hispanic people are often relegated to the realm of myth and legend, not to the truths of scholarship and academic facts. Only recently have museums made efforts to include these long-ignored voices in their exhibits. Recent authors of history books have also begun to expand their research to include the best primary sources of Indigenous and Hispanic lives: the voices of actual living Indigenous and Hispanic people.

An important example of this new approach to telling the stories is the collaboration between the Cheyenne and Arapaho nations in the Sand Creek Massacre exhibit at the Denver History Colorado Center. For decades the massacre, as written by the self-described "victors," had reported the events as a battle. Only much later did the truth of the events of the day, November 29, 1864, become recognized and rightly described as a massacre.

A recent installation of the exhibit, developed with close collaboration of the Cheyenne and Arapaho nations over several years, has all the exhibit signs in the first-person voice. The text of the signs reads I, We, and Us. It is the Cheyenne and Arapaho people telling their own story. It is a significant change in the telling of historical narratives.

It most importantly answers the question of whose story gets told and who gets to tell it. The Sand Creek Massacre is the story of the Cheyenne and Arapaho people, and they should be the ones telling their own story.

It takes a long time for history to find its true voice. As Martin Luther King Jr. said, "The arc of the moral universe is long, but it bends toward justice." Change takes a long time, but it does happen.

As an acknowledgment of asking the question of whose story gets told and who gets to tell it is chapter 5 of this book: Giving Witness: Latino/a Voices Speak Their Truth. This chapter includes voices of Colorado Hispanic leaders who have made significant contributions to American culture. They represent a range of lives lived: politicians, academics, educators, artists, and community activists. They are authentic voices of Hispanic people as they share their personal story of being Hispanic in America.

America's 250th anniversary, and Colorado's 150th anniversary as a representative of the borderland states of the Class of 1848, have provided a moment in time to reflect on the journey of Hispanos in the American Southwest. The essential questions are simple:

- Who are the Hispanos of the American Southwest?
- What were the historical events that shaped them?
- Who are they now?

The answer of whose story it is and who gets to tell it is a direct one. This is the story of Hispanos in America over four hundred years, and Hispanos themselves get to tell it.

CHAPTER 2

NAMING CULTURE

What Do We Call Ourselves?

Why Are the Words Hispanic, Chicano/a/x, and Latino/a/x Used in This Book?

It is very important to pay attention to the language used in describing a people and their culture, especially in our era of cultural and political sensitivity. There is often confusion about what to call the descendants of the Spanish colonists, especially those living in the American Southwest. Also, there are diverse opinions regarding the correct word to use: *Spanish*, *Hispanic*, *Mexican American*, *Chicano/a/x*, or *Latino/a/x/e*. Each term has its advocates and detractors. Each term has its historical origins, and each term has its proper application. Each term is a recognition of a person's desire to self-identify, to reject assigned labels, and to fight cultural erasure.

Of course, the real answer is to call people what they want to be called. Even within the Hispanic community, there is great divergence of opinion as to what is the correct term. Hispanic culture consists of many individuals, and one of its great beauties and strengths is its own diversity. The most important aspect of naming culture is to give individuals and groups the power of self-identification.

Historical Coda #3

My own life story illustrates the fluid and changing nature of language as it relates to naming culture. First, I was Spanish because my father and mother both had immense pride in their Spanish heritage. My father's Vigil line originated in Asturias, Spain, and my mother's Martinez line also has ancestral roots in Spain. Even though my family shares many aspects of Mexican culture—a language, a religion, a cuisine, and a belief in the importance of family above all—we are not Mexican because we were not born in Mexico and all our lineage roots are in America, specifically in northern New Mexico and Colorado. In truth, in spite of not being Mexican, I have often been called Mexican by folks who take a single glance at my brown skin, hear my name, hear my accent, and just assume, "There is another Mexican."

In a series of changes through the decades as language fashion changed, I became Spanish American, Mexican American, Hispanic, Chicano, Latino, and now occasionally Latinx and Latine, according to the audience I am addressing. I laugh about it now, but as a child in the Texas panhandle, I even heard the words *spic* and *beaner*. Once I was even called *pocho*, the Mexican slang term with various meanings but essentially a person with limited fluency in Spanish who is not really a Mexican. In the end, no matter what I am called, I have always been Angel Vigil, a person with great pride in my Hispanic heritage.

In truth, there is no one correct term. Sensitivity, awareness, and knowledge are the only true guides. Sensitivity reminds us that people value ethnic terms that accurately reflect their ancestry and personal values. Awareness teaches us that ethnic identification is affected by history and its fluid events. Knowledge gives us the understanding of why one term is preferable over another. So, let's wade into these turbulent waters of nomenclature and learn why all these terms are so important.

I will use the terms *Hispanic* and *Hispanos* predominantly, with *Latino/a/x* and *Chicano/a/x* used when it is appropriate and because they are also prevalent terms used in the common culture.

The word *Hispano* denotes people and communities who trace their heritage and cultural roots to the Spanish colonists from the earliest days of Spain's control of the southwestern part of the United

States. The following review of these terms is not only important for definition's sake and cultural understanding, but it also represents what I call language fashion. Just as clothing fashion can represent a historical era, language fashion changes as history, politics, and culture change. Each term originated in a specific historical era, and each represents the lives of the people of that era. These terms represent and reflect the changing nature of history.

Hispanic

Authors writing for the general public use this term most commonly. The word *Latino* is the only word that rivals it for common usage. It has been used by generations of scholars studying Spanish language and culture in the Americas. Advocates of the word support its use because it represents the concept of a cultural heritage, lineage, and language with its origins in Spain. As an adjective, it describes the numerous ethnic groups, especially in the American Southwest, that have Spanish surnames, heritage, and culture in common. For these reasons, I have chosen to use this word in this book.

Detractors of this term find offense with it for several reasons. One is that it does not allow for recognizing the importance of Indigenous cultures as influencing culture either in Mexico or the American Southwest. Another is that they view it as a governmentally mandated generic term that did not originate from within the culture itself.

This last contention is derived from the belief that the term *Hispanic* came into general usage because of its identification as an ethnic category in the 1980 US Census. The September 1996 issue of *Hispanic* magazine has an interesting article that describes and explains the events and reasoning that led to the selection of the word *Hispanic* as an ethnic designation category in the census. The article explains why, even with an awareness of the controversy over the term *Hispanic*, many people continue to support its use. Part of the reason is that it is the easiest term to use. The term has become generic in its description of the descendants of the earliest Spanish colonists.

Hispano

The term *Hispano* is the Spanish adjective for *Hispanic* or *Spanish*. This word is often used by Spanish-language speakers when referring to Spanish ancestry. It is also used as an indicator of cultural pride in Spanish ancestry.

Mexican

This term describes Mexican citizens who were born in Mexico. It is also used to describe Mexican citizens who work, live, or visit in the United States. *Mexican Nationals* is another term that describes Mexican citizens in the United States.

Historically, many American citizens of the Southwest can claim Mexican ancestry because the Southwest was part of Mexico from 1821 to 1848. A deeply held belief concerning the position of US citizens with Mexican ancestry, due to the Treaty of Guadalupe Hidalgo in 1848 that is discussed in greater detail in chapter 3 of this book, is that "I didn't cross the border. The border crossed me."

Recent political developments concerning immigration issues have made the term extremely negative for certain aspects of American discourse. The issue of birthright citizenship, border policies, immigration, and deportation demands have negatively charged the term in daily conversation.

Legendary golf pro Lee Trevino had a cutting but revealing remark when he said, as he became more successful on the professional golf circuit, "You're Mexican until you make money, and then you're Spanish."

Mexican American

This term describes US citizens who are of Mexican ancestry, descendants of Mexican parents, or naturalized citizens with origins in Mexico. This term is acceptable to many Mexican descendants. This term parallels the use of the terms *African American*, *Chinese American*, and *Japanese American* in American culture. As language fashion changed, it became more acceptable to attach the term *American* to several ethnic groups to recognize their historical ethnicity while diffusing their cultural heritage by reassuring everyone that they were also American. Certain groups see this description as a cultural sellout. It is assumed that people born in the United States are American citizens, American by birthright no matter their cultural heritage, and no further descriptor is necessary.

Spanish

This term describes a population who identifies primarily with the original Spanish settlers of the American Southwest. The strongest concentration of these people lives along the Upper Rio Grande Valley of New Mexico and Colorado. While they admit to a shared culture and language with Mexico, they view themselves as descendants of the original Spanish colonists and not as Mexican. In their daily language, they refer to themselves as Spanish or Hispano. Do not make the mistake of calling a Spanish-identified person a Mexican. They will always correct you.

Chicano/a/x

This term is a relatively recent word describing people of Mexican origin or descent living in the United States. There are several theories about the origin of this word. A widely believed source for the word stems from the pronunciation of the word *Mexican* by field laborers from Mexico working in the United States in the 1930s and '40s. Native Nahuatl speakers from the Mexican state of Morelos called themselves "Mesheecanos."

The pronunciation is derived from the Nahuatl language pronunciation of the "x" in *Mexico* as a "sh" sound. Nahuatl, like English, has a "sh" sound Spanish does not have. Early Spanish chroniclers used an "x" to render the sound in Spanish, as in *Mexico*.

Xicano is a Nahuatl word meaning "children of the earth." Eventually, this pronunciation evolved into *Chicano* and entered the general language. Since its origins were with poor laborers, its early use was often derogatory. It was often used as a racist and classist term against low-income Mexicans.

Activists in the 1960s who took part in the Brown Power movement in the US Southwest reclaimed the word *Chicano* to describe themselves. They believed that the use of the word *Chicano* was a statement of cultural pride, ethnic solidarity, and political empowerment.

Historical Coda #4

This historical coda is a personal reflection on naming culture, in that my own father and I were caught in a classic conflict between the older and younger generations. My father was a World War II veteran. His family proudly sent three sons to support the war efforts. My father served in the Pacific Theater, the Solomon Islands, and Luzon, eventually rising to the rank of Second Lieutenant. He was a proud American veteran who displayed the American flag every Fourth of July.

To his great dismay, his son—myself—began to call himself a Chicano during the power days of the Chicano Movement. He considered the term *Chicano* to be derogatory, along with the term *Pachuco* from the zoot suit era. It was a classic father-and-son generational disagreement as old as time. We never did come to a shared understanding, as he died before I was mature enough to understand his life history and why he believed what he did. He had experienced severe racism as a young person, which continued into his adulthood, but he saw himself as true and patriotic American who had served his country honorably in a World War. He was not a Chicano.

The word came into widespread usage to represent a positive cultural and political perspective about being of Mexican heritage, along with Indigenous and Spanish descent in the United States. Proponents of its use adopted it because its use included their Indigenous heritage, which had been unrecognized in other identifying terms.

Activists embraced the term because it identified them as a new mestizo people of mixed heritage living in two worlds and not being accepted in either one. On one hand, Mexicans did not accept them because they were born in America and were actually American citizens. On the other hand, they experienced the rejection of mainstream America because of their Mexican heritage.

The word *Chicano* has its strong advocates and detractors. Its advocates speak of its use as an important point of cultural pride and awareness and its recognition of Indigenous culture, especially Mexican Aztec culture. Its detractors are uncomfortable with its militant overtones and its former derogatory implications.

As political and personal awareness evolved, an additional version has recently been added to the traditional Chicano/a versions. The Spanish language is binary in its descriptions of male and female terms, as represented by the use of the "-o" word ending to represent masculine and the "-a" word ending to represent feminine word gender. Owing to awareness of the exclusionary limitations of binary naming, the term *Chicanx* developed as a nonbinary, gender-neutral version of Chicano/a.

Latino/a/x/e

This term refers to people having a heritage related to Latin American cultures. *Latino* is the Spanish word for *Latin*. The term *Latin* describes the origins of the romance languages, one of which is Spanish, the language spoken throughout most of Mexico, Central America, and South America. *Latino* has recently become widely accepted and is the preferred term for many people in place of either *Hispanic* or *Chicano*. Its advocates prefer it because it is a self-chosen term, it includes a larger cultural base than *Hispanic*, and it does not have the militant and derogatory associations of *Chicano*.

The term *Latino* has recently rivaled *Hispanic* in general usage. Many people who previously identified as Hispanic and even Chicano now call themselves Latino or Latina. The simplest reason is that as times change, so do people.

As previously discussed in the section on the term *Chicanx*, a similar development occurred with the term *Latino/a*. Evolving personal identification also required a gender-neutral term for *Latino/a*. The term *Latinx* became the preferred term for those seeking gender-neutral language.

The most recent term is *Latine*. It is another gender-neutral term used to describe people who prefer a gender-neutral, nonbinary identification. It developed because people believed it is more natural to pronounce in Spanish than *Latinx*.

Genízaro

A most interesting recent development in the naming of people of Spanish heritage is the term *Genízaro*. Genealogical and scholarship research has created a field of study into the history and facts of Genízaro ancestry.

The term reflects a particularly negative time in the relationships between Spanish colonists and native Indigenous populations. As research discovers overlooked aspects of the relationships between people in the Spanish/Mexican frontier, the revelations of history can be damning.

This recently acknowledged category of descendants of the Spanish colonists are the Genízaros. It was common practice during the Spanish colonial era for native Indigenous people to be attached to Spanish families. The term *attached* disguises the reality of the situation. The Indigenous people were sold to Spanish families as indentured servants, even though *slaves* is a more accurate term. The Indigenous people were captured in Indian wars or in raiding expeditions and then were sold to Spanish colonists.

The Wikipedia entry for Genízaros states the following:

> *Genízaros* was the name for detribalized Indigenous people from the 17th to 19th century in the Spanish colony of New Mexico and neighboring regions of the American Southwest. Genízaros were usually women and children who had been captured in war by the Spanish or purchased from Indian tribes who had held them captive as slaves.
>
> To circumvent Spanish laws forbidding slavery, the purchaser (or rescuer) of a genízaro had the obligation to introduce them to Christianity and Spanish customs. Genízaros worked as indentured servants, shepherds, and laborers. They occupied the lowest rung of status-conscious Spanish society in New Mexico but slowly assimilated and intermarried into Spanish and later Mexican (1821–1846) and American (1846–present day) society. The descendants of genízaros are also called genízaros and the word has become a term of pride for the descendants of the original Indian captives and slaves.

Historical Coda #5

In a DNA test, I discovered that I am 27 percent Native ancestry. This was news to my mother, who always prided herself as being of 100 percent Spanish heritage. She was so clear that she and her family were not Mexican or Indian. I must say that she took the news of her DNA Native ancestry very well. Some of my cousins came up with similar results and also had to break the news to their mothers. Instead of offering the expected denials, the older generation just sort of shrugged it off with a "What next?" attitude that must accompany the acceptance of life's vicissitudes as one ages.

My own family has a direct link to this Genízaro experience. A cousin of mine, Annette Vigil, is a dedicated genealogy researcher and has done deep family research into our genealogical lines. Her research discovered a fourth-great-grandmother, Maria de la Luz Rolen, who was an Ute Indian sold to a Spanish family.

The genealogy primary source documents record several Anglicized versions of her name. On June 26, 1842, she, along with two other Ute children, were baptized in Taos, New Mexico, into the family of Taos merchant John Roland and given the name Maria de la Luz. This distant grandmother, Maria de la Luz Rolens, lived a life that is a dramatic tale. Sold to a Hispanic family and later traded to a member of the Vigil family, she eventually married Antonio Basilio Vigil. They had ten children, and in that way, Ute ancestry—through slavery, marriage, and descendant children—was introduced into the Vigil family line.

I tell her story as an example of how difficult it is to weave together an accurate genealogical story going back multiple generations. A recent genealogical discovery has revealed that Maria de la Luz might not have been an Ute Native but rather a Pawnee. Sometimes the genealogical path comes to a dead end; sometimes it comes to a crossroads; sometimes the path leads to more uncertainty. As any genealogist will say, however: "Do the work. Keep on the hunt." Robert Caro, author of a magnificent three-volume biography of President Lyndon Johnson, offered a wonderful piece of advice for genealogical and historical researchers when confronted with a mountain of daunting paperwork: "Turn every page."

Manito

Manito is another term describing the descendants of the Spanish colonials of the Upper Rio Grande Valley, southern Colorado, and northern New Mexico. For those with a family legacy of these borderlands, it is a term of endearment and cultural pride formed from the contraction of *Hermanito/a*, little brother and little sister.

CHAPTER 3

HISTORY'S JOURNEY

We Have Been Here a Long Time—How Did We Get to Now?

No lo que fuiste, sino lo que eres.
Not what you were, but what you are.
We are our own history.

Querencia is a beautiful, poetic idea. It is the beloved homeland. It is a place where one feels safe, where one feels at home, where one draws strength of character. In the bullring, it is the place where the bull makes its final stand.

For Hispanos in the American Southwest, the land itself is their querencia. While the love of family is of primary importance to Hispanic culture, the Southwestern landscape is the homeland where the heart and soul of the people reside. The title of this book could easily have been *Stories from the Homeland.*

For Southwestern Hispanos, the land is where they create their lives, the place where they make their history, the place where they tell their story. The voices of their ancestors who have long lived on these lands speak to them over time. The sense of place is important in the telling of history.

This concept of land and its resonance with the heartfelt attachment to a place called home will be a continuing theme in this chapter. Together with the concept of family, it will be one of the two primary characteristics of Hispanic history and culture in the American Southwest.

For more than four hundred years, Hispanic culture has existed in the area now recognized as the American Southwest. Through centuries of exploration, conquest, settlement, war, perseverance, and resilience, Hispanic people have maintained their presence and culture in the American Southwest. Transported from Spain, evolved in Mexico, and adapted in America, Hispanic culture is a centuries-old experience continuing to animate the lives of Hispanic people throughout the Southwest. The truth is that we were here before America was here.

An important opportunity provided by the celebration of America's 250th and Colorado's 150th twin anniversaries is the challenge they present to examine and reflect upon the historical paths the Hispanos of the American Southwest have traveled in these years. While dates, names, places, and events dominate the study of history, it is also important to recognize patterns over time. It is a truism that one who does not study history is destined to repeat it. Patterns over time reveal the interconnected nature of events.

The true worth of the study of history is to recognize that what has happened before is still relevant to what is happening today. The past can be a mirror to the future. As mentioned previously, the famous quote of William Faulkner is the heart of this truth: "The past is never dead. It's not even past."

There are many patterns that repeat over time in the study of history. For our discussion, we will examine three specific patterns: (1) colonization, (2) assimilation, and (3) marginalization. These three patterns occur frequently in the history of Southwestern Hispanics. We can use classic definitions of these terms as our guides to understanding the historical events that critically affected the lives of Southwestern Hispanics. The details of the effects of each of these historical patterns on Southwestern Hispanic life reveal a compelling and dramatic history.

Colonization is the process of entering, or invading, another territory with the intent of gaining control of the territory's land, people, resources, and institutions. It also involves the imposition of the colonizer's culture. The most direct example of colonization in the Americas is the Spanish colonization that changed the lives of American Indigenous populations forever. One of the results of this colonization is the Spanish settlement of El Norte—its northern frontiers, the Southwest United States—that established a Hispanic population in the American Southwest that has endured four hundred years.

Cultural assimilation is the process through which a minority group or culture takes on the majority group's or culture's values and beliefs. This can happen either by willing choice or by forced compliance. The starkest example of forced cultural assimilation was the government movement of American Indigenous peoples onto the reservation system, thereby destroying their traditional ways of life. Another was the kidnapping of Native children and the relocating of them to government boarding schools in an effort to "take the Indian out of the child." For Hispanos, as well as all other cultures, the fundamental question has always been whether assimilation into American popular culture eventually results in losing your traditional heritage. Is it really possible to balance two identities and be true to both of them?

Marginalization is the act of treating someone or a group as if they are not important or of any significant value, accompanied by the denial of basic rights. The issue of cultural superiority has always raised the question of who is a "true American." Examples of marginalization are abundant in American history: the Three-Fifths Compromise, enshrined in Article I, Section 2 of the US Constitution, which stipulated that for the purposes of representation and taxation, enslaved people would be counted as three-fifths of a person; the denial of women's voting rights until the Nineteenth Amendment in 1920; the legal segregation of races in housing and public accommodations through Jim Crow laws until the passage of the Civil Rights Act of 1964; and the denial of equal voting rights requiring the Voting Rights Act of 1965.

The most powerful historical narratives are those of continual and rising improvement, in which a cultural group challenges the limitations and restrictions of these three historical patterns: colonization, assimilation, and marginalization. The most interesting historical studies are of the moments when life actually changed from one way to another. A saying about history is that its backward vision is always 20/20. Recognizing these moments as they are actually occurring is the gift of awareness that history is happening in the here and now.

A close review of Hispanic history of the American Southwest reveals a beautiful, proud people struggling in a harsh environment, overcoming racial and political barriers, and through perseverance and resilience keeping their culture alive and their families strong. They are a people who have fought discrimination and marginalization. They are a people who have made significant contributions to American society. They are a people who have of been in one place for four hundred years. They are a remarkable people who found their querencia and stayed there.

The challenge is to understand exactly how they did this. What were the historical patterns that had to be recognized, confronted, and overcome? What were the events that tested and strengthened their resolve and character? What were the moments when their path changed from one destiny to another? What were the signposts of the road traveled? Who were their Moseses leading them to the Promised Land? How did they get to now, and what have been the patterns over time that got them here? These are the questions that make the study of history so interesting.

First, a timeline will present the significant events in the Hispanic Southwest. Following the timeline, a short version of a long story will review the major historical events of the four hundred years of Spanish settlement in the American Southwest.

Following sections will examine the pivotal events and moments that shaped Hispano life forever. These are the stories of their history.

A Timeline: What Happened When?

The facts of history—the names, dates, events, and places—are the bane of the student facing the final exam. While they can seem a daunting task of memorization, timelines serve a valuable function in that they place events in relation to each other. They also present a sort of poetic flow of the passing of time. Years and centuries glide by. Most of all, they give images of time passing and the moments of importance in people's lives that made history.

Significant Dates Impacting Hispanic Presence in the American Southwest
(American historical dates listed for historical reference)

1492: Columbus arrives in America.

1565: St. Augustine, Florida, is established by the Spanish—the oldest permanently occupied European settlement in the United States.

1596: Explorer Juan de Zaldívar enters the San Luis Valley.

1596–1800s: Spanish explorers to the San Luis Valley encounter Indigenous peoples, including the Ute, Apache, and Navajo.

1598: Juan de Oñate establishes the first Spanish settlements in the northern frontiers of New Spain, present-day New Mexico.

1607: Jamestown, Virginia, is founded by the English.

1610: Santa Fe, New Mexico, the oldest state capitol in the United States, is founded by the Spanish.

1620: Mayflower arrives in Massachusetts.

1775–1783: American Revolutionary War

1776: US Declaration of Independence

1776: Domínguez–Escalante Expedition

1810: El Grito de Dolores—Mexican independence from Spain

1812: War of 1812 between United States and Britain

1832: Conejos Guadalupe Land Grant is bestowed by Mexico to fifty New Mexican families.

1842: Trappers, traders, and mountain men, along with Hispanic wives, establish Pueblo, Colorado.

1843: Sangre de Cristo Land Grant bestowed by Mexico to Narcisco Beaubien and Stephen Lee.

1846–1848: Mexican-American War

1848: United States defeates Mexico, Treaty of Guadalupe Hidaldo is signed.

1851: Settlement of San Luis, oldest Colorado town

1852–1870: Additional Spanish settlements in the Upper Rio Grande Valley of Colorado: San Pablo Garcia, San Pedro, San Acacio, Jaroso, Mesita, Guadualupe, Mogote, Conejos, Los Rincones, Las Mesitas, San Rafel, Cañon, Capulin, Los Cerritos, Los Sauces, La Florida, La Isla, Epinoza, El Centrito, Chama, and Los Fuertes. The names of these towns indicate the extent of Spanish settlement in Colorado before it even became a state.

1861: Colorado becomes a US territory.

1861: San Luis Valley becomes part of Colorado Territory.

1861–1865: US Civil War

1876: Colorado statehood is granted.

1910–1920: Mexican Revolution

1930s–1940s: Pachuco Era

1942–1964: Bracero Program

1950s–1960: Civil Rights era

1960s: Vietnam War

1962: United Farm Workers Union is formed.

1960s–1970s: Chicano Movement—El Movimiento

Present Time: Rising to positions of power and influence

La Historia: A Short Version of a Long Story

"In 1492, Columbus sailed the ocean blue." This little children's rhyme marks the beginning of traditional Hispanic culture in the New World. The history of Hispanic culture in the American Southwest is the story of centuries of blending the European Spanish culture the conquistadores brought with them with the Indigenous cultures that existed when they arrived.

Columbus's voyage of exploration represented the birth of European expansion in the New World. His discovery of a New World led to the conquest of Indigenous culture by European powers and changed the world forever. It was a short thirty years between Columbus's discovery of America and the defeat of the Aztec empire in Mexico. The original conquistadores who came to the New World in their *caravelas* (Spanish galleons) were explorers who came looking for gold and personal glory.

Later, missionaries would come with a religious mission. These military adventurers, colonists, and missionaries would create a New Spain, based upon the cultural heritage of the Spain of the Old World.

When the conquistadores landed in the New World, long-established cultures flourished in all parts of the New World. Of primary interest was the Aztec culture, the dominant culture of Mexico at the time of the Spanish arrival.

The Aztecs, or Mexica, arrived in the Valley of Mexico in the thirteenth century. A wandering band of nomadic people, their fabled history told of their origins in a mythical land to the north, Aztlán. The true location of Aztlán is lost in antiquity, but many Hispanic people believe that Aztlán was the northern frontier of Mexico, the land that is today the American Southwest. The legend of Aztlán is especially powerful for Chicanos living in the American Southwest, many of whom believe that the Southwest is the site of legendary Aztlán.

According to the legend of Aztlán, the Aztec god Quetzalcoatl had told his people to look in their wanderings for a lake with an island in the middle of it. On the island would be a cactus, and on top of the cactus would be an eagle with a snake in its mouth. By this sign they would know they had found the place to establish their empire. Legend, of course, has the Aztecs finding this island with the cactus, eagle, and snake. The Mexican flag has as its central image this miraculous combination: an eagle on a cactus with a serpent in its mouth.

The lake was Lake Texcoco, and in the center was the island Tenochtitlán. The Aztecs made Tenochtitlán the center of their empire, and the Spaniards built their capital, Mexico City, at the site of Tenochtitlán.

The Aztecs had a profound and complex culture that they had evolved during their nomadic wanderings from their mythical homeland of Aztlán. After they settled in Tenochtitlán, they established a culture that was the final culmination in a series of advanced cultures in the Valley of Mexico.

The Spaniards marveled at Tenochtitlán, for they had never seen a city of its size and complexity before. The city had a water system and parkways and was surrounded by ingenious canals and fields for

Figure 8—Cortés Meets Moctezuma

growing an abundance of food. They had evolved a sophisticated system of time measurement and kept accurate records of commerce and history. They also had an education system and an established literary tradition. Their cosmology was based upon myths of a pantheon of gods, most associated with their existence as an agricultural and warrior society.

The Aztec empire was at its zenith when the Spanish first encountered it. A Spanish soldier, Bernal Díaz del Castillo, gives us a stirring description of its magnificence in *The History of the Conquest of New Spain*, the University of New Mexico Press edition listed in the bibliography, his history of personal recollections written fifty years after the conquest.

> We saw so many cities and villages built in the water and other towns on dry land . . . we were amazed and said it was like the enchantment they tell of in the legend of Amadís . . . some of our soldiers even asked whether the things we saw were not a dream. . . . I do not know how to describe it, seeing things as we did that had never been heard or seen before, not even dreamed about . . . never in the world would there be

> discovered other lands such as these. . . . Gazing upon such wonderful sights, we did not know what to say, or whether what appeared before us was real. (2008, 156–157)[1]

His description of the great Aztec marketplace of Tlatelolco gives support to the belief that the Aztec empire was equal to any in Europe at the time of the conquest.

> We were astounded at the number of people and the quantity of merchandise that it contained . . . for we had never seen such a thing before . . . some of the soldiers among us who had been in many parts of the world, in Constantinople, and all over Italy, and in Rome, said that so large a market place and so full of people, and so well regulated and arranged, they had never beheld before. (2008, 173, 176)[2]

Unbelievably, in spite of their highly sophisticated culture, the dominance of their empire, and their great strength as a warrior culture, the Aztecs would not prevail against the Spanish. Hernán Cortés was the conqueror of the Aztecs. With little over five hundred men and aided by his consort and interpreter, the woman the Mexicans would later refer to as the traitorous La Malinche, he succeeded in defeating the glorious Aztec empire.

Several important factors contributed to the rapid conquest of the Aztec people by Cortés. One was the help of La Malinche, an Indigenous woman from the Mexican Gulf Coast and given to Cortés by the Tabasco tribe. Malinche spoke several native languages, and as Cortés's translator, she facilitated his first contacts with native populations. Another was the conquistadores' use of the horse, which had never been seen by the Aztecs. A third was the Spaniards' use of firearms and metallic armor, also never seen by the Aztecs. Also, the Aztecs had a sacred legend foretelling the return of their god Quetzalcoatl from the east. The Aztecs originally believed that the Spaniards were gods and that Cortés was their returning god, Quetzalcoatl. Finally, the diseases of Europe, especially smallpox, decimated the defenseless Aztecs.

With the conquest of the Aztecs, the Spanish were the dominant European power in the New World, and they began systematic colonization of its new territories. They set up governmental and economic systems in order to control the new lands and the people they found on those new lands. They established cities based upon the traditional Spanish city with a plaza at its center. Around the plaza were public buildings and the church.

The economic system was based upon the *encomienda*, a system of land distribution that allotted land and Native workers to Spanish settlers who had given governmental or military service to the crown. The land estates were *haciendas*, the land owners were *patrones*, and the native slaves were *peones*. The laws of the encomienda system were supposed to protect the Native workers, but there were common abuses resulting in a condition of almost slave servitude for the Native workers. This system and its harsh injustices eventually were replaced after Mexican independence from Spain in 1821.

Over time, there was intermarriage between Native people and Spaniards. A descriptive system of bloodline nomenclatures created classes within Spanish society. *Peninsulares* were pure Spaniards born in Spain, *criollos* were pure Spaniards born in the New World, *mestizos* were mixed Indian and Spanish, *mulatos* were Black and Spanish, *zambos* were mixed Black and Indian. During the colonial period, the greatest discrimination, after *Indios* and Blacks, fell on the people of *mestizo* and *zambo* bloodlines.

Missionaries from Spain came to the New World determined to convert Native people to Catholic Christianity. They established missions dedicated to educating the Native converts and teaching them the Spanish religion, language, and culture.

In addition to the immense task of establishing New Spain, the Spanish also continued their vast exploration of the New World. While Spaniards explored both North and South America, we are most concerned with the northern outposts of the Spanish empire. In 1539, explorer Francisco Vázquez de Coronado, under orders from the viceroys of New Spain, entered the northern frontier of New Spain searching for the legendary Seven Cities of Gold. His search was futile, but his explorations established the northern frontiers of New Spain for colonizing expeditions.

Figure 9—Francisco Garcés, a Spanish Missionary Priest, 1775

In 1598, Don Juan de Oñate led the first expedition to succeed in establishing a permanent colony in New Mexico along the Upper Rio Grande Valley. Soon after, the clergy and military followed, further colonizing the northern frontier of New Spain. These early Spanish settlers founded the first Spanish communities in northern New Mexico and southern Colorado in the Upper Rio Grande Valley and later the San Luis Valley. After twelve years, with the assistance of the San Juan Tewa Pueblo at San Gabriel, which the Spanish named San Juan de los Caballeros, Santa Fe was established as the administrative outpost of this area in 1610.

Another path of settlement was along the coast of the northwestern frontier. Father Junípero Serra was a Franciscan missionary in California in the 1700s. He was instrumental in the founding of twenty-one missions in California along El Camino Real, the Royal Highway, a road connecting all the missions along the California coast from San Diego to San Francisco.

Through the decades following the establishment of New Spain, the Spaniards founded missions and military settlements, followed by civilian settlements. As these civilian settlements expanded throughout the northern frontiers of New Spain, they contributed to the consolidation of Spanish culture in the New World.

Throughout the seventeenth century, colonists came into the northern regions and brought with them the Hispanic and Indigenous (or Indio-Hispanic) cultural elements of Spanish colonial society. These colonists represented the various groups present in Mexico at this time. These included Spaniards who had settled in Mexico, children of these Spaniards, mestizos of Spanish and Indian parentage, and Indians from various ethnic groups in Mexico.

For generations these communities developed, adhering to a Hispanic way of life. The early settlers brought with them the language, religion, and customs of Spain. These Spanish customs were somewhat modified and influenced by Indigenous culture.

Joined by these common cultural bonds, they forged a strong sense of community among themselves. Geographically and politically isolated in what would eventually become the American Southwest, isolated across hundreds of miles of barren frontier, distanced from the centers of Mexican political cultural life, they nevertheless maintained a culture with Spanish roots while adapting to their new land.

In 1810, after almost three hundred years of Spanish rule, the Mexican people began a fight for independence from Spain. On September 16, the most important national holiday in Mexico, Father Miguel Hidalgo rang his church bell in Dolores, Mexico, and thus began an eleven-year struggle for independence. Finally, in 1821, Mexico gained its freedom from Spain and became a sovereign nation.

Mexico's great victory of independence was short-lived, however. Mexico was soon to lose half of its lands to the United States, which was operating in the Americas under a policy of Manifest Destiny, a militant policy that had as its central image a country with borders spanning from sea to shining sea. This policy of Manifest Destiny empowered the United States to aspire to Mexican land.

In 1844, US President James K. Polk was elected on a policy of western expansion. In 1846, Polk confronted the Mexican army at the Texas-Mexican border and thus began the Mexican-American War.

In 1848, the Treaty of Guadalupe Hidalgo ended the Mexican-American War. This treaty ceded the northern portion of Mexico to the United States. The area containing all or parts of the states of Arizona, California, Colorado, Kansas, Nevada, New Mexico, Oklahoma, Utah, Texas, and Wyoming, all part of northern Mexico, became part of the United States.

A common sentiment about this political loss of Mexico's northern land is expressed in one item of folk legend that has a person from the time commenting about his sudden change from a Mexican citizen to a United States citizen: "I didn't leave my country. My country left me." A variation of this folk saying has the man saying, "I didn't cross the border. The border crossed me."

Even though these Hispanic communities of the northern Mexican frontier suddenly came under the jurisdiction of the US government, their way of life remained relatively unchanged in their remote villages. The traditional way of life in these Hispanic communities unfolded as it had for generations. Even though the people were now US citizens, culturally their life remained centered in the Hispanic traditions that had ruled Mexico for more than three hundred years.

The history of modern Hispanic life in the American Southwest is marked by a continuation of the centuries-old Spanish colonial culture combined with the influence of Mexican immigration in the twentieth century. Mexico experienced a revolution in 1910, and one result of its social disruption was the immigration of Mexican nationals to the United States.

Also throughout the twentieth century, Mexico has been a steady source of agricultural workers for the United States. This immigration of workers has been both legal and illegal. It has been legal under several US government-sponsored labor programs. However, when those government programs expired, the immigration and employment of Mexican workers in the United States continued. Illegal immigration continued to exist because of the desire of Mexican workers to seek work and increased prosperity in the United States and because of American employers' willingness to hire illegal workers because of their low wages.

In conclusion, we can view the history of the Hispanic Southwest as characterized by five distinct historical periods:

1598–1821: The Spanish colonial period—223 years of Spanish rule and influence. The year 1598 is the year Juan de Oñate established the first Spanish settlements in the northern frontiers of New Spain, present-day New Mexico.

1821–1848: A relatively short twenty-seven-year period of Mexican nationality. 1821 is the year of Mexican independence from Spain. 1848 is the year of the Treaty of Guadalupe Hidalgo.

1848–1910: American frontier settlement. A time of large immigration of Anglo Americans into the Southwest. The establishment of United States nationality.

1910–present: The Mexican Revolution of 1910 caused the beginning of large-scale Mexican immigration into the Southwest.

The twentieth and twenty-first centuries—a period of cultural struggle between assimilation and preservation, economic striving, and marginalization and accomplishment.

This historical overview reveals several important reasons for the existence of a continuing and strong Hispanic culture in the American Southwest. The simplest is that the people of the Hispanic culture have lived in the region for centuries. Their culture evolved as a result of several powerful influences:

- The continuous influence of Indigenous cultures existing in Mexico at the time of the arrival of the Spanish in spite of Spanish efforts to totally eradicate it.
- The Spanish colonial period of Mexican history secured Spanish culture, especially its language and its religion.
- The continuing revitalization of the culture in the United States by Mexican immigrants. Even the annexation of the northern Mexican frontiers by the United States and the dominant presence of American Anglo culture has not been enough to extinguish the Hispanic culture of the Southwest.

The Spanish presence in the Southwest has revealed that there is a wealth of history to be explored and examined. Many scholars and authors have written extensively about this history. The bibliography at the end of this book lists many excellent sources for further research and study.

The following sections will present in greater detail the critical historical moments that established and changed Hispanic life in the Southwest, with discussion about why these moments were of such importance. View these sections as a sort of "Greatest Hits of History."

If you are inclined to delve deeper into this history, I encourage you to read the many resources listed in the bibliography. You don't have to know everything about this history unless you are a dedicated history aficionado, but examining the following significant moments of history will give you a strong understanding of the historical patterns over time and how individuals affected the course of history, resulting in a Hispanized Southwest.

These sections cover the following significant historical moments that contributed to who we are now:

- Spanish Settlement in the Southwest—the True First Thanksgiving
- Mestizo Culture and Genealogy Discoveries—Cultural Blending
- Pueblo Revolt in 1680
- The Mexican-American War and the Treaty of Guadalupe Hidalgo
- Mexican Independence and the Mexican Revolution—the Creation of the Borderlands
- The Bracero Labor Program
- The United Farm Workers Movement
- The Pachuco and Zoot Suit Riots
- The Chicano Movement—Aztlán: A Lost Homeland
- The Poets of the Chicano Movement
- Students and Community Protests
- Los Seis de Boulder
- Unsung Heroes—Marginalization of Hispanic Leaders
- Rising to Positions of Leadership and Influence
- The Continuing Revitalization of Hispanic Culture

Spanish Settlement in the Southwest

Colonization from South to North and the True First Thanksgiving

Spanish explorers moving north from New Spain explored the northern frontiers of the Empire of New Spain extensively. Francisco Vázquez de Coronado in 1540–1542 explored what is now Arizona and New Mexico in search of the Seven Cities of Cíbola, the fabled Seven Cities of Gold. While he found no great wealth or treasure, he did encounter the Pueblo Native cultures of the region, and his men were the first Europeans to view the Grand Canyon and the Colorado River. His explorations did lay the groundwork for further explorations and the eventual Spanish colonization of the southwestern United States.

In 1598 Juan de Oñate, sometimes referred to as "the Last Conquistador," crossed over the Rio Grande River to what is now El Paso and claimed the land for the King of Spain. He led 129 soldiers and ten Franciscan missionaries, plus a large number of women, children, servants, slaves, and livestock.

The makeup of the expedition was a clear indication of the intent to set up a Spanish settlement. Phillip II of Spain had ordered Oñate to lead an expedition to colonize the northern frontier of New Spain. Oñate became the first colonizer of the vast northern frontier, and he later became the first colonial governor of the Province of Santa Fe de Nuevo Mexico.

History records that Oñate and his expedition celebrated the true first Thanksgiving in the Americas on April 30, 1598, twenty-three years before the Pilgrims celebrated their Thanksgiving at Plymouth Rock. Oñate's expedition celebration took place near present-day El Paso, Texas, after a hazardous and treacherous fifty-day journey across the Chihuahuan Desert and after surviving several near-death experiences brough on by isolation, heat, and the desert environment. They reported running out of food and water before they found salvation in the waters of the Rio Grande River.

Finally finding safety and refreshing waters, Oñate and his contingent of soldiers, Franciscan missionaries, and colonists celebrated. Oñate called the site of this celebration "El Paso del Río del Norte." The celebration included a feast, a Catholic mass, and a declaration of "La Toma," the traditional claiming of the land for Spain. The feast consisted of game and fish that the local Native tribes provided for the Spanish. The celebration also included the first recorded theatrical performance in America, a play by Captain Marcos Farfán de Godos. This was the first true Thanksgiving celebration in America.

While Oñate's historical reputation remains complicated and controversial for his subjection of Native peoples, he does receive the recognition of leading the first colonizing settlers into Southwestern America. After the first Spanish explorers traveled north in search of God, glory, and gold, colonists and settlers migrated north to establish new communities in the northern frontiers of New Spain and later Mexico. Many more would follow.

Santa Fe, New Mexico, became the first permanent European settlement in the Southwest in 1610. In 1769, the Spanish established Mission San Diego de Alcala, the first of twenty-one missions to be established on the coast of California. In 1851, New Mexico settlers moving north established the town of San Luis de la Culebra, the first permanent settlement in Colorado. The Spanish settlement of the American Southwest had begun.

Mestizo Culture and Genealogy Discoveries: Cultural Blending

As the Spanish colonized the American Southwest, a blending of Spanish, Mexican, and Indigenous cultures created a new racial category of people—the *mestizo*. In the Spanish colonial world, a strict hierarchical caste system existed. At the top were the *peninsulares*, Spaniards born in Spain. Next were the *criollos*, people born in New Spain of Spanish parents. Third were mestizos, people of mixed European and Indigenous ancestry. Following these first three groups were *mulatos*, people of mixed European and African ancestry; *zambos*, people of mixed Indigenous ancestry; Indigenous peoples; and finally African peoples. This racial caste system allowed the Spanish to maintain their power and superiority over other racial groups in New Spain.

Mestizos became the Hispanos of the American Southwest. This blending of Spanish and Indigenous cultures is the center of today's Hispanic southwestern culture.

A recent development has been a deep interest in the nature of this blending of racial and cultural categories. The study of genealogy has moved from being a hobby to a true scientific exploration of family genealogy and the hidden connections between the various people living in the American Southwest. The Genealogical Society of Hispanic America has as its mission the promotion of genealogical and historical research and education. With the proliferation of internet genealogical sites, the task of discovering and studying ancestral roots has become common and readily accomplished.

While the relationships between Spanish and Indigenous people have long been recognized, two additional areas of study have recently developed. One is the existence of Genízaros, and the other is the discovery of Jewish ancestry in Hispanic families.

As the Spanish colonized New Spain's northern frontier, they encountered Native tribes that had been on the land since the beginning of memory. The conflicts between the Spanish and the Native tribes resulted in a class of people who were captives of the Spanish. The Spanish developed a system in which they sold these captured Native People to Hispanic families. *Indentured servitude* is one way to describe this situation, but *slavery* is a more accurate term.

The Royal Crown had outlawed slavery, but the Spanish created systems around that prohibition. One was that the captured Native could pay tribute in the form of goods or products such as blankets or corn. If the Native captive was unable to pay any tribute, then the Native had to work off the debt owed to the Spanish captors. From this situation came the selling or trading of Native captives to Hispanic families to work off their debts. These labor service relationships introduced Natives to Spanish traditions and culture.

The extent and nature of Indian enslavement is a fact of history. The Natives placed in Hispanic families became detribalized, Hispanized, and Christianized. Indigenous captives placed in Hispanic homes received Spanish or Anglo names to present the appearance that they had been adopted when in fact they were enslaved. If they eventually married the family line and produced children, it introduced Native ancestry into the eventually genealogical record.

Genízaros were the Natives sold or traded to Hispanic families. They are also the present-day descendants of these original Genízaros. Recent genealogical research has revealed the history of Genízaros in many Hispanic families. Families have embraced these discoveries as they add a fascinating complexity to family genealogy that had not existed before the research.

One of the best references to examine the little-known Genízaro story is *Identifying Captivity and Capturing Identity: Narratives of American Indian Slavery, Colorado and New Mexico, 1776–1934* by Estévan Rael-Gálvez, a dissertation submitted in partial fulfillment of the requirements for the degree of Doctor of Philosophy (American Culture) at the University of Michigan, 2002. Another is *Plains Indians in New Mexico: The Genízaro Experiance* by Russell M. Magnaghi, published by the University of Nebraska Press.

Another recent discovery that has emerged from the increased interest in Hispanic genealogy is the recognition of Jewish ancestry in families in the Upper Rio Grande Valley of New Mexico and Colorado. The origins of these Jewish roots are in late fifteenth-century Spain. In 1492, the Alhambra Decree by the Catholic Monarchs of Spain called for the expulsion of Jews, leading to a combination of internal and external migrations, mass conversions, and executions.

Many Jews became *conversos*, Jews who converted to Christianity in order to escape the harsh decrees. These conversos often lived a secret life: Christian in public but retaining Jewish practices in secret, preserving their heritage. Today, these people are known as "crypto-Jews": Jews or people descended from converted Jews who continue to practice Judaism in secret.

The Spanish Inquisition was the result of this development. The Inquisition was instituted to identify heretics who converted from Judaism to Catholicism. The Spanish decree and the Inquisition created a mass exodus of Sephardim populations from Spain. Finding a safe place to live became more and more difficult in Europe as many countries adopted decrees similar to Spain's. This situation created a diaspora to the New World, Mexico, and other countries. Many Jews fled to Mexico, where they could remain Spanish subjects while practicing Judaism in private. When the Inquisition later came to Mexico, those Jews migrated north, eventually settling in the Upper Rio Grande Valley of New Mexico and Colorado.

The conversos in the New World continued to practice Judaism in secret out of fear of the consequences of the Spanish Inquisition. Over time, many conversos lost connection to their original Judaism, and their descendants forgot their Jewish ancestry.

Genealogy research, however, has revealed this Jewish heritage to many Hispanic families. These discoveries have added valuable additional elements to the story of Hispanos in the American Southwest. The original mestizo category, simple in its Spanish and Indigenous definition, now has additional layers of cultural blending. The cultural mix is even richer now.

Historical Coda #6

While doing research for my book *The Corn Woman: Stories and Legends of the Hispanic Southwest*, I was fortunate to receive grants to travel to the Upper Rio Grande Valley of northern New Mexico and southern Colorado to do research. I spent many wonderful hours recording conversations as I asked elder Hispanos about the traditional cuentos, stories of their childhood. I also often asked them about the games they played as children. One elderly man told me of his favorite game, *Saca y Pon*, to take and give. I asked him about it, and he said he hand-carved the pieces to play the game out of pine wood. He then went into another room and brought out one of the pieces and gave it to me and said I could keep it. It was a four-sided spinning top piece with *saca* and *pon* written on the four sides. We then played the game. I immediately recognized the piece as a dreidel. The game his family played was similar to the dreidel game of putting and taking items out of the pot on the table, only it was the Spanish words of *saca* and *pon*, for *give* and *take*, instead of the Hebrew symbols for the same actions. I was astounded to find confirmation of Jewish customs in a little farmhouse in the San Luis Valley. I asked him how he learned the game. He casually shrugged and said they had always played it in his family. I still have the game piece he gave me.

Figure 10—Hand-carved Saca y Pon, *a game piece for a children's game played in the San Luis Valley. Handmade by a Hispano elder for his children in the San Luis Valley. Photograph by Angel Vigil.*

Pueblo Revolt in 1680

To further understand the persistence and dedication to the task of the Spanish as they colonized their northern frontier, it is important to examine the only time in history Native people overthrew their Spanish oppressors: the Pueblo Revolt of 1680. The Pueblo Revolt was a revolt against the political, religious, and cultural domination of the Spanish over the Pueblo people of New Mexico. It was the only successful uprising of Native people against a colonizing power in North America. It represented a rare successful resistance against European colonization.

Prior to the revolt in 1680, the Pueblo people had endured decades of economic exploitation, forced conversion to Catholicism, and cultural suppression. With the establishment of the first permanent settlements in 1598, the Spanish began their complete subjugation of the Pueblo people. Pueblo Natives were forced to pay tributes to their Spanish rulers in the form of labor, corn, textiles, and other goods. The Franciscan missionaries took on the task of eliminating "pagan" religious practices and forcing Catholicism upon the Natives. They outlawed Native practices and burned all objects of religious observations.

Especially brutal was the Spanish oppression of Native resistance in the Pueblo of Acoma. In 1599, the Spanish put down a revolt at the Acoma Pueblo with brutal and murderous tactics that included the burning of the Pueblo to the ground. The Acoma Massacre created anger toward the Spanish for years afterward.

The toll of this total oppression of the Pueblo Natives eventually led to the Pueblo Revolt in August 1680, under the leadership of Po'pay, or Popé, a Tewa leader and medicine man. Po'pay, who also had suffered decades of Spanish oppression, had a desire to restore Pueblo tradition and cultural practices. History recognizes him as the leader of the Pueblo Revolt. With other Pueblo leaders, he was able to develop and coordinate the revolt among Pueblo villages in the province of Santa Fe, Nuevo Mexico. Po'pay promised that once the Spanish were killed or expelled, the ancient Pueblo gods would reward them with health and prosperity.

In a carefully organized plan, runners traveled through the villages carrying a knotted cord. As each day passed, they spread the word of the planned attack against the Spanish. Each day, they unknotted one knot on the cord. When the last knot was undone, it was time for the coordinated attack.

Pueblo warriors attacked Spanish settlements, killing Spanish settlers and Franciscan missionaries and burning churches. The Spanish were forced to flee to El Paso.

The revolt killed four hundred Spaniards and forced two thousand settlers to flee. The revolt was a total victory for the Pueblo people. They regained control of their territories and were able to re-establish their religious and cultural practices.

In the years after the success of the revolt, Po'Pay's promised return to prosperity did not materialize. Drought destroyed Pueblo crops, and food grew scarce. Raids became common as attacks by the Apache and Navajo continued. Po'pay eventually was disposed of his leadership by the Pueblo people and is said to have died before the reconquest by the Spaniards, and, like so many other historical figures, he disappeared into history.

In 1692, twelve years after the revolt, the Spanish began their reconquest of the Pueblo people. Through successive encounters with Pueblo leaders, the Spanish made the Puebloans agree to peace. The Spanish leaders promised the Puebloans clemency and protection if they swore allegiance to the King of Spain and returned to the Christian religion. While a temporary peace was realized over the next several years, instances of resistance to Spanish rule and oppression continued among the Pueblo people. The Spanish responded with military force and either killed or imprisoned the remaining resisters. By the end of the century, the last Pueblo villages had surrendered, and the return of Spanish control was complete.

While the era of Pueblo revolt ended, the episode changed the power dynamic between the Spanish and Pueblo people. It could be said that the Spanish had learned their lesson, and they adjusted their practices with the Pueblo people. They gave land grants to each Pueblo and appointed a public defender to argue their legal cases in Spanish courts. Puebloans were also able to continue to practice their traditional religion in spite of the Franciscan efforts to convert them to Christianity.

The end result of this dramatic episode of history was the continued expansion of Spanish colonization of the American Southwest. The history of New Spain and Mexico would contain many more upheavals. History never stops moving forward.

The Mexican-American War and the Treaty of Guadalupe Hidalgo: Its Causes and Consequences

Causes: Sometimes a Nation Just Wants a War

The Mexican-American War, 1846 to 1848, was one of the most important and primary events affecting the lives of Hispanos in the American Southwest. It was a war of imperialistic aggression based upon the United States' belief in Manifest Destiny. That belief was based upon the idea that America had a God-given providence to expand its territory from sea to shining sea. The phrase *Manifest Destiny* first appeared in an article written by John L. O'Sullivan in the *Democratic Review* in 1845, in which he stated it must be our "manifest destiny to overspread the continent by Providence for the free development of our yearly multiplying millions." Western expansion was America's divine right.

Historians and scholars have deeply studied and documented this war. It is multi-layered in all its aspects and complications. Our examination of this war will review the primary events leading up to the war, the significant events of the war, and the consequences of the Treaty of Guadalupe Hidalgo for the Hispanos in the American Southwest.

In 1844, President James K. Polk ran on a democratic platform that supported Manifest Destiny. His desire was for the United States to have the land encompassing territory from the disputed land of Texas all the way to California, land now recognized as the southwestern United States.

The country had previously been successful in purchasing land from a foreign power with the Louisiana Purchase in 1803. The United States paid France $15 million for land from the Mississippi River to the Rocky Mountains, thereby nearly doubling the size of the nation. This purchase opened up vast territories for western expansion.

Following this earlier success of purchasing land for western expansion, Polk sent American diplomat John Slidell to Mexico with an offer to purchase the land, offering Mexico $25 million for the land. Mexico refused the offer and in fact refused to even meet with Slidell. Polk, however, was determined to acquire the land for the United States. In pursuit of this goal, in January 1846 he sent four thousand American troops under the command of Zachary Taylor to Texas to the land between the Nueces River and the Rio Grande River, land Mexico claimed as its own, to provoke a war with Mexico.

In order to understand the disputed territory of Texas that was claimed by both the United States and Mexico and led to war between the two nations, we must take a few backward steps in the history of the Texas territory. Mexico's northern territory included land that eventually would become the state of Texas. In a strategic error, Mexico invited settlers from the American states to come into Mexican territory and act as a buffer against further encroachment of America in the Mexican territory.

Over time, however, these American settlers retained their allegiance to the United States. This eventually resulted in conflicts between these Texas settlers and the Mexican government. Texas would go on to declare itself an independent nation in 1836 with the desire to join the United States.

Texas's bid for statehood met several roadblocks. The first was that it was a large slaveholding state, and many felt its admission would upset the delicate balance between non-slaveholding states and slaveholding states. Also, many did not want to provoke a war with Mexico. Mexico had outlawed slavery and declared that the Texas territory was its territory.

Texas eventually gained admission to the United States in 1845, becoming the twenty-eighth state. Mexico refused to recognize Texas's independence and considered the annexation of Texas by the United States as a potential act of war.

In response to this act of territorial aggression, Mexico sent its own troops into the disputed territory. The stage was set for war. On April 25, 1846, Mexican troops fired on United States troops, thereby giving Polk the opportunity to declare, "Mexico has invaded our territory and shed American blood on American soil." He then sent an order of war to Congress. On May 13, 1846, Congress declared war on Mexico.

This act of war created a widespread antiwar movement in the United States. Political opponents labeled Polk's aggression as an unprincipled land grab, and abolitionists viewed it as a scheme by Polk, a southerner, to add more slave states to the Union. One opponent was freshman Illinois congressman Abraham Lincoln. He introduced a series of resolutions maintaining that Polk had provoked the battle on Mexican land and that Polk was a seeker of military glory. Supporters of the war opposed Lincoln's efforts, and it damaged his reputation with the pro-war constituents.

As in any war, there were also many human-interest side stories. One notable fact of the war was that it was the first combat experience for many future US leaders. These included future presidents Zachary Taylor and Franklin Pierce, as well as future Civil War generals Ulysses S. Grant, Robert E. Lee, and Stonewall Jackson.

Another interesting story of the war that has been lost in the passage of time is the heroic action of Los San Patricios. The desertion of the St. Patrick's Battalion was one of the most defiant acts of the war. The two-hundred-man battalion consisted mainly of Irish Catholics and other immigrants who resented the prejudice they received from Protestants in the United States. The rejection of foreign immigrants to the United States is one of the most recurring patterns that have plagued US history.

These Irish soldiers understood the effects of racial and religious prejudice, having experienced it previously from the English in their own country. They also understood what it was like to have a more powerful country attack a weaker country, once again through their country's relationship with England. Their sympathies were with the weaker and Catholic country of Mexico.

Under the leadership of Irishman John Riley, the San Patricios became Santa Anna's elite artillery force serving with distinction at the battles of Buena Vista and Cerro Gordo. As the war concluded, the US Army captured and, following a court martial, executed by hanging fifty of the soldiers. Others were whipped and branded with a D for "deserter." Even though the San Patricios were seen as traitors in the United States, Mexico views them as national heroes and celebrates them every St. Patrick's Day.

Another legendary story of the war involved six Mexican teenage military cadets at the Battle of Chapultepec. The cadets remained at their posts after their fellow soldiers had abandoned the battle. The legend tells how one of the cadets prevented the capture of the Mexican flag by wrapping it around his body and leaping to his death off the castle wall. Even though the battle of Chapultepec was lost, Mexicans called the cadets Niños Heroes—heroic children. They later honored the cadets with a monument in Mexico City.

Over the two years of the war, battles intensified in many fronts on Mexican land. As in any war, the tides of the battles ebbed and flowed. The war's end was initiated by America's first major amphibious attack when General Winfield Scott invaded the Mexican port city of Veracruz. After he captured Veracruz, Scott led his troops in a six-month, 265-mile march to Mexico City. His capture of Mexico City in September 1847 marked the end of the war. Polk's original intent of a quick, easy victory over a weaker nation had turned into a long and arduous conflict on Mexican soil.

President Polk sent State Department clerk Nicholas P. Trist to negotiate a peace treaty with the conquered Mexican government. The negotiation stalled, and Polk ordered Trist to return to the United States. Trist, however, felt that a successful concluding negotiation pact was near, and he refused to return. Even though Polk tried to have Trist removed from the negotiations, and did fire him when he returned to the United States, Trist eventually concluded the negotiations in the Mexico town of Guadalupe Hidalgo, and the United States and Mexico on February 2, 1848, agreed in principle to the Treaty of Guadalupe Hidalgo, thus ending the Mexican-American War.

The war was a major catastrophe for Mexico. While the terms of the treaty had the United States paying Mexico $15 million, Mexico lost over half of its land. The United States gained what would eventually become the whole southwestern United States: all or parts of California, New Mexico, Nevada, Utah, Arizona, Colorado, Wyoming, Oklahoma, and Kansas.

One continuing question about the conclusion of the war is that, with its complete victory over Mexico, why did the United States not annex all of Mexico? The answer is another of the repeating patterns that appear throughout history: the aversion of people against the perceived "other." As Congress debated the possibility of annexing all of Mexico, the discussions centered on racial grounds.

South Carolina Senator John C. Calhoun argued that annexing all of Mexico would threaten the character of the country. He stated, "We have never dreamt of incorporating into our Union any but the Caucasian race—the free white race. To incorporate Mexico, would be the first instance of the kind of incorporating an Indian race; for more than half of the Mexicans are Indians, and the other is composed chiefly of mixed tribes. I protest against such a union as that! Ours, sir, is the Government of a white race."

Rhode Island Senator John Clark also objected to the annexation of Mexico, stating that "To incorporate such a disjointed and degraded mass into even a limited participation with our social and political rights would be fatally destructive to the institutions of our country. There is a moral pestilence to such a people which is contagious—a leprosy that will destroy [us]."

As odious and hateful as these statements appear today, these sentiments carried the day, and Mexico was not annexed. The United States did not want to incorporate a Spanish-speaking and Catholic population. As history's patterns reveal over time, this was just the first of many conflicts over these issues.

Consequences

It must have been quite a shock. One day you are living in Mexico, and the next day you are living in the United States. Meanwhile, you never moved. This was the reality experienced by those living in the annexed northern frontiers of Mexico after the conclusion of the Mexican-American War and the signing of the Treaty of Guadalupe Hidalgo. The experience is best expressed in the common refrain: "I didn't cross the border; the border crossed me."

While the history of the Treaty of Guadalupe Hidalgo has been eclipsed by the momentous events of the Civil War, the effects of the treaty have left a long-lasting impression in the lives of southwestern Hispanos on the negative consequences of America's quest for its Manifest Destiny. It was the key nineteenth-century event that produced the first Mexican Americans.

For Hispanos, life did change drastically in the annexed territories, the land encompassing the totality of the American Southwest. We shall explore these changes in relation to three important aspects: citizenship, land grants and land ownership, and water rights.

Citizenship

The treaty offered Mexicans living in the annexed territories one year to accept US citizenship or to retain their Mexican citizenship and return to Mexico. More than 90 percent of the Mexican population chose American citizenship. This population is the one that most accurately could call themselves Mexican American.

This offer of citizenship was compromised, however, as the United States ceded the authority to grant citizenship to the states. Within a year, states in the annexed territories passed laws that banned all Mexicans living in Arizona, California, New Mexico, and Texas from US citizenship except white male Mexicans, thereby denying the rights of citizenship to any Hispanic with Indigenous heritage. This is a good time to remember the previous discussion on racial categories stating that most Mexicans were of mestizo ancestry, a combination of Spanish and Indigenous ancestry. In addition, non-white Mexicans, meaning those of Indigenous heritage, lost citizen rights to vote and to hold government positions.

These direct government infringements on the supposed rights of citizenship created immediate distrust among the Hispanic population. The border had crossed them, and their new life in the United States would be one of repeated discrimination and limitations based upon race.

Property Rights, Land Grants

Mexico had long issued land grants in the northern frontiers to Mexicans and others to encourage settlement in its northern frontiers. For Mexico, the main threat in its northern frontiers was the rising influence of the United States, and Mexico felt it needed to secure its borders with its land grant policies.

They did this in order to populate these sparse territories and to create a populated buffer zone against the encroachment of other foreign governments with interests in these territories. The treaty stated that Mexicans who chose to remain in the United States would retain their property rights "as if the property belonged to citizens of the U.S. according to the principles of the Constitution." The direct language was as follows: "In the said territories, property of every kind, now belonging to Mexicans not established there, shall be inviolably respected." This quote is a clause in Article X of the Treaty of Guadalupe Hidalgo. As with the promise of the benefits of granted citizenship, these promises of the recognition of Mexican land grants and property ownership were quicky broken.

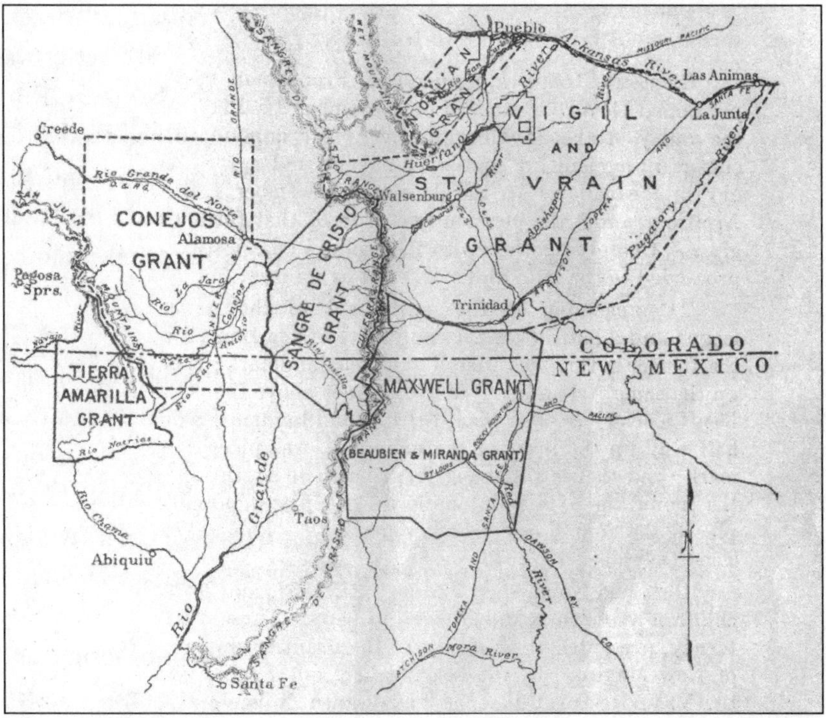

Figure 11—Mexican land grants in northern New Mexico and southern Colorado. This image also shows the Tierra Amarilla land grant as it crosses over into Colorado.

The United States did not honor the guarantees of the treaty that obligated the American government to honor all Spanish and Mexican land grants. As a result, many Hispanos lost their land. According to the terms of the treaty, Mexican land titles should have been sufficient to establish land ownership. In practice, however, the guarantees were not reliably enforced. Upon ratification of the treaty, the US Senate deleted the entirety of Article X, a section meant to guarantee land rights for citizens living within the new borders.

Various tactics were used to deny land grant claims. Hispanos had to appear in English-speaking courts to establish their claims. If the travel was too great or Spanish interpreters were not available, their claims were denied. Also, a difference existed between Mexican and American legal documents, and Mexican documents were often dismissed in courts. In New Mexico, the government recognized only 6 percent of the land grants.

Land grants were also lost due to illegal appropriations, deceit, and fraud. One of the most notorious of these land grab tactics was the work of the Santa Fe Ring in New Mexico. The Santa Fe Ring was a group of Anglo lawyers and politicians who gained land titles through manipulation of the legal system and later sold the land at a profit. The Ring specifically targeted Hispanos and their small, village-based farms for land grabs through legal manipulation, political influence, and fraud.

An additional aspect of this denial of land ownership claims as US laws went into effect after the treaty was that under the English law of coverture, women surrendered their legal claims and rights to their husbands. Under Spanish and Mexican civil law, women could own property in their own names. As the treaty resulted in the denial of Mexican property rights, women who owned land under Mexican civil law saw their claims to land ownership denied. Often, marriage facilitated the transfer of land ownership to Anglo men.

This denial of land ownership has resulted in Hispanos losing land that had been in their family for generations and creating a poverty and discrimination experience that continues to this day. The result has been a long series of conflicts between Hispanos and land speculators, ranchers, and developers over land rights and land access.

The most famous was the Tierra Amarilla land rights conflict in 1967. The land encompassed 524,215 acres of the Tierra Amarilla Land Grant.

Community leader Reies López Tijerina founded the Alianza Federal de Mercedes (Federal Alliance of Land Grants) to reclaim land grants that had been expropriated by the federal government and private landowners. His central claim was that, according to the original terms of the treaty, the land of Tierra Amarilla belonged to the descendants of the original Mexican land grant owners.

Tijerina and his followers raided the Tierra Amarilla courthouse to protest the denial of these land grant claims and to raise public awareness of land rights abuses. The raid resulted in a shootout with law enforcement and the kidnapping of a deputy and court reporter. Needless to say, this was the lead story in the newspaper the next day, and it ignited national attention to the issues of historic Hispanic land rights in the Southwest.

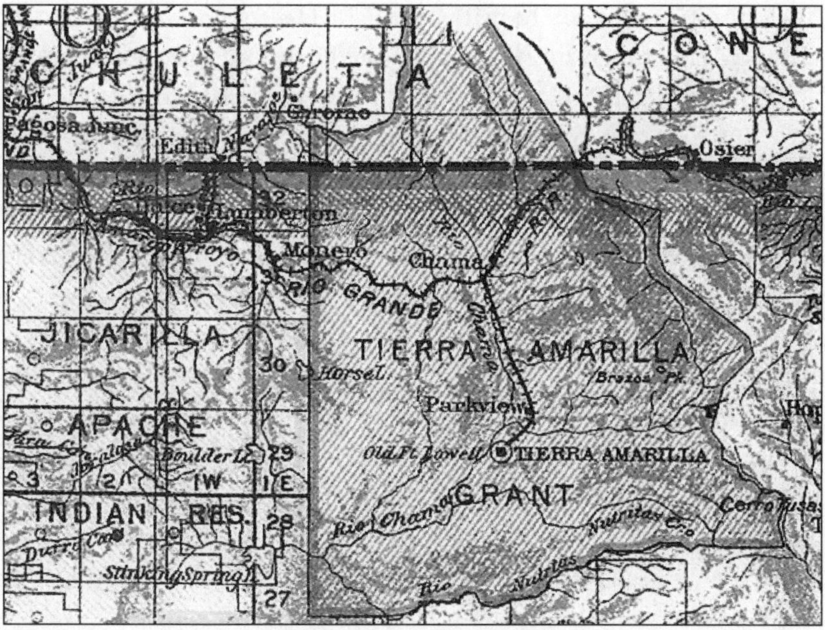

Figure 12—An enlargement of the map of the Tierra Amarilla Land Grant in New Mexico and Colorado, showing its position adjacent to the Jicarilla Apache Indian Reservation and crossing into Colorado.

The end result of this raid was the arrest of Tijerina and his followers. At his trial, he was convicted of the charges directly related to the raid.

The legacy of Tijerina's actions are multifold. The Chicano movement at the time used this issue to highlight the continuing challenges of land rights and civil rights for Hispanos in the American Southwest. His efforts also brought to public attention the issues of historic discrimination, denial of first-class citizenship, the right to speak Spanish, and the efforts to preserve Hispanic culture. The story of Tijerina's actions also continue to serve as a source of cultural and political pride for the people of northern New Mexico.

Land rights disputes continue to this day. A Colorado example of this issue is the decades-long dispute over land, water, and grazing rights on the Taylor Ranch in the San Luis Valley. After years of legal disputes, in 2002 the Colorado State Supreme Court ruled in the case of *Lobato v. Taylor* that the heirs of the 1844 Sangre de Cristo Land Grant, an eighty-thousand-acre land area known as La Sierra, retained their historic rights according to the original land grant provisions to the disputed land for grazing livestock, gathering wood, and water access. In 2005, more than 350 families gained access to their historic land.

This Colorado battle over land rights, while seemingly resolved in 2002, has recently ignited anew as of 2024. Another billionaire landowner has begun to construct fences limiting access to this traditional land for both valley residents and wildlife now restricted from their traditional migratory routes. The 150-year battle for recognition of and respect for the legal land rights of the heirs of the original land grants is far from over.

Water Rights

Water is the lifeblood of a community. It provides the essential sustenance for all that exists. The history of the American Southwest is written in water. It is an arid land perpetually in a state of drought, and water rights issues dominate the political and legislative landscape, for land without water is worthless.

As in so many other aspects of their life, the Treaty of Guadalupe Hidalgo radically changed Hispanos' relationship with water, especially in New Mexico and Colorado. For centuries, southwestern Hispanos utilized water under the acequia system. After the treaty, that all changed.

The acequia is a community-based water irrigation system based upon a simple idea: Water is like air; no one can own it. It is a shared resource to be used by all. It is both a practical and a philosophical approach to water management.

The Spanish introduced the acequia to the American Southwest. While Native culture also had well-developed strategies to manage water scarcity, the Spanish established the acequia system, a system they had developed over centuries in Spain.

The word *acequia* comes from the Arabic *as-saqiya*, meaning "water carrier" or "water conduit." The Moors had ruled Spain from 711 to 1492, and many aspects of their culture became central to Spanish culture, including the acequia irrigation system developed in Spain and North Africa. Spanish settlers introduced the system to the American Southwest in the 1600s.

Acequia systems rely on gravity for the natural flow of water. Mountain snowmelt flows into valleys where farmers divert and direct the

Figure 13—Acequia System of El Rancho de las Golondrinas, New Mexico. Listed on the National Register of Historic Places in the United States. Photo by Archinia.

water through a system of ditches to their fields. A community member who holds a position of leadership, the *mayordomo*, or ditch boss, regulates the shared use of the water supply. Community members regulate the use of water, and each community member has an equal voice in the decisions around water distribution and usage.

In this way, acequias are not just irrigation systems; they are also a reflection of community values and the traditions of the farmers who depend on a reliable water source during the growing season. Acequias use ancient technologies to distribute water equitably and in a sustainable manner that benefits all involved.

The treaty, however, changed this centuries-long tradition of the acequia system. With the introduction of American laws, many aspects of Spanish and Mexican laws and practices evaporated. One of these was the nature of water usage.

US water laws, especially the Law of Prior Appropriation, came to rule the issue of water rights and who gets to use water. The law had a simple rule: "First in time, first in right." The law stated that the first person to use the water in a beneficial manner, based upon first use, was the senior water rights owner, and this right is protected against later users. Beneficial use included irrigation, mining, or domestic use.

In practical terms, the senior water rights holder can use all the water they need, and junior water rights holders will have to wait in line, if they get any water at all. Senior water rights holders can make a "call on the river," which requires junior water rights holders to stop diverting water, thereby ensuring the water goes to its rightful owner. Many western states, including Colorado, New Mexico, Idaho, Wyoming, Nevada, Montana, and Utah, use the prior appropriation doctrine.

Under the senior water rights system, water is a commodity that is property that can be bought and sold. The complication of the system is that water rights are separate from land ownership, but land ownership is often the requirement for water usage.

In the Southwest, Hispanic communities face water rights challenges stemming from historical injustices over land ownership; legal complexities remaining from disputed Spanish, Mexican, and American laws; and competing claims over limited resources, leading to concerns about water access and sustainability. Competing claims over water usages create conflicts among legally entitled water users including Native tribes, Hispanic communities, and other water users.

For Southwestern Hispanos, the loss of land ownership also meant the loss of water rights usage. Even though they had been on the land for centuries before American settlers, and had ownership of the land under Spanish and Mexican land grant ownership, the consequences of the treaty stripped them of land ownership. The new landowners, the American settlers, claimed they had first use rights of the water on their newly acquired land and that under the law they were the senior water rights owners.

American laws clashed with the traditions of Spanish law. The perpetual scarcity of water created legal disputes over water rights. In the Southwest, all discussions about water end in one comment: "I'll see you in court."

Three wonderful resources can help to gain a better understanding of the historical complications surrounding water rights in Southwestern Hispanic communities. One is John Nichols's novel *The Milagro Beanfield War*. The novel also became a movie by the same title. The book and the movie tell the story of the struggle in the 1960s and 1970s by Hispanos in northern New Mexico to restore ancestral land and water rights taken from them by Anglos.

A second resource is the book *Water in the Hispanic Southwest: A Social and Legal History, 1550–1850* by Michael C. Meyer. The book explores the social and legal history of water rights in the region, particularly focusing on the period from 1550 to 1850.

A third resource is the book *Acequia Culture* by José Rivera. Its subtitle tells you all about the book: *Water, Land, and Community in the Southwest.*

A concluding reflection on these complicated issues of land ownership and water rights is given by Dr. Devon G. Peña, a local farmer, president of the Acequia Institute, and former officer with the Sangre de Cristo Acequia Association in Colorado, as quoted in *La Jicarita: An Online Magazine of Environmental Politics in New Mexico* (August 29, 2018):

> For the local acequia farmers who are land grant heirs, some of the most important rights tied to La Sierra are the oldest water rights in the state of Colorado. That mountain is our watershed and protecting the forest is vital to the survival of the oldest family farms in the state, especially in a time of climate change. It is astounding that we have a newcomer speculator who ignores legal precedent and the rights of the local people to continue sustainable use. The community has been a good

Historical Coda #7

Once while visiting an aunt of mine, she casually revealed that my grandfather, her father, was mayordomo of the local acequia system. She said he would go around on horseback informing the farmers of the days they could access the acequia water. I am always so surprised and pleased to learn lost bits of family history. This revelation rivaled the time she told me that the men in the family had all been members of the Penitente Brotherhood, the lay brotherhood providing religious services and community assistance in the isolated regions of northern New Mexico and southern Colorado. These discoveries made history not only something interesting to learn; they made it deeply personal. My own male relatives played significant historical roles in their communities.

> protector of the land grant despite abuses by an ever-shifting cast of rich men seeking a prestigious playground. We advocate for a co-management plan that focuses on creating jobs for local people to work restoring the ecosystem of La Sierra that was so badly damaged by decades of excessive logging by private land speculators with no ties to the community.[3]

Mexican Independence and the Mexican Revolution: The Creation of the Borderlands

Borderlands are an ancient crossroads. They are boundaries with lives on one side and lives on the other. Sometimes the borderlands are designed as political separations. Sometimes they are natural boundaries, insurmountable except by the most adventurous travelers. Most of all, they are boundaries separating people, lives, and cultures.

The borderland between Mexico and the United States has been all of these: a political boundary, a natural boundary, and a cultural boundary. A conflicted war, the Mexican-American War, resulted in the political boundaries of the two countries being redefined. Once the Arkansas River was the boundary between the two countries; now it is the Rio Grande River. As for cultural boundaries, some towns in America along the border appear to be Mexican towns, the immersion of language, food, and music are so similar. Border towns are always a reflection of both sides of the border.

At several moments in history, these borderlands have split apart, allowing the flow of lives and cultures to cross over. The oft-mentioned refrain "I didn't cross the border; the border crossed me" is the most direct statement about the impact of borders on the lives of those living in the changing borderlands.

Borderlands define where you can live and where you can't live. They define literally who you are. In this case, are you Mexican or American? Are you legal or illegal? Are you an immigrant, or has your family been here since before the border crossed them?

Mexican history has two seminal events that created a borderland mentality between Mexico and the United States and that continues to resonate across the centuries: the Mexican War of Independence from Spain in 1821 and the Mexican Revolution in 1910. While separated in time, both of these events created new relationships with the United States.

An enduring impact of these two events was the integration of Spanish and Mexican people and culture into the land and psyche of the United States.

With each of these two events, America had a new neighbor just across the river. History separates these two stories, but for our purposes, they are the same event with the same result for America. Mexico had an interior violent convulsion that redefined itself and its people. In both instances, Mexico began a new relationship with El Norte, the American Southwest.

The Mexican War of Independence

The Mexican War of Independence was a revolutionary war, a decade-long struggle to liberate Mexico from Spanish rule. For years, resentment about Spain's domination of ruling positions, its imposition of its own rigid version of Catholicism, and economic inequality between the sharply defined classes under Spain's rigid caste system eventually created a crisis of revolution in the country. The growing resentment among the criollo, mestizo, and Indigenous classes created the unstable conditions leading to the overthrow of Spanish rule.

In 1810, the Spanish had ruled Mexico for three hundred years. During that time, they had instituted a tribute system and land ownership system that put *peninsulares*, pure-blood Spaniards born in Spain, in the elite ruling class. *Criollos*, pure-blood Spaniards born in Mexico, were second-class citizens in their own country. Also, a system of slavery existed for Mexican Indians.

During the nineteenth century, criollo priests led the movement for Mexico's independence from Spain. They were educated members of colonial society, and they were aware of Enlightenment ideas of individual worth and freedom from autocratic governments. France's defeat of Spain in 1808 filled the criollos with the French ideals of *liberte, igualite*, and *fraternite*—freedom, equality, and fraternity. They resented peninsulares who kept them from rising in the church hierarchy. Even though they were criollos, they viewed themselves as equals to the peninsulares. They also held grievances against the church, which favored peninsulares. Finally, they were in sympathy with the plight of the Mexican Indians.

The area of Querétaro was one of the centers of the independence movement. Its conditions as a mining area and the harsh treatment of the Indian laborers in the mines contributed to the Querétaro people's aggressive stance toward independence. The leaders of the independence movement formed the Querétaro Society.

Father Miguel Hidalgo y Costilla, a criollo Catholic priest, was born in 1753 near Guanajuato. As a priest, he worked in Dolores and eventually became involved with teaching the Indians. He had mastered the Otomí Indian language of his parishioners and worked hard to improve their lives. He also was a member of the Querétaro Society and shared the belief that Mexico had a right to independence.

Father Hidalgo was an active participant in a plot to gain Mexico's independence from Spain. The plotters planned on forming an army, seizing towns, and expelling the peninsulares. The members of the Querétaro Society chose Father Hildalgo to lead the independence movement.

Their plan was discovered on September 15, 1810. Father Hidalgo, along with three other independence leaders, decided to immediately begin the fight for independence. On September 16, Father Hidalgo

Figure 14—Statue of Father Miguel Hidalgo y Costilla in Dolores, Mexico. Photograph by Adam Jones.

rang the church bells at Dolores to gather his parishioners. He called for the expulsion of the peninsulares, the independence of Mexico, and the end of the Indian tribute system. His followers went on to capture Guanajuato and other small towns, eventually marching on Mexico City.

On September 16, Father Miguel Hidalgo y Costilla gave the now-legendary *Grito de Dolores*—the Cry of Dolores: "*¡Viva Mexico! ¡Viva La Independencia!*"—Long live Mexico! Long live independence! Father Hidalgo y Costilla's Cry of Dolores urged his parishioners to take up arms against their Spanish oppressors, overthrow the existing power structures, and establish an independent Mexico. This rallying cry sparked a decade-long struggle that ultimately led to the establishment of the independent country of Mexico in 1821.

Father Hidalgo is known as the father of Mexico, and *El Diez y Seis de Septiembre* is celebrated as Mexican Independence Day. Father Hidalgo, however, did not live to see Mexico's independence, for he was captured and executed before Spain recognized Mexico's independence. Mexican independence fighters struggled eleven years to defeat royalist forces and establish an independent government.

The United States no longer had the Empire of New Spain as its closest neighbor on its southern border. It now had a new country as its neighbor, Mexico. And Mexicans had an eye on El Norte, the American Southwest.

On both sides of the border were people with Mexican heritage, Spanish language, familial connections, and a Spanish and Mexican cultural heritage. Cultures merged, collided, and shaped identities. The borderlands created a powerful blending of cultures—Spanish, Mexican, and Indigenous. It also was the beginning of cultural conflicts in this borderland, the American Southwest, that continue two hundred years later.

Another result of the Mexican War of Independence was Mexico opening up to American trade. Trade routes such as the Santa Fe Trail not only brought American goods to Mexico; it also brought Americans to this newly opened-up land.

This migration of Anglo settlers across borders, both historical and political, also resulted in the devastating genocide and displacement of Native populations. The resulting Indian Wars of the 1800s have been explored in great detail in other books, and they are not the subject of this book. An acknowledgment is necessary, however, for many of the issues that have historically affected Hispano lives also affected the lives of Native populations, often to catastrophic consequences for Native peoples.

Mexico opening its borders for trade is a clear example of unintended consequences. The new Americans on Mexican soil acted as if the land should be theirs. They were not visitors or tourists exploring a new land. They were settlers making homes, setting up businesses, and creating lives. Mexico actually invited and encouraged them to move into Texas and set up their lives. This single act of invitation was one of the instigating causes of the Mexican-American War.

The Mexican-American War was the end result of Americans crossing the borders of Mexico. The land did become the property of America. We now understand that the result was generations of people with Mexican cultural heritage living in the American Southwest. These people were the ancestors of today's Southwestern Hispanos.

The Mexican Revolution of 1910

A second historical event resulted in mass immigration into the United States by Mexican citizens. The Mexican Revolution of 1910 impacted the United States by leading to increased immigration and border tensions that continue to the present day.

As with all histories, especially those involving armed battles, the Mexican Revolution was the result of long-developing social, political, and economic tensions in Mexican society. The Mexican Revolution, beginning in 1910, was a decade-long struggle that overthrew the long-standing dictatorship of Porfirio Díaz and led to a period of significant social and political upheaval.

The violence and instability in Mexico caused Mexicans to seek refuge in the United States. El Paso, Texas, dubbed the "Mexican Ellis Island," became a major port for entry into the United States. Between 1910 and 1930, the United States census recorded a tripling of Mexican immigration from 200,000 to 600,000. During this period, many Mexicans also migrated to the United States to fill labor shortages caused by the United States' participation in World War I and quotas limiting immigration from Eastern and Southern Europe.

This use of a migrant labor force is one of the repeated patterns that has caused immigration issues to flare up continually in American history. One of the most direct examples was the use of Chinese immigrant labor to construct the Transcontinental Railroad. At the peak of construction, Chinese workers composed approximately 90 percent of the workforce that built the Central Pacific Railroad, the western leg of the Transcontinental Railroad, between Sacramento, California, and Promontory, Utah. A second example is the Bracero Program of the 1940s to 1960s.

In both of these instances, immigrant labor forces provided necessary labor support for the United States. But when Mexican laborers entered the United States workforce during World War I, the United States expected them to be temporary residents and to return to their native lands when the need for them had ended. That is not, however, how human nature works. These laborers tended to remain in the United States to set up their lives and begin their families. The complications of these historical forces have caused continuing turmoil and conflicting issues for the United States over immigration and the definition of who is an American.

These two Mexican events, the War of Independence and the Mexican Revolution, resulted in an increase in populations with Spanish and Mexican heritage in the American Southwest. While the United States and Mexico are separated by defined borders, in reality these borders are political and psychological barriers that people cross in both directions as necessary. Border control is a pressing issue worldwide, but the human impulse for migration has always been a part of human history. The creation of barriers at borderland sites will not stop the human impulse for migration in search of a better life. Borderlands exist because people create them, but they also create blended cultures that only propel the human story forward with all its conflicts and beauties.

The Bracero Labor Program

The United States has regularly sponsored special programs to meet its labor needs. One of the consequences of these programs was that they created opportunities for immigrant populations to establish roots in America.

An additional complication to this situation is the Fourteenth Amendment to the Constitution, which confers birthright citizenship to any child born in the United States. While these original immigrant laborers were foreign immigrants to the United States, their children born in America were US citizens. While this issue of birthright citizenship is presently a targeted and debated issue, it remains the law of the land enshrined in the Constitution.

This is how families, individuals, and a complete culture cross borders and become part of the fabric of a nation. People come here to work by invitation; they stay; they begin families; their children are American citizens; they become American.

The Bracero Program is an example of this historical phenomenon. The program imported Mexican laborers between the years 1942 and 1964 to work seasonally on short-term contracts in the US farm and railroad industries. Originally designed to fill labor shortages during World War II, as had been done during World War I, the Bracero Program continued after the end of World War II. Offering employment to over five million braceros, it was the largest guest worker program in US history. It was named the Bracero Program because the Spanish term *bracero* means "manual laborer."

While the program did accomplish its goals of providing America with a critically needed workforce, it had both its supporters and detractors. On the positive side, Mexican men gained legal access to a life in America that provided them with employment and wages. They also were able to send money back to support their families in Mexico.

The negative aspects of the program, however, far outnumbered its positives. Critics in Mexico decried the disruption of Mexican families

Figure 15—Mexican agricultural workers topping beets. Stockton, California, 1943. Photograph by Marjory Collins.

by having men separated from their families for extended periods. Also, they pointed out that by having millions of working men go to America, Mexico was deprived of its own necessary labor force.

American critics of the program stated that by importing such large numbers of low-wage workers, the program depressed the wages of American farmworkers. There were also issues around exploitation of farmworkers isolated in labor camps, unsanitary housing and work conditions, and substandard wage theft and discrimination in food, housing, and other aspects of their lives in America.

Another critical consequence of the program was that it actually increased illegal immigration. Workers who did go back to Mexico would illegally return to America in hopes of finding more work. Workers who did not find contract work would then illegally stay in America and take "under-the-table" work, exposing them to further discrimination and abuse. After the program ended, American growers continued to employ immigrants, legal or illegal, to do the backbreaking work of American agriculture.

The Bracero Program is now recognized as a precursor to the later work of the United Farm Workers Union under the leadership of Cesar Chavez and Dolores Huerta. The program contributed to the development of migrant networks and farmworker activism. Labor strikes for better farmworker conditions became common, and the work of the United Farm Workers Union joined the other civil rights movements of the 1960s, working for societal changes in America for those at the bottom of the American dream.

The long-term result of the Bracero Program was that it brought Mexican workers into America and was yet another instance of the successive waves of immigration populations into the United States. Once established in America, especially the American Southwest, Mexican immigrants built communities, extended their American families, and laid down generational roots with their children being American citizens. Many also developed networks north of the border that allowed them to transition away from farmwork into the urban service sector industry.

Historical Coda #8

I have my own memories of the Bracero Program. During the late 1950s and early 1960s, my father worked for the US Department of Labor. Stationed in the Kansas City regional office, he had assignments monitoring the Bracero Program in Kansas and Texas. He would be gone for long periods of time as he traveled to the various farm labor camps. Since Spanish was his first language, his ability to speak directly to farmworkers, most of whom only spoke Spanish, was immensely advantageous to his work. My most common memory was of him and my mother talking about his trips and what he observed in the camps. It often fell to him to send back to families the personal items of farmworkers who had died while working in the farm camps. Our house would have boxes of these treasured items awaiting shipment back to the grieving family in Mexico. I would look through these boxes and see the final reminders of lives that ended on American soil doing the backbreaking work of feeding America.

The United Farm Workers Movement

The Bracero Program introduced many of the factors leading to the development of the United Farm Workers Union. In 1962, Cesar Chavez, Dolores Huerta, and Gilbert Padilla founded the United Farm Workers Union (UFW). The purpose of the UFW was to advocate for the rights and welfare of farmworkers in California and throughout the Southwest. The UFW formed from the merger of the National Farm Workers Association led by Cesar Chavez, Dolores Huerta, and Gilbert Padilla and the Agricultural Workers Organizing Committee led by Larry Itliong. While there were others central to the founding of the UFW, over time Cesar Chavez and Dolores Huerta became the recognized leaders of the UFW.

Cesar Chavez admired the work of Mahatma Gandhi and his philosophy of nonviolent protest to achieve societal change. Because of this the UFW utilized principles of nonviolent protest as it campaigned for

Figure 16—Cesar Chavez speaking at the Delano UFW rally in Delano, California, June 1972. Photograph by Joel Levine.

improving farmworkers' rights. The primary issues of the UFW were improving farmworkers' wages and working conditions, as well as promoting nonviolent strategies and educating the general public about the conditions on America's agricultural farms.

Cesar Chavez grew up in Yuma, Arizona, in a farming community in the 1930s. He began working in the farm fields at age eleven and experienced the injustices, discrimination, and harsh working conditions farmworkers endured in the field firsthand.

In 1952, Chavez began to organize farmworkers to advocate for the reform of labor laws in order to provide safer working conditions and fair wages for farmworkers. His initial efforts centering on labor laws were necessary because while the 1935 National Labor Relations Act gave employees the right to join unions to collectively address labor issues, it excluded farmworkers and domestic workers, positions primarily held by minorities.

Chavez's famous rallying cry, when he and his followers were confronted with the difficulty of their goals, was *"¡Sí, se puede!"* "Yes, we

Figure 17—The flag of the United Farm Workers Union, containing the UFW eagle on a white disc on a red field.

can!" The UFW later trademarked the saying, and it has become the rallying cry for many other movements.

In 1962, Richard Chavez, Cesar Chavez's brother, created the international symbol of the UFW. The symbol is a combination of images, and its origin story is inspirational. Cesar wanted an Aztec eagle on the flag in order to show the connection the union had to migrant workers of Mexican American descent, though not all UFW workers were of Mexican American descent. After several iterations, Richard designed a flag with a red background and a white circle with a black Aztec eagle on it in the center. Richard designed the eagle with squared-off wings so union members could more easily draw it in their handmade flags. Cesar later said, "A symbol is an important thing, and that is why we chose an Aztec eagle. It gives pride. . . . When people see it they know it means dignity."

Figure 18—Dolores Huerta holding a UFW huelga (strike) sign.

Dolores Huerta, like Cesar Chavez, had an early childhood that shaped her later activism. Born into a farmworker family in New Mexico, she experienced discrimination that helped shape her social consciousness. A schoolteacher, prejudiced against Hispanics, accused Huerta of cheating because her papers were too well written. In another episode, her brother was brutally beaten by white men for wearing a zoot suit, a popular Mexican American pauchuco fashion style.

Together Cesar Chavez and Dolores Huerta founded and led a movement that inspired farmworkers nationwide to protest and advocate for themselves. At the time of the beginning of the UFW, California corporate farms exploited farmworkers by hiring low-wage workers from Native, Asian, and Mexican populations. The workers endured harsh working conditions that included exposure to deadly chemicals, inadequate food and shelter, sexual harassment, and low wages. Workers who protested were replaced by workers contracted under the previously discussed Bracero Program. When the Bracero Program ended in 1964, the work of the UFW began in organizing farmworkers for their basic rights.

The primary nonviolent strategies and tactics of the UFW were the boycott and the strike picket line. The union also built partnerships with religious organizations, student and civil rights activists, and politicians, including Martin Luther King Jr. and Robert Kennedy.

The UFW gained national attention with the Delano Grape Strike and boycott from 1965 to 1970. California grape pickers initiated a strike and boycott of California grapes. The strike and boycott eventually were successful and led to union contracts and improved working conditions for farmworkers.

In the following years, the strike and boycott strategy grew to include strikes and boycotts against lettuce and strawberry growers. These actions often led to confrontations with law enforcement representing the interests of the growers. Farm workers and strike supporters experienced beatings, jail time, and replacement by nonunion workers.

The strikes and boycotts and the national attention they brought to the work of the UFW eventually resulted in the UFW realizing success in its goals. Dolores Huerta successfully negotiated labor contracts providing farmworkers with improved lives and working conditions. The list of the UFW accomplishments is significant. It includes changed labor laws, improved working conditions, fair wages, collective bargaining agreements with large farm owners and other large farm businesses, union contracts, an end to discriminatory practices in hiring and worker treatment, and immigration reform.

Today the UFW continues its work advocating for the rights of farmworkers. It has contracts protecting thousands of farmworkers. Through a separate organization, the UFW Foundation, the UFW

Historical Coda #9

While I was living in Kansas City, I was one of the coordinators of the boycotts in support of the UFW. We spent endless hours discussing the best tactics to support the national boycotts. We focused on four boycotts: grapes, lettuce, Safeway stores, and Coors beer.

The grape and lettuce boycotts were both national boycotts. The Safeway boycott was because the stores sold nonunion grapes and lettuce. The Coors boycotts were in support of workers at the Coors brewery in Golden, Colorado, at a time when Coors was charged with its own unfair labor practices discriminating against its Hispano workforce.

The actions consisted of weekly standing in front of the Safeway stores in Kansas City distributing leaflets explaining the positions of the UFW in relation to the national boycotts. We asked people not to support Safeway and not to shop at the store. If they decided to continue to shop at Safeway, the leaflets asked them not to buy the boycotted products.

The experiences on the line in front of the stores were as varied as could be expected. While we were never directly threatened with violence, it was a regular occurrence to be yelled at as "dirty hippies," which we were neither; to be told "to go back to where you came from," even though we were all American citizens and where we came from was where we were at; and to "love it or leave it." Really nothing too unusual considering what was going on in America at the time.

Of course, there were also folks who took the leaflet and said they would read it and think about it. That was probably the best that could be hoped for at the time.

works to spread its founding mission of empowering communities and individuals to advocate for equitable labor policies and providing supportive services to farmworkers.

The legacy of the UFW, which began at the same time as the Civil Rights Movement and Chicano Movement of the 1960s, continues from that dramatic era into the present time. The issues of fair labor practices are ever-present, and the true legacy of the UFW, Cesar Chavez, and

Dolores Huerta is in the multitudes of people who keep the faith and hope that through advocacy and unified effort, Hispanos in America can make progress toward the promise of the American dream.

The Pachuco and Zoot Suit Riots

The Pachuco era of the 1940s was one of the most interesting times in the long history of Hispanos in the Southwest. It was the precursor to so many aspects of Hispano life that followed. It was the beginning of a through line that gave us the spirit of the Chicano Movement, the low-rider phenomenon, the era of *cholos* and *cholas*, *vatos* and *vato locos*, and other aspects of Chicano youth street culture. The Pachucos established the pattern of Hispano youth developing their own subculture as a form of resistance to the rigid restrictions of the dominant culture.

The term *Pachuco* refers to the Chicanos and Mexican American youth in Southern California and Texas who developed a highly personalized lifestyle involving dress, language, music, dance, nightlife, and street attitude in response to living their lives between two cultures: the culture of their Mexican parents and the culture of white America. Pachuco style was a vibrant expression of their urban Mexican American identity. Feeling rejected by both cultures, they developed their own. It was a way for young Mexican Americans to express their identity

Figure 19—West Side Dreams: Zoot Suit Pachucos, the National Chicano Dance Theater, 1979. Photograph by Daniel Salazar.

and resist assimilation into an American society that was discriminating against them and rejecting them.

The defining feature of Pachuco style was the zoot suit. A flamboyant and exaggerated fashion style, it featured high-waist pants, sharply pleated with pegged cuffs, long jackets, expressive colors, large dramatic fedora hats, often with a feather in them, and various other stylistic flourishes, such as long, side-draped pocket watch chains. In music, Pachucos favored jump blues, jazz, and swing. They also developed their own street language, caló, a mixture of Spanish and English particular to them. Caló was their own invented language for insiders only.

The zoot suit era could be considered as just another example of youth forging their own identity and path had it not been for the Zoot Suit Riots and the Sleepy Lagoon murder. These two incidents fueled the image of Pachucos as a rebellious, defiant, and dangerous gang of criminals.

The Zoot Suit Riots occurred in Los Angeles June 3–8, 1943, when US Marines and sailors attacked Mexican American youth in a bloody brawl. The servicemen, stationed in Southern California, attacked Mexican Americans identified as Pachucos and beat them, stripped them of their clothes, and burned their tattered clothes in a pile. Media coverage sensationalized the events and encouraged others to join the brawls. Witnesses to the events described thousands of soldiers and civilians marching through the streets and targeting and beating up any "zoot suiters" and Mexican American youth they could find.

Eventually military authorities, in order to quell the riots, made the city off limits to military personnel. The newspapers lauded the riots as having a cleansing effect to rid Los Angeles of miscreants and hoodlums.

The precipitating events leading to these incidents were many. The first was the influx of Mexicans and Mexican Americans over a decades-long immigration of people from Mexico to work in the California fields and farms. The second was the racist reactions of the Anglo culture to the presence of so many "foreigners" on American soil. The third was the general atmosphere of the times, as the country was in the midst of World War II. The presence of the Mexican Americans and their children generated an opinion that the foreigners were anti-American.

One particular resentment was the zoot suit itself. During a time of war rationing, including fabric required for military uses, the excessive fabric used in the zoot suit attire was determined to be unpatriotic and detrimental to the country's war efforts.

The Sleepy Lagoon murder added an additional hysteria to the times. In the morning of August 2, 1942, police found José Gallardo Díaz stabbed and dying at a reservoir known as Sleepy Lagoon. He had been involved in an altercation between two rival gangs that resulted in his death.

The media called for the arrest of "zoot suiters," who were convicted in the press before a trial was even held. The Los Angeles Police Department quickly arrested seventeen Mexican American youth and held them for trial. Despite insufficient evidence, the young men were held in jail, without bail, on charges of murder.

The trial ended on January 13, 1943. Twelve of the defendants received sentences and served time in San Quentin. The remaining defendants received lesser charges and served time in the Los Angeles jail system.

The convictions were reversed on appeal in 1944, and all those convicted were declared not guilty. The trials exposed the extent of discrimination against Mexican American youth, even in the courts of law.

The movie *Zoot Suit* by Luis Valdez and starring Edward James Olmos is an excellent resource to further understand the historical complications and consequences of these two events. The movie portrays the many challenges Pachucos faced as they tried to navigate a life

Figure 20—"Although jazz enthusiasts favored the more outlandish Zoot Suit, this young man models the drape style that was popular among Mexican Americans in Los Angeles: double-breasted jacket cut to the finger tips, in a conservative color and pattern, topped with a porkpie hat." Caption from Eduardo Obregón Pagán's book Murder at the Sleepy Lagoon.

Historical Coda #10

I grew up in a barrio of Albuquerque, New Mexico. My father's family home was in Barelas, the historical Mexican American community of Albuquerque. It is the oldest neighborhood in Albuquerque, established as a ranching settlement in the late 1600s, predating even Historic Old Town. As a young boy, I was exposed to the street life of the neighborhood. I have even seen pictures of my father and his brother Alonso cruising the streets dressed so sharply with creased pleated pants and rolled-up shirt sleeves, affecting their own version of Pachuco cool and full of youthful confidence and bravado. One day I came home with my collar turned up, as I had seen the cool guys in the neighborhood and school wearing their collars. My father took one look and commanded that I turn my collar down and never to turn it up again. He sharply said, "None of that Pachuco style in the house. No son of mine is going to be a Pachuco!"

between two cultures and presents the injustices they experienced in the Zoot Suit Riots and the Sleepy Lagoon trials. The movie is almost a documentary of the times, and it also delves into the personal struggles of Pachuco youth. It is often said that movies are a terrible way to learn about history, but this movie is an exception.

The legacy of the Pachuco era continues to influence Mexican American culture, and the zoot suit fashion has become its own cultural icon. The defiance of the Pachucos and their stance of self-definition in the face of discrimination and rejection also contributed to the spirit of the following Chicano Movement.

An interesting and unexpected side note of Pachuco history is that Cesar Chavez, cofounder of the United Farm Workers, was a Pachuco. The PBS television special *American Masters* revealed that "labor leader and civil rights activist Cesar Chavez expressed an interest in music from an early age. He grew up identifying as a Pachuco, a young Mexican-American who wore zoot suits and listened to jazz, blues and swing music." Filmmaker Luis Valdez, the celebrated Chicano director of the movie *Zoot Suit,* said in a PBS *American Masters* program describing Chavez's love of jazz and Pachuco culture, "A lot of people have no idea that the leader of the Farm Workers Union was this guy that had this urban soul inside him."

The Chicano Movement

The Chicano Movement, El Movimiento, is one of the most powerful and complicated eras of Hispano history in the Southwest. Its elements are vast, and it would take books and books to cover all of its aspects. It is a rich area of study for historians because of the fascinating number of events that occurred in such a short time, really one decade, 1965–1975.

The movement coincided with a tumultuous time in American history. Major events included the United Farm Workers movement, the Civil Rights Movement, the March on Washington and the "I Have a Dream" speech, the Vietnam War, the assassinations of national leaders, a president not seeking re-election, the hippie and youth countercultural movement, riots in the streets, the Kent State shootings, and so much more. The Chicano Movement was central and adjacent to all of these events.

In its simplest assessment, the Chicano Movement was a movement of cultural pride for Mexican Americans in the Southwest. It was a movement of social, political, and cultural resistance against discrimination and racial injustices. It was a movement seeking social justice. It was a movement of community building and empowerment. It was a movement of cultural revitalization. It was a movement of self-definition. It was a movement of education about one's lost heritage. It was a movement in creation of a homeland. It was a movement bringing into national conversation the issues of workers' rights, voting rights, education equality, police brutality, and land rights. It was a movement rejecting assimilation.

The very word *Chicano* was originally a racial slur targeting lower-class working Mexican Americans. As the Pachucos in a previous era took a racially charged term and reclaimed it as a term of racial solidarity and pride, Mexican Americans took the term *Chicano/a* and transformed it into *chicanismo*, a term of pride in one's heritage and culture. With the rise of chicanismo in the 1960s, the term *Chicano/a* also became a term to express pride in one's Indigenous heritage and to express the resistance to the assimilation implied by the term *Mexican American.*

The foundations of the Chicano Movement were laid by the defiant attitude of the Pachuco generation, in the work of the United Farm Workers Union under the direction of Cesar Chavez and Dolores Huerta, and the early Mexican American organizations created to fight discrimination, such as the League of United Latin American Citizens (LULAC).

Other events defining the Chicano Movement era were the land grant work of Reies López Tijerina in northern New Mexico and the founding of the La Raza Unida Party, a Hispanic political party, in South Texas. Another significant organization of the Chicano Movement was the Crusade for Justice in Denver, Colorado, under the leadership of Rodolfo "Corky" Gonzales.

While there is literally too much history to cover, a closer examination of several key moments in the history of the Chicano Movement will give us a deeper understanding of this momentous time in history.

Aztlán: *A Lost Homeland*

One of the most enduring myths of importance to the Chicano Movement was the story of Aztlán, the mythical homeland of the Aztec people. At the heart of the Chicano psyche was the importance of homeland, the *querencia* previously discussed. Querencia is the beloved homeland. It is a place where one feels safe, where one feels at home, where one draws strength of character.

The Chicano Movement had the rediscovery of one's Indigenous heritage as one of its most important features. The recognition and embracing of Chicano Indigineous Aztec roots empowered the myth of Aztlán.

According to ancient myth, the Aztecs originated in the northern lands of Mexico. Chicanos claimed that the American Southwest, the very land Mexico lost in the Treaty of Guadalupe Hidalgo, was the site of Aztlán, the lost homeland. This shared belief gave the Chicano Movement a mythical and even mystical origin story. Chicanos were literally fighting for their homeland, the lost homeland, the land they had lived on since the beginning. The rallying cry was "Somos Aztlán!" We are Aztlán!

The Mestizo Face

The mestizo face became a central image for the Chicano Movement. People debate its origins, and many people claim to have been its original designer. The strongest case for the originator of the mestizo face is that Emanuel Martinez of Denver, Colorado, was the Chicano artist who first drew the design.

*Figure 21—*Somos Aztlán *with Mestizo Face by Emanuel Martinez*

Figure 22—Mestizo face representing Spanish and Indigenous heritage by Al Cardenas

The face represents the racial category developed by the Spanish in their rigid racial category system of identification. Mestizos were people of mixed heritage, part Spanish and part Indigenous. The category represented children of a Spanish father and an Indigenous mother.

The face had three faces on it. On one side in profile was a fair-skinned Spanish person. On the other side, also in profile, was a dark-skinned Indigenous person. In the middle, in between the two side faces and facing forward, was at third face, a face with skin tones and blended features representing the mix of both parents' heritage.

The mestizo face was a powerful symbol of the blended heritage of Chicanos, Spanish, and Indigenous. The symbol recognized a new race of people: the Chicano.

The Crusade for Justice

Colorado was the one of sites of the beginnings of the Chicano Movement. Rodolfo "Corky" Gonzales established the Crusade for Justice in Denver, Colorado, and the work of the Crusade spread nationally. Through his work at the Crusade, Gonzales became one of the most prominent leaders of the Chicano Movement.

Figure 23—Rodolfo "Corky" Gonzales, addressing demonstrators at the Colorado State Capitol, Denver. Photograph by Juan Espinoza.

The Crusade for Justice, founded in 1966, was a community-based civil rights organization formed to fight for Chicano political, education, and employment rights. During a time of systemic racism against Mexican Americans, the Crusade's work advocating for cultural pride, self-determination, and social justice energized Chicano youth and elders to join the work of the Crusade. In addition to its work in the political arena, the crusade also was a community outreach program offering job training, a food bank, and a bilingual school.

In 1969, the Crusade hosted the First National Chicano Youth Liberation Conference. The conference, as the title describes, was the first

Figure 24—Chicano Youth Liberation Conference Announcement, published in the newspaper El Gallo, *January 1969.*

Historical Coda #11

In the spring of 1969, I was already becoming immersed in the civil rights movements of the time. These were heady times for young social activists. The Vietnam War protests, the Civil Rights protests, the hippie and youth countercultural movement, and the various boycotts of the United Farm Workers all provided a rich environment for almost daily involvement in the activist challenges of the era.

I, along with a small group of fellow activists, had been following the work of the Crusade for Justice from our outpost in Kansas City, working for the United Farm Worker boycotts. We, as so many other Chicano youth, had been energized by the poem "I Am Joaquin" by Corky Gonzales.

Reports back from the conference from friends who had attended it said that without a doubt the highlight of the conference for them was the poet Alurista. On everyone's mind was "Have you heard Alurista?" While Corky Gonzales was the recognized leader of the Crusade for Justice and the leader of the Chicano Movement, Alurista was the rock star of the conference. With the publication of Gonzalez's "I Am Joaquin" and followed by Alurista's readings at the Conference, poets attained the highest stature and respect in the Chicano Movement. Today we call it "spoken word," but back then, it was poetry!

What a great time to be young and involved in the defining issues of the time. As with so many youth movements of the era, we actually believed we could change the world.

nationwide gathering of Chicano youth for the purpose of community building and celebrating Chicano pride. The conference also presented workshops for building awareness of cultural pride and preservation, political empowerment and activism, and social justice.

An additional powerful aspect of the conference was the workshops for Chicana women, in which they articulated their own vision of their role in the Chicano Movement. Their position stated their commitment to the goals of the Chicano Movement while developing a Chicana perspective on the work of the Movement and the ideals of Chicana liberation.

At the conference, Gonzales presented the Chicano Movement's manifesto, the *Plan Espiritual de Aztlán*—the Spiritual Plan of Aztlán. The plan was a call to action for Chicanos around the issues of Chicano nationalism and self-determination for Mexican Americans in the face of racial discrimination. The plan detailed Chicano political, social, and economic goals.

The preamble of *El Plan Espiritual de Aztlán* reads as follows:

> In the spirit of a new people that is conscious not only of its proud historical heritage but also of the brutal "gringo" invasion of our territories, we, the Chicano inhabitants and civilizers of the northern land of Aztlán from whence came our forefathers, reclaiming the land of their birth and consecrating the determination of our people of the sun, declare that the call of our blood is our power, our responsibility, and our inevitable destiny.

The Poets

The Chicano Movement is primarily recognized for its work in the political arena and its commitment to social activism. It was, however, also a cultural and artistic movement. Especially important was the work of the poets in the Movement. They gave voice to people's thoughts and emotions at a time when many felt they were voiceless and unrecognized in America. Their poems gave strength and encouragement during times of resistance against discrimination and racial injustice. They also created a solidarity bond that made people feel they were not alone, but rather that they were part of an important historical moment.

Corky Gonzales

The most significant poem of the Movement was "Yo Soy Joaquín" ("I Am Joaquín"), written by Rodolfo "Corky" Gonzales. In 1967, Gonzales published in both English and Spanish an epic poem that became recognized as the defining poem of the Chicano Movement. In the poem, Gonzales recounts the dramatic history of the Chicano people and how they have endured mighty struggles to attain their cultural identity and cultural pride. The poem is literally a history following the development of the Chicano people from the earliest days of the Aztecs to the contemporary time.

The poem also details the Chicano fight for equality and recognition in America. The poem became a manifesto of the Chicano Movement, a call to action, and a celebration of Chicano history and culture. This single poem is an excellent introduction to understanding the long history of the Chicano people.

Its final lines, excerpted below, are a stirring celebration of victory over insurmountable odds:

Yo Soy Joaquin—I Am Joaquin

And now the trumpet sounds,
The music of the people stirs the
Revolution.
Like a sleeping giant it slowly
Rears its head
To the sound of
Tramping feet
Clamoring voices
Mariachi strains
Fiery tequila explosions
The smell of chile verde and
Soft brown eyes of expectation for a
Better life.
And in all the fertile farmlands,
the barren plains,
the mountain villages,
smoke-smeared cities,
we start to MOVE.
La raza!
Méjicano!
Español!
Latino!
Chicano!
Or whatever I call myself,

I look the same
I feel the same
I cry
And
Sing the same.
I am the masses of my people and
I refuse to be absorbed.
I am Joaquín.
The odds are great
But my spirit is strong,
My faith unbreakable,
My blood is pure.
I am Aztec prince and Christian Christ.
I SHALL ENDURE!
I WILL ENDURE!

—

Alurista

One of the highlights of the First National Chicano Youth Liberation Conference in Denver in the spring of 1969 was the poet Alurista. Born in Mexico but raised in San Diego, Alurista was later deemed the "Poet Laureate of Aztlán." Also a political activist, Alurista through his poetry helped popularize the idea of Aztlán and added a spiritual dimension to the concept of Aztlán, the Chicano homeland. His poetry also is a powerful combination of English and Spanish, with references to the Indigenous languages of Mexico, often presented with a challenging nontraditional poetry structure. This is a poem of his about Cesar Chavez and Corky Gonzales:

Pa' Césary Corky

what for the rush and bloody pain
what for the blooming and the rain
what for the quest and odyssey

what for the swimming and the sea, see
there b no shore or beach that anyone
can reach
and breathe, inhale, exhale, and love
all seems to ooze the stress that greed has carved in us
surely our species should be meek
before our motherearth's volcanoes
storms and huracanes
tornadoes, floods and tremors
and there we b secreting poisons for all leggeds, wingeds,
fish and even trees

what for the rush and bloody pain
we'll surely die, but then

we dig deeper in our heartmindspiritbody
and nurture glow and warmth
and light and peace and patience
and gladness and gardens
and gather all in oneness
and end the pain and bloody rush
desiring naught
expecting naught
missing naught
simply being being

we truly have no choice…though

we imagine, dream, hope, want
being all that we are we are all that is
and that is all there b

césar and corky
this b my writ to chávez y gonzález
carnales de las sonrisas grandes
de las carcajadas llenas

de murales
de cuadros, ensayos
matadors de pendejadas
terminators of guandajos and juanabees
    hermanos, jefes
your "death" is but our "birth"
    porque amasteis
        entregasteis
y hoy, como siempre,
    sois imprescindibles

—

Abelardo "Lalo" Delgado

There were two great, distinctive voices of the Civil Rights and Chicano Movements. One was Dr. Martin Luther King Jr., with his sonorous voice and preacher's rhythmic cadence lifting the spirits of a nation with his soaring rhetoric. The other was the deep, powerful, booming, room-filling voice of Lalo Delgado.

Abelardo "Lalo" Delgado was a Denver poet who wrote many impactful poems that have been anthologized in poetry collections, yet he specialized in improvisational poems. He would show up at Movement events and create a poem on the spot about the event he was attending. His poems were electrifying. They galvanized the spirit of the moment. His booming voice filled the room, and people were transfixed by both the power of his words and the power and joy in his voice.

His poem "stupid america" became his most well-known poem. It has been included in many poetry collections. While it is a short poem, its message is direct and powerful. It laments all the lost possibilities that discrimination and racial prejudice create. It is a cry for America to recognize that genius can exist in the most unexpected places. It first appeared in his poetry collection *Chicano: 25 Pieces of a Chicano Mind.*

stupid america

stupid america, see that
chicano
with a big knife
on his steady hand
he doesn't want to knife you
he wants to sit on a bench
and carve christfigures
but you won't let him.
stupid america, hear that
chicano
shouting curses on the street
he is a poet
without paper and pencil
and since he cannot write
he will explode.
stupid america, remember
that chicano
flunking math and english
he is the picasso
of your western states
but he will die
with one thousand
masterpieces
hanging
only from his mind.

—

Historical Coda #12

I went to Lalo's funeral. It was a traditional Catholic service at Our Lady of Guadalupe Church in the Mexican community of Denver. After the service, we were standing outside the church in the shade of the trees, everyone in their own silent reflection. As the coffin was being put into the hearse, the priest called out, "Goodbye, Lalo!"

A great voice of the Chicano Movement was silenced.

Figure 25—Lalo Delgado mural. Carlos Frésquez, Professor Emeritus of Art at Metropolitan State University of Denver, and eight of his students painted this mural in honor of poet, civil rights activist, and Metro professor Lalo Delgado. The painting was unveiled at the first Lalo Delgado Poetry Festival in 2008. Photo courtesy of Carlos Frésquez.

Viola Correa

Viola Correa is a Chicana poet who wrote *La Nueva Chicana*. She was a member of the Brown Berets, the Chicano community support organization, in California.

Unfortunately, she has disappeared into the fog of history making it impossible to obtain permission to reprint her poem. I encourage your own internet search for *La Nueva Chicana*. It will be worth the effort to discover her powerful words. They still speak to us today.

Figure 26—Brown Beret women march in step, 1970. Photo by Patricia Borjon-Lopez. Wikimedia Commons, public domain.

Student and Community Protests

As the Chicano Movement developed and gained momentum across the nation, especially in the Southwest, student and community protests gained strength and effectiveness. The goals of the protests were to bring attention and awareness to the issues in Chicano communities. They also served the purpose of mobilizing communities to advocate for their issues and to create community bonds.

National protests included two significant protests in Los Angeles: the East L.A. walkouts in 1968 and the National Chicano Moratorium march in 1970. During the Chicano Moratorium march, held on August 29, 1970, in Los Angeles, over 30,000 protesters demonstrated against the Vietnam War. These protests were part of the turbulent times of the 1960s and 1970s. They empowered people to address historical injustices and to build communities of solidarity with other cultural and political activists.

Hispano soldiers were overly represented in the armed forces because of unjust draft policies at the time. During the draft era, a person was exempt from the draft if they were attending college. This automatically exempted those in more privileged situations. It was often said about the Vietnam War that it was *campesinos* (poor farmers) from one country fighting *campesinos* from another country, because Vietnam had a similar privileged-class exemption rule for its own armed forces.

Violence broke out at the Chicano Moratorium demonstrations, and civil rights activist and *Los Angeles Times* reporter Ruben Salazar was killed when a tear gas canister hit him. His death was another defining event in the history of the Chicano Movement, further galvanizing the Chicano community to honor his memory by continuing the work of the Movement.

Any discussion of these protests and marches must include a description of the work of the Brown Berets. Founded in the barrios of Los Angeles in 1967, the Brown Berets were a community organization modeled in a similar manner as the Black Panthers. The Brown Berets focused on combating racism and police brutality while providing community support through demands for education, jobs, and housing equality. Their imposing stances at protests and marches as they lined up

Figure 27—Cesar Chavez flanked by two Brown Berets, speaking at a Los Angeles peace rally, May 3, 1971.

in military precision with their iconic brown berets brought a security presence to these events. The idea of the Brown Berets caught on, and chapters formed in cities across the Southwest.

The West High Walkouts in Denver, Colorado, in 1969 became a pivotal event in the Chicano Movement in Denver and served as an instructive example of all the issues around the student and community protests nationwide.

On March 20–21, 1969, students at West High School in Denver, which had a large Mexican American population, walked out of school in protest of racist comments from a teacher. Standing for an end to racist treatment in school and for better educational opportunities, they demanded the firing of the racist teacher, more bilingual classes, and the inclusion of Chicano history and literature in their classes.

Students began to walk out of classes on March 20, and the protest soon expanded in size as other students joined the walkout. The protesters walked to nearby Baker Junior High, where other students joined the march, then returned to West High School. As they returned to the school, police met them in full riot gear. An altercation broke out that resulted in police pepper-spraying the students and eventually in arrests.

The police actions have been described as a police riot. As reported by the History Colorado Center on its information page on the Chicano movement, an observer, Jim Hall, wrote in the neighborhood newspaper *West Side Recorder*: "Everything broke loose—night sticks started swinging and cops were pulling girls' hair by the handful. Nearly every cop I saw had a mindless look and was beating kids savagely."

On the next day, March 21, students from other junior high and high schools joined the protests, and eventually more than twelve hundred marched in support of the student demands. They marched to nearby Lincoln Park, where protesters and police clashed again.

Corky Gonzales and others from the Crusade for Justice assisted the students in organizing the marches and joined the marches themselves. Gonzales marched with the students as a sign of his support for their efforts and the rights of the Chicano community. Other adults from the community also joined the students in demonstration of solidarity and support.

The legacy of the West High Walkouts continues to this day. The walkouts demonstrated broad community support for actions against racism and injustice, and they highlighted the struggles and demands of the Chicano community for equality and justice. The walkout also inspired similar activism throughout the Southwest.

Los Seis de Boulder: *The Boulder Six*

The story of Los Seis de Boulder is one of the most tragic stories in the history of the Chicano Movement. Its facts are debated to this day, as the case has never been solved, and it continues to be memorialized in history.

The facts of the case are stark: On May 27, 1974, a car bomb exploded at Boulder's Chautauqua Park. Killed in the explosion were Alamosa attorney and University of Colorado (CU) Law School graduate Reyes Martinez, age twenty-six; Ignacio High School homecoming queen and CU junior Neva Romero, twenty-one; and CU double major graduate Una Jaakola, twenty-four, Martinez's girlfriend. Then, on May 29, another car bomb exploded in a Burger King parking lot in Boulder. Killed in this explosion were Florencio Granado, thirty-one, who once attended CU; former CU student Heriberto Teran, twenty-four; and Francisco Dougherty, twenty, a pre-med student from Texas. One survivor, who was outside of the car at the time, lost a leg and suffered severe burns.

The explosions and deaths traumatized the Boulder community. During this time, the cities of Boulder and Denver were communities struggling with racial tensions and protests. In Boulder and Denver, there were at least ten bombings, primarily directed at public buildings such as schools, police stations, and courthouses.

The Boulder Six were active in United Mexican American Students (UMAS), a Chicano student organization at the University of Colorado Boulder. Originally focusing on education issues, student groups such as UMAS later expanded their activities to include protests against racial injustice, police brutality, and the continuing involvement of the United States in the Vietnam War. Student groups such as UMAS also organized to address issues of institutional racism and discrimination on campuses. University officials targeted students participating in these organizations as disruptive elements on campuses because of their activities.

Investigations about the bombing never did come to a clear conclusion. Police authorities claimed that the Boulder Six were political activists and blew themselves up with poorly constructed bombs intended for further destruction in the Boulder and Denver area.

Chicano activists, aware of the government's infiltration of Chicano organizations through efforts like the controversial FBI program COINTELPRO, have always believed that the bombings were targeted actions by government operatives against identified student activists. In the face of these sharply divided theories, the fact is that the bombings have never been solved.

In recent years at the University of Colorado Boulder, theaters, art centers, and filmmakers have memorialized the lives and deaths of the Boulder Six. In 2017, filmmaker Nicole Esquibel directed the documentary *Neva Romero: Jamas Olvidados* (*Never Forgotten*). In 2014, the Denver theater company Su Teatro hosted a fortieth anniversary event commemorating the deaths of Los Seis. In 2020, the University of Colorado installed on its campus a permanent community-created sculpture designed by CU alumna Jasmine Baetz.

These art and media recognitions of Los Seis de Boulder are part of the efforts to never forget the lives of the Boulder Six. Honoring their lives in this way is part of the Chicano Movement's continuing work to address issues affecting Chicano students and communities.

El Movimento Sigue: *The Movement Continues*

The Chicano Movement was an incredible time in American history. Coinciding with so many other social, political, and cultural events, it marked a moment in history when Chicanos took control of their own destiny and through courageous leadership and community action changed their own lives by organizing and advocating for their rights as Americans.

A fitting closing motto for this section on the Chicano Movement is *El Movimento Sigue*—the Movement Continues.

Unsung Heroes: Marginalization of Hispanic Leaders

It is cliché to say that history is written by the victors, but it is true all the same. The idea of whose story gets told and who gets to tell it remains a challenge to history narratives. Recent developments in history recording and museum studies have expanded this idea to include a more diverse set of histories and a more diverse set of opinions and viewpoints on the story of the West. In order for this story to be more accurate and truthful, it has to become more inclusive of a much larger set of stories.

The traditionally accepted narrative of the settlement of the West is one of heroic settlers braving a wild, empty territory to bring civilization to the land. Today's perspective is that the West was never empty and uncivilized. It held multitudes of Native people with mature and established civilizations that had existed for thousands of years. The false story of an unpopulated and uncivilized land directly resulted in the forced removal of Native populations from their sacred homelands. From the Native perspective, a more accurate description of the settlers is that of invader.

The stories of history really are a matter of perspective. The challenge of the stories of American history is how to answer the question "Who is an American?" If the stories only give one perspective, then the history we learn is not complete.

It is more than a rhetorical question to ask, "Who gets to be an American hero?" The unwritten stories of America contain the lives of many who should be considered heroes. There are many untold stories of Hispanos who lived epic, even heroic lives in the exploration and settling of the West. Here, a presentation of five historical Hispanos will represent the many Hispanos whose stories have been forgotten, erased from history, or marginalized. These Hispanos were never recognized by history as American heroes, but they made significant contributions to the history, exploration, and development of the West. Their stories deserve to be told, for they are American heroes as much as the legendary names we learn in the study of history.

The Hispano heroes are

- El Vaquero—America's first cowboy
- Manuel Lisa—trapper, trader, and explorer—the equal to Lewis and Clark

- Mariano Medina—the founder of Loveland, Colorado, and the equal to John Frémont, Jim Bridger, and Kit Carson
- Olibama Lopez Tushar—scholar and author—a Latina pioneer and the equal to any scholar
- Teresita Sandoval—cofounder of Pueblo, Colorado, the equal to all the men

El Vaquero: *America's First Cowboy*

Figure 28—The Vaquero *by James Walker.*

> *Here was the original native-son vaquero of our United States, another of those picturesque types that mushroomed to glory, did their bit in the building of our history, and then were properly labeled and stored away in the museum cabinet of our glorious Western Americana.*
>
> —*Jo Mora,* Californios, The Saga of the Hard-Riding Vaqueros, America's First Cowboys, *published by Stoecklein Publishing, 1994, 86*

El Vaquero, the Spanish colonial cowboy, is a true American hero. He was the first cowboy to ride the open ranges and sleep under the stars. He was the first cowboy to tame the wild horses of the plains and deliver vast herds of cattle across great distances. He was the first master of the basic and eternal cowboy skills: riding and roping. He was the repository of highly practical and effective Spanish wisdom and experience in the ways of horses and cattle, developed over generations on the open plains of European Spain and New Spain in the Americas. His language gave us the words we now accept as common cowboy lingo: *rodeo*, *chaps*, *wrangler*, *lariat*, *hoosgow*, *lasso*, *mustang*, *corral*, *dally*, *buckaroo*, *bronco*, *stampede*, and *ten-gallon hat*, to name a few.

Without the Spanish Vaquero, there would be no John Wayne, no Gene Autry, no Roy Rogers, no Dale Evans, no Lone Ranger, no Annie Oakley, no Cisco Kid, no Hopalong Cassidy, no rodeos, no Stetson cowboy hat, no cowboy boots, no horses, no cattle, no trail drives, no cowboys singing around the campfire, no country western music, no Hank Williams, no Willie Nelson, no "Black Hat" modern country western singers, no Grand Ole Opry in Nashville, no "Mama, Don't Let Your Babies Grow Up to Be Cowboys," no Buffalo Bill's Wild West shows, no National Cowboy and Western Heritage Museum in Oklahoma City, no mythos of the cowboy at the heart of America's self-identity believed at home and exported worldwide—no western ranch, rodeo, and cowboy culture at all. El Vaquero is a seminal figure in the creation of western arts and culture. His story is the story of the creation of the American West.

From his humble beginnings as a Spanish mission Indian tending to the mission's cattle herds to his glory days before the legendary American trail drives, El Vaquero was the primary character in the story of the establishment of cowboy and ranching culture in the American West. His story begins with the introduction of horses and cattle to the New World by the Spanish and continues uninterrupted to his critical tutelage of American cattle men as they began to establish the great cattle industry of the nineteenth century.

The story of El Vaquero begins in 1492, when Columbus sailed the ocean blue. When the Spanish came to the New World, they brought their whole world with them. They brought their language, their cultural practices and traditions, their food, their practices of governing, and their religion.

They also brought two important animals with them: cattle and horses. As unbelievable as it seems, there was not a single head of cattle or horse in the New World when they arrived. The Spanish not only brought the animals; they also brought something even more important. They brought centuries of knowledge developed in southwestern Spain—Andalusia—of how to work with large animals in wide open spaces.

They brought the vaquero, the Spanish colonial cowboy. They brought the clothes for the work; they brought the hat for the work; they brought the tools for the work; they brought the knowledge of animal psychology; and they brought the language to describe the work. Every single aspect of rodeo, ranch, and cowboy practices came from one place and one place only: El Vaquero.

As the Anglo cowmen came into South Texas, the cradle of cowboy and ranch culture in the Southwest, they encountered El Vaquero. In a very short time, they adopted the work practices of El Vaquero, and as they say, the rest is history.

The American cowboy story is writ large with the exploits of John Wayne, Roy Rogers, and innumerable other movie and television cowboy heroes. They are the American image of the heroic cowboy. The only Hispanic cowboy hero was the Cisco Kid. It is past time for El Vaquero to take his rightful place in the pantheon of American cowboy heroes, for without him there are no American cowboy heroes.

His story is the living history of the origins and development of traditional cowboy practices in the American West. El Vaquero's clothing, tools, and way of life are a direct line identifying his traditional Spanish practices as the source of the daily activities of today's ranch worker. His stories illuminate the contrasts between the romanticized Hollywood depiction of the cowboy with the realities of the real working cowboy. With stories ranging from the tedious, dust-filled miles on the trail, to the lonely beauty of a starlit night riding herd as he sings to slumbering cattle, to the stark, death-filled panic of a stampede, El Vaquero's life is a firsthand account of what it was like to make both myth and history.

The stories of El Vaquero explain the origins of the most powerful and enduring American myth: the cowboy on his horse, riding tall in the saddle, his self-reliant, independent spirit representing all that is good in the American character. The stories of El Vaquero are the stories of America. His story is the story of the American West.

Manuel Lisa: Trapper, Trader, Explorer—The Equal to Lewis and Clark

Figure 29—Manuel Lisa

Manuel Lisa roamed and explored the Northwest Territories during the same era as did Lewis and Clark in their famous expeditions of 1804–1806. Manuel Lisa was a merchant, fur trader, explorer, and US Indian agent who led the first trading expeditions up the Missouri River and opened up the region to white men in the early nineteenth century. He dominated the fur trade from 1807 to 1920. Lisa, in the words of a true hero, told William Clark, "I go a great distance while some are considering whether they will start today or tomorrow."

A Wikipedia search reveals these life facts:

- Manuel Lisa was born in 1772 in New Orleans to a Spanish father and an American-born mother of Spanish heritage.
- In 1802, prior to the Louisiana Purchase, Lisa had obtained a trade monopoly from French officials.
- In 1807, blocked in his efforts to open trade along the Santa Fe Trail, he began explorations up the Missouri River.
- In 1807, Lisa established the trading post Fort Raymond, named after his son, later known as Fort Manuel, at the mouth of the Bighorn River in present-day Montana, the first trading post in the upper Missouri region.
- Married Mitane, a daughter of Big Elk, the principal chief of the Omaha people. Lisa also had an Anglo wife in St. Louis at the time. It was common practice for Western explorers of the time to take Native wives as part of securing alliances with Native tribes. They often had what they called "city wives" as well as "country wives."

- In 1808, he established the Missouri Fur Company in St. Louis along with several other men, one of whom was William Clark of Lewis and Clark fame.
- In 1809, Lisa built Fort Lisa near what is now Bismarck, North Dakota.
- He was appointed US Indian agent during the War of 1812.
- During the War of 1812, he helped pacify the Teton Sioux, Omaha, and Ponca Nations and keep them loyal, in wartime, to America. Lisa had a strong, excellent reputation with the tribes. The tribes perceived him as always being an honest man with them,
- In 1813, Lisa established another Fort Lisa near the area now known as Omaha, Nebraska, and became the first known settler of Nebraska.
- In all, Lisa established seven forts as trading posts in the Northwest.
- Because of his strong relationships with Omaha, Ponca, Yankton and Teton Sioux, Mandan, and Arikara tribes, he extended the development of commercial interests to the Yellowstone and Bighorn Rivers.
- In 1815–1817, Lisa hosted sixty-seven Native chiefs in St. Louis for treaty signings.

As these significant accomplishments record, Lisa, adventurous and courageous mountain man, explored all the important beaver streams in the Rocky Mountain West. He also built the first trading posts in the region and established tremendously helpful relationships with the Native tribes of the region. His Missouri Fur Company was one of the first major fur trading businesses in the era. Without a doubt, Lisa was a major figure of the early West and lived the life of a true American hero.

Figure 30—Mariano Medina

Mariano Medina: Founder of Loveland, Colorado—The Equal to John Frémont, Jim Bridger, and Kit Carson

In the annals of Western explorers, the names of John Frémont, Jim Bridger, and Kit Carson reign large. An equal to them in the explorations of the West and in his significant role in the founding of Loveland, Colorado, Mariano Medina, mountain man extraordinaire, deserves a reconsideration in the listing of American heroes. He was a trapper, trader, bounty hunter, interpreter, guide, mountain man, ranchman, businessman, and city founder.

A Wikipedia listing of his life accomplishments will document a heroic life worthy of its own dramatic tale:

- Mariano Medina was born in Taos, New Mexico, in 1812, the son of a French trapper and a Jicarilla Apache mother.
- In the 1830s, along with Charles Autobees, he ran "Taos Lightning" whiskey from Taos to the South Platte River.
- In the 1840s he was a free trapper along the Snake River.
- In 1848–1849 he was a guide, interpreter, and runner for the John Frémont Rocky Mountain Expeditions.
- In the 1850s he was trading along the Oregon Trail.
- He gained a reputation as a respected mountain man and associated with other mountain men and frontiersmen, including Jim Bridger, the Bent Brothers, and Kit Carson.
- Because of this reputation built upon Medina's vast knowledge of the wilderness, famed explorer John C. Frémont employed Medina in one of his many explorations of the West.
- In 1857, through heroic efforts, he saved the lives of Captain Randolph Marcy and his men, who had become stranded in a mountain snowstorm and were starving to death. Marcy was impressed

with Medina's skills as a guide and described him in his book *Thirty Years of Army Life on the Border* as a "peculiar specimen of the mountaineer genus who accompanied me over the mountains. . . . I found Mariano's experiences in the high northern latitudes and the ready resources which he had at hand for every emergency, of great service to me." (1866, pp. 411–412)

- In 1860, after the beaver trade died off and his years as a guide came to an end, Medina homesteaded land along the Big Thompson River in Colorado.
- On the Big Thompson River, he established a trading post and a river crossing known as Mariano's Crossing, an area that later became the city of Loveland, Colorado. Medina is recognized as the founder of Loveland.

Medina is another unsung Western hero who lived an epic hero's life only to be forgotten by history. A mighty adventurer in his youth, he later became a respected elder statesman of a disappearing American West.

Historical Coda #13

I have created living history reenactments of El Vaquero, Manuel Lisa, and Mariano Medina as part of the national Chautauqua programs. The Chautauqua programs give scholars the opportunity to present first-person portrayals of historical figures to communities for both education and entertainment. I developed programs on these three Hispanic characters in order to bring their stories into the historical narrative of America presented at these Chautauqua programs. Their lives were so epic and heroic that they deserved a wider recognition. A common sentiment I have heard expressed at these events is that after years, even decades of these programs, I was the first to present a Hispanic character. I viewed it as bringing honor to my people and sharing our stories and heroes.

Olibama Lopez Tushar: Scholar, Author, Latina Pioneer—The Equal to Any Scholar

Figure 31—Olibama Lopez Tushar

Olibama Lopez Tushar was an American scholar of Hispanic heritage. She was born in the San Luis Valley, Colorado, community of Los Rincones in 1906. Both sides of her family were founders of Colorado's first towns, schools, and churches. Her ancestors were Spanish settlers from New Mexico who later migrated to the San Luis Valley as part of the Sangre De Cristo Land Grant.

Lopez Tushar was valedictorian of her class at Belleview High School. Despite facing gender and racial discrimination throughout her life, she eventually succeeded in her dream of becoming a teacher and earning a college degree. She was one of the first Latina graduates from the University of Colorado Boulder in 1930. She later earned a master's degree from the University of Denver in 1941, being the first Latina to earn that degree from that institution. She also was one of the first Latina members of the women's business sorority Phi Alpha Kappa.

She later expanded her master's thesis on the history of the San Luis Valley into *The People of El Valle: A History of the Spanish Settlers in the San Luis Valley*, a book documenting three hundred years of Spanish settlement, culture, traditions, and genealogy in the San Luis Valley. Unable to find a publisher, she self-published the book and sold over five thousand copies. The book eventually became an accepted scholarship text on the history and genealogy of the San Luis Valley. Numerous colleges and universities have used the book in history courses, and the Colorado Centennial Commission endorsed the first edition of the book as part of Colorado's centennial celebration.

Lopez Tushar spoke six languages: Spanish, Portuguese, Italian, Latin, French, and English. The Olibama Lopez Tushar Hispanic Legacy

Historical Coda #14

I was once on an author's panel with Rudolfo Anaya, the acknowledged maestro of Chicano literature. He had written the foreword to one of my books, and I was greatly honored to share the panel presentation with him. Olibama Lopez Tushar was also on the panel.

The panel moderator began the event by inviting Rudolfo to make the opening remarks. In a moving moment of respect, courtesy, and acknowledgment of our literary debts to her, Rudolfo graciously deferred and invited Olibama to be the first to speak. His deference and respect to her were an example to all present. I was in the presence of two literary and personal heroes of mine.

Olibama and I lived in the same neighborhood. She and I had enjoyed many warm conversations about life and Chicano literature. I once was also honored to give the presentation speech for her induction into the Colorado Latino Hall of Fame.

My two daughters were young teens at the time, and I felt that they just had to meet her. So I invited myself and my daughters over to visit with her. My daughters dutifully went along with the idea because it was part of my practice of giving them "life lessons."

Olibama was so happy we came to visit and to have young girls in her house. She was so gracious and welcoming. She shared stories of her own youth in the San Luis Valley.

Olibama lived to be ninety-eight years of age. Her life encompassed the history of her people. In her last years, she welcomed the next generation of Chicana girls, my daughters, into her house and shared her spirit with them.

It is a saying that you should not meet your heroes, because the cynic once observed that even the gods have clay feet, and you might be disappointed. But if you choose the right heroes, in this instance Rudolfo Anaya and Olibama Tushar, meeting your heroes who have lived and made history large will be a life blessing.

Research Center in Denver is named after her. In 2019, she received the Legacy Award from the Latino Hall of Fame. She passed away in 2004.

Lopez Tushar is an example of the power of perseverance and strength of character in the face of gender and racial discrimination that was pervasive during her lifetime. Her deep scholarship was at the service of her love for her *querencia*, her homeland, the San Luis Valley.

Teresita Sandoval: Cofounder of Pueblo, Colorado— The Equal to All the Men

Born in 1811 in Taos, New Mexico, Sandoval was a trader, homesteader, and pioneer in nineteenth-century Colorado. Sandoval was one of the first women of European descent to live in the Colorado Arkansas Valley.

Figure 32—Teresita Sandoval, sketched by Alexander Barclay in 1853.

Her life eventually saw her moving to Fort El Pueblo, a trading post along the Arkansas River. During a time when women's roles in the West were very constrained, Sandoval was a true pioneer woman whose work and accomplishments were equal to men's. She was one of the founders of Fort El Pueblo and was central to the construction and the daily operations of the fort. She lived at the fort with her children and parents.

As a trading post, the fort was an important regional hub for the trading of goods such as furs, tools, weapons, and food. It was here that Sandoval's life included connections with other pioneers, businessmen, travelers, mountain men, notable Western frontiersmen, and Indian traders.

Sandoval later joined many other Hispanic women who saw their rights limited after the Mexican-American War. Mexican law previous to the war allowed women to inherit and purchase land and livestock, to share ownership with their husbands, to establish their own businesses, and to begin divorce proceedings. After the war ended in 1848 and the Treaty of Guadalupe Hidalgo ceded the northern lands of Mexico to the United States, the new United States laws deprived women of these rights.

A fitting memorial to the pioneer life of Teresita Sandoval is a historical marker near the El Pueblo History Museum in the city she cofounded. It reads:

> Teresita Sandoval was one of the daring souls that arrived at the Pueblo settlement in 1841. Like other women of that time, she would witness and be partner to changes in her country. She departed from her traditional life as the wife of Manuel Suazo and followed her heart and Mathew Kinkead to the Arkansas River, where her extended family endeavored to establish life at El Pueblo Trading Post (1842). Described as "pretty as a peach," Teresita captivated another Englishman, Alexander Barclay, who wrote of "TS" in his journals. From his diary a glimpse of their grand undertakings emerges as does her role and contributions. Her life affirms that women moved between cultures, strengthened family and trade alliances, exercised rights under Mexican Law and ventured north for the freedom the frontier promised.

Rising to Positions of Leadership and Influence

The centuries-long journey of Hispanos in America has resulted in the present era of individuals rising to positions of recognized leadership and influence. Rising from the era of unsung heroes, we segue to individuals who have risen to positions of leadership not only in the Hispano community but also in larger American society. While each individual's accomplishments are significant, they represent so many who have brought hope to their communities and who have strengthened their communities. Collectively, they represent a people's centuries-long journey for recognition and the generations of Hispanos who have given so much to America.

Every state of the Class of 1848 has individuals who have broken through barriers. Each state could compile its own list of Hispanos who serve as role models for succeeding generations. We have become governors, senators, congressional representatives, mayors, city council members, business leaders, educators, scientists, business leaders, sports heroes, popular music icons, and significant artists.

By example, they are the Moseses leading Hispanos to the Promised Land, a land of equal opportunity and access to the American dream. The journey has been long, the sacrifices many. But as Dr. Martin Luther King Jr. stated so eloquently, the Promised Land is within sight: a land of full and equal rights and recognition of the strength and beauty of Hispanic people in America.

Our historical leaders are a pantheon of individuals who answered the call of history to improve the lives of their people. Three dominant historical leaders are Cesar Chavez, Dolores Huerta, and Rodolfo "Corky" Gonzales. These three are representative of the many who have stepped up and become leaders. We have had the benefit of so many leaders rising up to positions of power and influence that they have created a map for the way forward.

As we enter America's 250th year, the dream for Hispanos of an equal share of the American dream has been achieved by many, but is beyond reach for many others. The motto of the Chicano Movement still rings true: El Movimento Sigue: the Movement continues.

The Continuing Revitalization of Hispanic Culture

As we come to the end of this chapter of the book, its title, "We've Been Here a Long Time . . . How Did We Get to Now?" is a challenge to make sense of and understand the epic and dramatic history of the Hispanic people of the American Southwest. We have covered four hundred years of Southwestern Hispano history. We have explored the journey of a people who have been here longer than America has been here.

We have learned the facts of history: the dates, names, and events that define historical eras. We have explored the issues of cultural pride and cultural retention. We have identified a culture that has contributed to the multicultural fabric of the United States, enriching its diversity.

The historical roots of the Hispanic Southwest continue to influence the region's culture, its bilingual essence, its bicultural spirit, its immigration patterns, its artistic expressions, its festivals and celebrations, its religious practices, and its shared heritage with Mexican, Hispanic, and Indigenous communities.

The story has also told of the struggles to maintain cultural integrity and identity while facing the challenges of assimilation into the greater fabric of American culture. Historical patterns over time have shown that stereotypes, discrimination, hostile immigration policies, harsh border policies, language resentment, and deportation threats are all challenges to the preservation and continuation of a Hispanic culture that has existed for centuries.

While traditional Hispanic culture has a strong legacy in families and communities, the negative aspects of urban life have placed a litany of ills upon Hispanic culture that is lamented by parents and educators alike. Even a cursory survey of these ills reveals a culture under stress: the breakup of the extended family, the weakening of the church as a centering spiritual force in communities, the crisis in education, the loss of Spanish as a primary language, the xenophobia of forces devaluing Hispanic culture's contributions to American society, the troubling questions about race and culture in American society, the ills of social media and toxic internet culture, the brutality of forced immigration deportations, and, lamentably, the loss of cultural traditions among Hispanic youth today. Often it appears as if Hispanic culture is at its greatest crisis just as the Hispanic community has become the largest American minority group and its language is the second-most-spoken language in America.

Even with the stark realization that Hispanic culture is threatened from both external and internal forces, there are positive signs of the culture's vibrancy and perseverance, of its continuing revitalization. One reassuring aspect of Hispanic culture is that, in spite of its present struggles, Hispanic culture is a centuries-old presence in America. Its roots are old and deep. Its traditions are strong because they developed over centuries and through generations. Its cultural practices remain within the experiences of the family.

Another positive development is the deliberate effort communities throughout the Southwest are making to reestablish traditional practices. Communities, families, and individuals are searching for ways to maintain a historical cultural heritage in the environment of twenty first-century America. Their efforts are not only to preserve cultural traditions, but to create them anew with new meaning in a modern cultural context.

A third sign of the culture's enduring spirit is the development of curriculum in schools that is more culturally sensitive and inclusive of diverse American experiences. In school, students can learn about cultural traditions in classroom activities, and this learning can help reinforce and extend family experiences.

Churches, community centers, and art centers are leading the way in sponsoring culturally based activities, both religious and artistic, as a strategy to strengthen and support individuals, families, and communities. Visual, performing, and literary artists are building upon the works of the past to give new voices to their cultural heritage. And schools are realizing the value of recognizing the beauty, wisdom, and contributions of diverse student populations.

Like a story unfolding through time, Hispanic culture endures, growing and changing as each new generation makes its own contributions. The story begins in the daily living experiences of the family, continues out to the shared life of a community, and returns confirmed and strengthened to the family and individual. Culture and tradition are a never-ending story. The childhood memories of one adult are part of a mosaic of shared memories and family practices, the whole of which forms the culture of a people.

I hold a deep belief that Hispanic culture has great contributions to make to American society. I also hope that the story about the Hispanic Southwest will help people of all cultures recognize part of themselves in the practices of the Hispanic culture and thereby recognize that we are all part of a greater spirit, the human culture we all share.

CHAPTER 4

CULTURAL TRADITIONS

This Is Us: Who We Are in Our Hearts and Souls

A cada tierra, su uso.
Every land has its own customs.

The Spanish sayings before each section of this chapter are *dichos*, folk proverbs. Hispanic culture is especially rich in dichos as part of its oral traditions. There are dichos for almost every possible situation. The dichos open each section as a reflective bit of folk poetry and wisdom.

Hispanic culture is a profound living culture with traditions of folklore given to us by our ancestors. It is a culture of rich traditions, vibrant celebrations, and a deep sense of family and community heritage.

Folklore is a vast experience in people's lives, and a review of its many facets will present its profound penetration into the mythos of the Hispanic Southwest, timeless in its historic appeal.

As we begin to explore the folklore and traditions of the Hispanic Southwest, our main questions are the inquiries of the scholar, the historian, and the folklorist:

- Why does this folklore exist?
- Who are the people who live this folklore?
- What are the origins of the folklore?
- Why is this folklore important?
- What does the folklore look like?
- Do you have to forfeit your culture, traditions, and language to assimilate and succeed in Anglo culture?

A mere mention of the Hispanic Southwest conjures a multitude of images: its arid, dry desert landscapes; its vast, desolate vistas; a large, solitary saguaro cactus; towering buttes in a John Ford movie; the magnificent, breathtaking Grand Canyon. These images give the Southwest its character and provide a landscape that has for centuries been the home of Hispanic life and family existence.

Another set of images will begin to ignite the imagination of Southwestern Hispanic life through the centuries: Spanish explorers searching for God, Glory, and Gold; Hispanic farmers diligently cultivating their crops; Hispanic artisans creating enduring images of devotional art; lowriders slowly cruising and hopping in bedazzling artistic automobiles; vaqueros busting broncos and roping cattle on the open range; a farmer enchanting a ring of children around the coal stove and the winter's fire in the family farmhouse, telling them stories from his own childhood; a mariachi band entertaining a crowd at a community celebration; Hispanic artisans selling their wares at a Spanish market. The list of images is almost unending, but it give a glimpse into the diversity and range of cultural expression in the Hispanic Southwest.

Folklore exists in any particular region because it is important in people's lives. Wherever they settle, they use their cultural practices to give meaning to their daily activities, to enrich their spiritual lives, and to celebrate who they are.

Whether you call it arts and crafts or folklore, the objects and activities of cultural life are clear representations of a people's spiritual and community life. An interesting fact of early folklore is that its creators would never call themselves artists. True to the rural roots of Hispanic life in the Southwest, they were farmers, coal miners, sheepherders, storekeepers, vaqueros, and family members. A folk proverb of these early times states that they had no arts or artists because everything they did was artistic.

Only later, as Hispanic life transitioned into an urban experience, did the creation of the tourist industry, the development of folk art as a collectable market, and the emergence of museum collections result in specific individuals becoming identified as cultural artists. These modern cultural artists have, however, dedicated themselves to re-creating important cultural rituals and keeping traditional knowledge alive. They also serve to help families and communities preserve their cultural practices, thereby sustaining the spiritual connections families and communities have with each other.

The Hispanic Southwest is home to many of the richest cultural traditions in America. These traditions have sustained generations of families and individuals as they search for meaning in a demanding and ever-changing America. For them, folklore is a deeply personal experience. Their cultural activities keep alive the memory, heritage, and values of their ancestors. At the same time, these cultural traditions give a heart and soul to modern life that so desperately strives to find meaning in its daily lives.

Now let us examine the beginning of Hispanic culture in the American Southwest. When the Spanish explorers arrived in the New World, they brought many aspects of their culture with them. They imported their whole culture: their religion, their government and laws, their food, their animals (especially cattle and horses, which were nonexistent in the New World at the time), and especially, for our discussion, their folklore and cultural traditions. Original settlers in the Southwest, Hispanic people never lost their Spanish cultural heritage, and they nurture their folklore to preserve this heritage.

Most importantly, the Spanish brought their concept of *la familia*, the family, to the New World. The family was the most important part of Spanish life. A large, extended family gave support and guidance to every member. The importance of family life is one of the defining characteristics of Hispanic life.

La familia, the family, is the heart of it. It is sustained by our faith and family traditions. La familia is our sustaining force because the heart of the family gives strength to the individual.

The oft-quoted aphorism "It takes a village to raise a child" is especially realized in Hispanic culture. With the family being the most important aspect of Hispanic life, extended Hispanic families serve as the "village," providing a supporting and nurturing environment for both children and adults. Before the urbanization of Hispanic life in this century, rural families lived close to each other, sharing the work and resources of the family farm. Even with the urbanization of Hispanic culture, families often live in the same neighborhood, thus facilitating regular contact between family members.

A unique system in Hispanic culture that further enhances the extended family and its role in nurturing and raising children within the culture is the system of *compadrazgo* (compaternity). Parents select a child's *padrinos* (godparents) at the time of a child's baptism or confirmation. The padrino can be either a family member or a nonfamily member. The padrinos become godparents to the child and *compadres*, or co-parents, to the parent. This special honor gives parents lifelong compadres and gives children lifelong padrinos. The padrinos become second parents to the child, and the parents have another set of adults to assist with the raising of their children. Compadrazgo contributes to the extended family by extending and strengthening the family. And even though family members could be padrinos, the frequent choosing of nonfamily members results in whole communities being related by marriage, blood, or the system of compadrazgo. With la familia being the central aspect of Hispanic culture, the system of compadrazgo strengthens the culture by creating communities with close family ties, common values, and shared responsibilities.

The greatest benefit of the Hispanic extended family experience is in the intergenerational exchanges that are possible with relatives living either in the home or nearby. In the extended family, children know their grandparents. Aunts and uncles know their nieces and nephews, and cousins are each other's playmates. Within the experiences of the extended family, parents find support from other family members for the responsibilities of raising their children. Each family member has a life centered in la familia. Each gives to la familia, and in an elegant reciprocity, la familia nourishes each member.

That the family is at the center of Hispanic culture is a truth all Hispanics know in their heart. Culture is created and continued in the crucible of the family. Generation after generation has passed on the wisdom of the elders, the deep appreciation of spirituality, the love of the land, and the lore learned from years of experience. Culture flourishes because families have continued to practice the traditions of previous generations.

A people's celebrations are representations of their spirituality, their artistry, and their communal rituals. In the beginning, these celebrations were for the interior life of families and communities. Today, many of these celebrations have moved out of the life of the family and have transitioned into larger public and community events. Many of them are staged for the purpose of tourism and economics. The challenge of these modern celebrations is to somehow bridge the worlds of traditional ritual and modern commerce in order to give its participants and witnesses the transcendent experience at the heart of all communal ceremonies.

Historical Coda #15

As a child, I grew up in an extended Hispanic family, enhanced by the system of compadrazgo, in New Mexico. My daily life was filled with the activities of childhood—school, play, and family. My own family of parents, two sisters, and a brother was the center of my world. My extended family of grandparents, aunts, uncles, cousins, compadres, and padrinos was also at the center of my childhood experiences.

My most common childhood memories involve family gatherings—large family gatherings. Birthday parties, weddings, baptisms, Easter, Christmas, church, picnics, and, yes, even funerals. My playmates were not my friends from school but rather my cousins. Two of my cousins, Frankie and Danny, and myself were the Three Musketeers, inseparable, one for all and all for one.

My childhood memories are filled with details of this extended family. Even the passing of the years and the dimming of adult memory have not faded these early memories. A simple recitation of a few of these memories reveals a rich life centered in family experience and strong in folklore heritage.

- I remember going to my grandmother's farm and eating a delicious white homemade goat cheese with heavy, sweet molasses poured on it.
- I remember stories of my father singing an old, joyous Spanish song, "Amapola," at a wedding.
- I can taste the fresh, warm, just-off-the-griddle, jam-covered tortillas my aunt made especially for me whenever I came for a visit.
- I can feel the small, hard beans under my little fingers as I sort them from one pile to another, carefully completing my childhood job of cleaning the beans by separating them from the rocks before they are cooked.
- I can see my mother kneeling and praying, eyes closed, hands folded, before the altar to la Virgen she kept in her bedroom.
- I can hear my mother sternly admonishing me not to turn around in church or I'd turn to stone.
- I can hear the rustle of my sister's fancy, lacy white First Communion dress.
- I can see my parents, aunts, and uncles sitting around a large, round kitchen table at my grandfather's house, sharing a pot of posole with red chile, telling cuentos, laughing and reminiscing about the good old days, their own childhood.
- I can hear the hushed, droning, muffled voices of my aunts saying the rosary at a velorio, the wake before a funeral.
- I can feel my parents' warm and firm hands on my head as they gave me their blessing when I left home.
- I remember the family gathering at my sister's house to make tamales for the holiday season.
- I remember my mother using remedios, traditional natural cures, when I was sick.
- I remember the family gathering to say the rosary at a funeral memorial.
- I remember the annual slaughter of the pigs, the matanza, with my grandfather and my uncles and my dad all taking part in the ancient ritual.
- I remember my mother making capirotoda, traditional New Mexican bread pudding, for a special dessert.

Figure 33—The matanza at the Martinez family farm outside of Springer, New Mexico. The matanza is the ancient ritual slaughter of pigs to provide meat for the family. I am the little boy with the men of the family: my dad, my uncles, and my grandfather.

- I remember my mother encouraging me to go to the seminary to study to be a priest because a Spanish family that has a priest in it has a special blessing from God.
- I remember my sister and I buying and roasting the bushels of chile to put up this year's supply of fresh chile.

These memories and many more reveal a truth about my family. My own family was a source of folklore. This realization that my own family was a living example of Hispanic cultural practices changed the way I viewed my childhood. As an adult, I now look back on my childhood memories and realize that living in an extended Hispanic family meant much more than just having a lot of relatives and seeing them often.

My own memories confirm that my family itself was a repository of generations of Hispanic culture. Without consciously determining their purposes, my grandparents, parents, aunts, and uncles had passed on the traditions of Hispanic culture to the following generation simply by continuing the family practices as they had experienced them in their own childhood.

I came to appreciate that all my cultural awareness about myself as a Hispanic person originated with my family. I realize that I am a member of the ever-growing Hispanic community in America and that we are the repository of Hispanic cultural traditions and practices. Each and every family passes on its culture to their own children.

This Is Us

The following sections are the primary cultural practices that give us our cultural identity. They identify us to ourselves, providing cultural solidarity and pride. They also give us insights into the outside world. These cultural practices are available to everyone and anyone. Many of them have become shared community experiences and celebrations.

The cultural practices covered are as follows:

- This Is Us: Spanish—We Speak Two Languages
- This Is Us: *La Familia*—Family Celebrations
- This Is Us: *Nuestras Raíces*—Family Genealogy
- This Is Us: *La Iglesia*—Religious Celebrations
- This Is Us: *Remedios*—The Healing Arts
- This Is Us: *Las Artes*—The Arts
- This Is Us: *La Cocina y la Comida*—Traditional and Celebratory Foods.
- This Is Us: *Cinco de Mayo*—A Redefined Cultural Celebration

Spanish: We Speak Two Languages

Quien sabe dos lenguas vale por dos.
He who knows two languages is worth two persons.
Recommends knowing more than one language.

Southwestern America is a dual-language country. While English is the dominant language, of course, Spanish is ever-present throughout the region. In addition to Hispanos who have lived in the region for generations and have retained their Spanish language, the language is continually reinforced by Mexican immigrants.

The president of the United States has recently issued a directive to make English the official language of the country. This directive is in response to the realization that many languages are spoken in the country, with Spanish being the second-most-spoken language after English.

Recent data states that there are 41 million Spanish speakers in the country who speak Spanish as their first language. There also are almost 12 million bilingual speakers of Spanish. Data also states that Hispanics are the largest minority population in the country. The fact of these statistics is that Spanish will continue to be an active and prevalent language in the country.

The erasure of one's language is equated with the loss of one's culture. The United States has a long history of its attempts at cultural erasure of targeted groups. The most direct example is the removal of Native children from their families and the forced placement of these children in government schools far away from their families. At these schools, children were punished for speaking their Native languages in an effort to eradicate the Native languages. Native activists have long recognized the tragic effect this had on their culture.

Spanish-speaking Hispanos are very aware of this effort to diminish their language, and they resist this movement in recognition of its end result of cultural erasure. Cultural activists and artists have led the efforts to ensure that Spanish remains a central aspect of Hispanic culture.

Su Teatro theater company in Denver, Colorado, produced a play titled *La Carpa Aztlán Presents: I Don't Speak English Only*. Presented in the style of the Mexican vaudeville tent (carpa) show tradition with minimal props and a satirical tone, the play directly tackles the sensitive social issue of speaking Spanish in an English-dominant America.

The play begins by relating that, in 1988, the Colorado government passed an amendment to the Colorado Constitution making English the official language of the state. This, for the state of Colorado, meant that in order for their government to communicate legally, it must be done through English, and no one had the right to demand government-provided services in any other language. It also severely limited bilingual education programs. This law and its consequences are then explored in the action of the play and its effect on its characters' lives.

The fact of this law existing in Colorado is contradicted by the fact that in 1876, when Colorado became a state, the state constitution was written in three languages because the framers of the constitution believed it was important that the people in the three most common language groups at the time—English, Spanish, and German—be able to read it.

Spring forward 150 years, and it is common to see the state's institutions offer their services in both English and Spanish. It is easy to devise a list of how deeply penetrated Spanish is in America's daily life throughout the Hispanic Southwest. One common example is that museums throughout the Southwest have display signs in both English and Spanish. In addition, product labels are in dual languages, and it is common for television ads to be in Spanish. Business advertisements of "Se Habla Español" or "We Speak Spanish" to inform customers that staff can communicate in Spanish are common throughout the Southwest.

Figure 34—Ranger sitting with a sign at the visitor center, Joshua Tree National Park, Photo by Robert Zuniga, NPS.

Also, despite the official English language designation, southwestern states are committed to language access for individuals with limited English proficiency, ensuring meaningful access to services in state courts. You can pass a law, but its application and enforcement are very nuanced and variable in daily life.

As for individuals, there are three categories of Spanish speakers. One is the native speaker, for whom Spanish is a first language and also the language of the home. This person very often also speaks English. The second category is the person who speaks English as a first language but is also fluent in Spanish, as referred to in the title of Su Teatro's play, *I Don't Speak English Only*. The third category is the Hispanic person who, while familiar with the Spanish language, is not conversationally fluent in Spanish.

The third category has two interesting aspects. One is that older Hispanics who do not speak Spanish usually never learned it because their parents made a deliberate decision not to speak Spanish at home. Having experienced racism in their own lives over speaking Spanish at school or in public, they made a choice that their children would be "American" and only speak English. Another is the common cultural phenomenon among all immigrant groups that the second and third generations lose the original family language.

Of critical importance is this question: If you lose your traditional language, do you lose your culture? This is almost a rhetorical question because the answers are so complicated. It is true that at one time all Hispanos in the American Southwest spoke Spanish as their only language. The cultural traditions they practiced were all spoken in Spanish. Over time, the dominating presence of English came to the cultural practices. Does this fact invalidate the cultural traditions? Do the cultural traditions have no value if the practitioners speak only English? Is speaking Spanish a cultural requirement to be a true Hispanic? Or do the traditions still have value and relevance in the lives of Hispanos in the Southwest even though English is now the dominant language?

This book is an example of this situation. Even though it is written in English and intended for English-reading audiences, it is impossible to write about Hispanic culture without the Spanish language. For example, every section of this chapter begins with a Spanish dicho. Also, since almost all of these cultural traditions originated in Spanish and

Spanish colonial culture in Mexico, the native language of all these traditions is Spanish. The passing of the years, however, has seen English also become the language of these traditions.

The real truth is that Hispanic culture in the American Southwest is a dual-language culture. This is part of its history and tradition. It is also what gives it its beauty and resonance in the larger culture. Laws or no laws, Spanish remains at the heart of Hispanic culture.

Those who do speak Spanish are the carriers of Hispanic culture in its oldest forms. Those Hispanos who do not speak Spanish are also carriers and repositories of the century's old cultural traditions of the Hispanic Southwest. What is most important is that people carry the traditions in their heart and soul and are dedicated to keeping the traditions alive in their own generation, then pass it on to the following generation. That is how culture remains a living presence in the lives of its people, no matter what language they are speaking.

La Familia: Family Celebrations

Contra amor y fortuna no hay defensa alguna.
There is no defense against love and fortune.
Love will find a way.

La familia, the family, is at the center of Hispanic life. Even as many of the old traditions are changing or fading away, the family continues to be of central importance to Hispanics. The family provides a home for each member and gives meaning to each member's life. Hispanic people always have the family as their central reference point and value.

The most important work a family does is emotionally support its adults and nurture and raise its children. Additionally, it is within the family that people experience cultural traditions and pass on cultural practices from one generation to the next. Each time a family gathers for a family celebration, its culture is reinforced and continued.

The great strength of the Hispanic family is that it is more than the nuclear unit of parents and children. Uncles, aunts, grandparents, cousins, godparents, and in-laws all form a large extended family for each other. Even deceased family members and their memory remain a positive presence in the family. Within this extended and intergenerational family, people share the experiences of their lives.

The study of family genealogy, *nuestras raíces* (our roots), is a renewed activity in Hispanic families and communities. For these families and communities, the researching of heritage and lineage is a source of cultural pride and knowledge.

In addition, three key Hispanic cultural events especially reveal the importance of family in the celebration of life. These experiences are the coming of age celebration *quinceañera*, the wedding ceremony of *la entriega de novios,* and the memorial of *el Día de los Muertos.*

The following discussions of these family cultural traditions are drawn from traditional practices. While they appear to represent the accepted standard for the traditions, they are meant only to illustrate the major and common aspects of the tradition. There are as many variations of these practices as there are families. As with any family event, every family adapts the celebration to its own needs, available resources, family history, and preferences.

One of the hallmarks of true folklore is the existence of these variations, because they indicate that the cultural practices are alive within the traditions of family life. The history of folklore is marked by the evolution and adaptation of cultural practices to fit the changing needs of families and individuals.

Nuestras Raíces: *Family Genealogy*

Hispanic educators, scholars, researchers, and community leaders founded the Genealogy Society of Hispanic America (GSHA) in 1989. Its mission statement says that the purpose of the GSHA is to promote Hispanic genealogical research, thereby expanding awareness and knowledge of Hispanic culture and Hispanic historical contributions. As a national organization with local chapters spread throughout the Southwest, GSHA works with libraries, schools, museums, and historical associations to provide support to institutions and individuals requiring assistance with genealogical research.

GSHA sponsors an annual convention, a speaker's bureau, and an active query service. Its quarterly journal, *Nuestras Raíces,* contains a wide diversity of articles for both the beginning and the professional genealogist: scholarly research, personal heritage stories, how-to-begin guides, and numerous other topics of historical and cultural general interest. The journal supports the idea that genealogical research is more than just constructing lineage charts. Its articles introduce the genealogist to the greater awareness of cultural history as an important part of any genealogical research, discovery, and knowledge.

GSHA is an invaluable aid to anyone wanting to begin a genealogical study and to introduce the study of Hispanic heritage and lineage to families, children, and communities. Its web page address is https://www.gshaa.org.

While genealogical research is rewarding for adults with a growing awareness of ancestry and a need for a "roots" journey, it is especially important for families striving to establish cultural awareness and pride in children. The knowledge and appreciation of one's ancestors has long been a basic tenet of traditional cultures. As today's families struggle with the stresses of modern life, children need more than ever the grounding security of a strong family. The shared discovery of a family's heritage and lineage is an extremely positive strategy for enhancing family and individual knowledge and pride. In addition, genealogical research is an intergenerational family activity that can be shared by both adults and children.

There are many resources for the beginning genealogist. Many cities have genealogical societies that can offer support and information. Local libraries also have a genealogy section, which is always a good place to start. Below are several helpful reference books available at libraries:

- *Spanish and Mexican Records of the American Southwest: A Bibliographical Guide to Archive and Manuscript Sources* by Henry Beers. A survey of records available for Arizona, California, New Mexico, and Texas.
- *The Source: A Guidebook of American Genealogy*, edited by Arlene Eakle and Johni Cerny. An excellent introduction to genealogical research tools, with a chapter on research in the Spanish and Mexican Southwest.

- *Tracing Your Hispanic Heritage* by George R. Ryskamp. Discusses techniques and principles of research and specific types of records found in Hispanic research.
- *Ethnic Genealogy: A Research Guide*, edited by Jessie Carney Smith. Includes a chapter on Hispanic genealogy.
- *Romance of Spanish Surnames* by Charles R. Maduell. Gives the meaning and geographic origin of approximately 1,500 common Spanish surnames. Worth the effort to find.
- *A Dictionary of Surnames* by Partick Hanks and Flavia Hodges. The title says it all. An interesting place to look up the origin and meaning of your family name.
- *Origins of New Mexico Families: A Genealogy of the Spanish Colonial Period* by Fray Angélico Chávez. The classic genealogical study of original New Mexico families in the seventeenth and eighteenth centuries.
- *V. & H. V. Rolland's Illustrations to the Armorial Général* by J. B. Rietstap. The best place to look up your family crest.

The Southern California Branch of the Genealogical Society of Hispanic America, https://www.gsha-sc.org, is another site for excellent information on Hispanic genealogical research.

Happy hunting!

Figure 35—Vigil family crest from Asturias, Spain, carved by Vigil family Santero, my uncle Pat Vigil.

Coming of Age: Quinceañera

Many cultures have a coming-of-age ceremony to mark the passage from adolescence to adulthood and to initiate the adolescent into the adult world. This rite of passage is an important part of the structure of a society, for it establishes membership in the adult society. It also is important because it conveys to the adolescent the responsibilities of adulthood. These celebrations also signal to all witnesses that the culture will continue as one generation joins another in keeping the traditions alive.

Cultures throughout the world have various rites of passage. In the Jewish culture, it is the bar mitzvah and bat mitzvah. In the Navajo culture, it is the kinaalda. In American Anglo culture, it is the debutante ball. In Hispanic culture, it is the quinceañera, the celebration of a young girl's fifteenth birthday. The name *quinceañera* is a combination of two Spanish words, *quince* for fifteen, and *años* for birthday.

The quinceañera is an affirmation of religious faith, and it signifies the entrance of a young woman into adulthood in society and the church.

The quinceañera has strong roots in both Mexican culture and in Southwestern Hispanic culture. It is common to find both Mexican and Mexican American families celebrating the quinceañera.

The preparations for a traditional quinceañera often take months. The planning can be as involved as a formal wedding, and the celebration itself can be as expensive as a wedding. In older, more traditional times, the girl's parents determined many of the decisions concerning the quinceañera, but in modern practices, the girl has more say in the decisions. Typical decisions involve the buying or making of the fancy dress to be worn, the date of the celebration, the guest list, the banquet menu, the arrangements for the mass, and the members of the attendant court. The extended family is especially important in these decisions, for they often are responsible for various aspects of the celebration and help with the expense.

The celebration of the quinceañera consists of two parts. The first is the church ceremony. During the church ceremony, the girl is escorted by a court of honor. The court consists of fourteen *damas*, young women, each one representing a year in the honoree's life. Fourteen *chambelánes*, young men, escort the damas. The honoree herself represents the fifteenth year and is escorted by the *chambelán de honor*.

The church mass is a continuation of the religious events the girl has previously experienced. The mass serves as a rededication to the religious faith expressed in the girl's baptism, Holy Communion, and confirmation. The mass also is the girl's rededication to the spiritual aspects of her life. Often the mass includes a sermon stressing the values of family and the religious life and asking for the blessing of the girl's patron saint. The priest instructs the young woman to seek positive role models, noting that the Blessed Virgin Mother is an excellent role model for religious women.

After the mass, the quinceañera moves to its second part, the fiesta! Either after the mass or later in the evening, the family hosts a reception in honor of the young woman. The reception begins with the introduction of the parents and the honoree, as well as members of her family. In this manner, the quinceañera is the introduction of the young woman to society. The first dance is a waltz in which the young woman dances with her father. Next she dances with her chambelán de honor. Then the celebration continues with toasts, food, music, and more dancing.

The quinceañera can vary from an event as simple and modest as the repeating of one's baptism vows to a celebration rivaling the grandest formal wedding. The young woman's padrinos often help the parents with the expenses and the arrangements of the quinceañera. In some quinceañeras, the padrinos each provide one element of the event, such as the cake, flowers, and so on.

The heart of the celebration is the rite of passage of a young woman into the adult world of the church and society. One often-performed quinceañera ritual is for the young woman to throw a doll into a crowd of young girls, symbolizing her departure from childhood.

The quinceañera serves to confirm the importance of the family and the culture that sustain the family. Its final message is the affirmation of the adult role the young woman is to play in her family, the church, and society.

Marriage: La Boda y La Entriega

De amor y amor, sólo amor.
From love comes only more love.
La vida de los casados los ángeles la desean.
The angels envy the lives of married people.

The traditional Hispanic courtship and wedding consist of several clearly defined cultural practices. These traditions serve as the anchors of this most important rite of passage as young people leave home to begin families of their own. The traditions of courtship and the wedding ceremony ensure that the individual marries with respect and integrity within the community.

The practices of the marriage rite of passage also serve to confirm the cultural values of the community. With their message that marriage is a sacred sacrament, these traditions contribute to the strength and importance of the family, the center of Hispanic culture.

In the "olden days," marriages followed these traditional practices strictly. Courtship was a very closely chaperoned experience. Often, young women had little say in the choice of their husband. Families guarded their young women carefully, as a courtship outside the accepted cultural practices would bring shame upon the young woman, and thus also the family. Parents and the extended family had clear roles and responsibilities in courtship and wedding activities. Of most importance was that the courtship and wedding be honorable in the eyes of the church and the community.

Today, as with all modern cultural practices, the courtship and wedding ceremony are as varied as families themselves. Also, modern life has greatly freed young women from the strict control of their families. In addition, modern culture has influenced the Hispanic wedding ceremony, sometimes in ways as simple as the bride wearing "something borrowed, something blue," as well as the wedding activities of the bridal shower, the bachelor party, and the rehearsal dinner. The constant influence of Mexican culture also continues to be a part of evolving cultural practices in the Southwest. Traditional Hispanic families, however, still practice many of the "old ways." The honor of the young woman and young man are still of central importance. The wedding ceremony still reflects the important role of religion in Hispanic life. In addition, respect for the family and its traditions still determine individual choices about the wedding ceremony.

The following description of traditional Hispanic courtship and wedding practices represent traditions that have been passed down through families in the Hispanic Southwest for centuries. While not many families still adhere to all of these traditions, the modern wedding ceremony of Hispanic families is based upon these traditions and is a blend of traditional and modern customs. In many aspects, the ceremony retains the most important cultural elements from the past and continues to reflect important Hispanic family values.

The traditional Hispanic courtship and wedding consist of five phases. The first is *el pedimiento*, the proposal. Next is *el prendorio*, the engagement. *El casorio*, the wedding, is next, followed by *el baile*, the reception and dance. The last part is *la entriega de los novios*, the presentation of the bride and groom.

El pedimiento de mano, the proposal by hand, the asking of the father for the bride's hand in marriage, was the beginning of the courtship process. In stricter times, families controlled the contact between young men and young women. Young people had no casual social contact. Young women especially were always accompanied by a family member. A traditional dicho, or folk saying, humorously describes this situation:

Adonde va el violín, va la bolsa.
Wherever the violin goes, the case goes.
(Said about mothers who always chaperone their daughters.)

If a young man wished to marry a young woman, he first told his own family of his intentions. His parents, or the oldest male sibling, representing the young man, would in turn approach the young woman's family, or oldest patriarchal figure, and ask for the young woman's hand in marriage and for permission for the courtship to proceed. This formal request for marriage could also be presented to the young woman's parents in a letter of proposal. The groom's parents would write the letter and hand-deliver it to the parents of the bride. If the family accepted the marriage, the marriage *banns*, or church announcements, were posted in the church bulletins, and plans were made for the engagement party.

If a family refused the petition of marriage, they could convey the rejection with an especially colorful folk expression. Families referred to the refusal with the saying *darle las calabazas*, translated loosely as "giving him squash or pumpkins." Sometimes, in order to signal a rejection, the bride's family would place squash, pumpkins, or even a pumpkin pie, on the doorstep of the hopeful but rejected groom. The family could also convey the rejection with a more conventional letter delivered within three or four days of the proposal.

After the pedimiento, the next step was el prendorio, the engagement party. The word *prendorio* comes from the word *prenda*, or jewel. A traditional part of the engagement party is the father of the bride introducing her to the groom's family with the words *Aquí tiene a la prenda que usted busca.* (Here is the jewel [prenda] you seek.)

In more traditional times, this party took place the day before the wedding. Some family traditions had the party eight days before the wedding. In modern times, with families scattered throughout the country, families hold el prendorio at a time that allows for important family members to be present.

The bride and her parents invited the groom and his family to their home. The engagement party's most important activity was to present the bride and groom to each other's families. Even though they already knew each other, this ritual formality served to express and affirm bonds between the two families. Family members would begin to call each other *compadre*—technically the godparent of one's child. In general usage, however, compadre refers to a special relationship in Hispanic culture, for a compadre is a close friend and part of one's extended family.

When the father of the bride introduced her to the groom's family at el prendorio, he began by referring to the bride as "the precious jewel you claim." The bride and groom then each presented themselves to each other's family with the formal phrase "consider me at your service." Then the bride and groom exchanged gifts, usually small gifts such as a rosary, shawls, or jewelry, and the two families would present gifts to the bride. The party then continued with a dinner celebration.

El casorio, the wedding, was a religious ceremony. A Holy Mass of Matrimony sanctified the wedding vows between the bride and groom. During the mass, the bride and groom dedicated their vows to each other, and the priest gave the church's blessing to the marriage. The bride and groom were accompanied by the *padrino*, the best man, and the *madrina*, the maid of honor.

After the wedding, a procession led the bride and groom to a reception hall for el baile, the dance party following the wedding. Musicians, typically a guitarist and violinist, traditionally led the processional march of the newlyweds, playing "La Marcha de los Novios." The traditional order of the procession has the musicians first, followed by the bride and groom. Next came the padrinos, family, and guests.

Two traditions still practiced at modern dances are the marcha dance and the dollar dance. At the reception hall, after the procession, the wedding party would begin the reception with the La Marcha de los Novios dance. In the dance, couples march around the room and then form an arch with their arms, under which the bride and groom dance through.

Modern custom has a flower-decorated car leading the procession to the reception, with the horn blaring all the way. It is also common for modern wedding parties to have a mariachi band as musical entertainment.

The final part of the traditional wedding ceremony was the entriega de los novios, a ceremony particular to Colorado and New Mexico, in

Figure 36—The wedding couple dances through the arch formed by the arms of the wedding guests.

which the bride and groom are given to each other by their parents and family and given final advice and blessings. In the olden days, the wedding party returned after the reception to the bride's home. The padrinos—the bride's and groom's attendants—would present the newly married couple to their parents. In modern wedding ceremonies, la entriega takes place at the reception near the end of the wedding dance.

Dr. Lorenzo Trujillo describes one theory of the origins of la entriega that supposes it became part of the wedding ceremony because priests were scarce in colonial times.[5]

La entriega, therefore, served as a matrimonial service for a couple wanting to be married. It provided a public ritual and religious ceremony for families and communities to mark the rite of passage from single to married life. Dr. Lorenzo Trujillo has written extensively about these wedding traditions, and his work is listed in the bibliography.

The *entregador*, or *poeta*, of the village would sing a long set of verses to the married couple on the sacredness of marriage. The music was in the form of a waltz, and the verses were a combination of traditional and improvised stanzas. The role of the singer was a special role in the community. The singer was a poet who wrote poems for the occasion. The best singers could improvise verses specially for the occasion.

The verses began by invoking the teachings of the church as spiritual guides to the couple. Verses followed that presented more secular but nevertheless important lessons for a successful, spiritually based marriage. The verses began with the singer apologizing for their lack of skill as a singer. Next came verses reflecting religious teachings. The final verses admonished the padrinos to assist the bride and groom in fulfilling their marriage vows and bless their marriage.

At the end of la entriega, the couple's parents, godparents, and relatives lined up and gave their own blessings to the marriage.

One colorful tradition has the couple kneeling on the floor on a white sheet. People throw money on the sheet for verses they particularly like. The money goes either to the wedding couple or to the entregador. Traditionally the money went to the musicians, but today it usually goes to the wedding couple.

A similar modern tradition is the dollar dance, a favorite part of the modern wedding reception. The bride and groom dance with guests who each pin money onto the bride's and groom's clothing. The money collected is an additional gift to the wedding couple to help begin their marriage in prosperity.

Marie Oralia Durán Trujillo in her book *Autumn Memories, My New Mexican Roots and Traditions* (1999, 85, 86) presents a version of *La Entriega* with a translation by Eva Nuanez.

La Entriega[4]

Translated by Eva Nuanez
A few of the typical verses are as follows.

Atencion pido senores *y a todos los ilustrados* *para explicares un poco* *tocante a los esposados*	Your attention I ask of you and all of the learned to explain to you a little regarding the newlyweds
En nombre de Dios comienzo *y de la Virgen Maria* *para entregar estos novios* *que se esposan este dia*	In the name of God, I begin and of the Virgin Mary to hand over these newlyweds that were married this day
El estado no es por un rato *ni por un dia ni dos* *es por una eternidad* *hasta darle cuenta a Dios*	The state of matrimony is not for a while nor a day or two is for an eternity until you give accounting to God
El padre les pregunto *si quiren casarse di* *y la iglesia los oyo* *que los dos dijieron si*	The priest asked them if you want to marry, say so, and the church heard them both say yes
Parece que esta lloviendo *confetti desde el cielo* *y han de ser las benediciones* *de nuestro padre eterno*	It seems like it's raining confetti from heaven it must be the blessing of our heavenly father

Death: La Ofrenda y el Día de los Muertos

La vida es sueño.
Life is a dream.

El Día de los Muertos, the Fiesta of the Day of the Dead, is a celebration during which families remember and honor relatives who have died. The celebration of the Day of the Dead is a blending of religious practices of two major cultures: the Mexican Aztec and the Spanish Catholic.

The Aztecs believed death and life were closely intertwined. They believed that the dead were an important part of the world of the living and that the spirits of the dead could affect the living. They had a complex cosmology that reflected their beliefs about the afterlife. According to this cosmology, a dead person traveled through a nine-level underworld, *Mictlan*, and faced many dangerous trials. In order to aid the spirit in its underworld journey and trials, the Aztecs had the practice of burying the dead with many objects from the dead person's life that would be useful in the long and dangerous journey through Mictlan. They placed both personal and household objects in the grave to help the departed spirit.

Other beliefs reflecting the cosmology of the afterlife included the paradise of Tlaloc, called *Tlalocan*, where those who drowned could enjoy a life of singing, games, and other pleasures. Warriors who died in battle and mothers who died in childbirth assisted the sun in its daily journey through the sky. For the Aztec, death was a mere passing from one world to another.

When the Spanish arrived in the New World, one of the Aztec customs they encountered was the celebration of the dead. Over time, the Aztec calendar had evolved to include celebrations in honor of the dead. On these dates, the dead returned to earth to visit family and friends and to see that they were remembered. In turn, families would hold celebrations to pay their respects to the dead. These celebrations included the preparation of favorite foods in order to make an offering to the visiting family members.

The Spanish brought their own customs to the New World. One of these was the custom of All Saints' Day and All Souls' Day. These

European and Catholic customs were religious days dedicated to praying for the souls of departed family members and friends. November 1 was All Hallows, or All Saints' Day, a day to honor the saints of the Catholic church. November 2 was All Souls' Day, a day to pray for departed souls. All Hallows Eve, October 31, eventually became secularized into Halloween.

It was one of the coincidences of history that the customs from two such different cultures overlapped on the calendar. In time, the ancient Aztec and the Spanish Catholic customs merged in the New World into the Mexican celebration we know as the Day of the Dead.

It is easy and common to confuse Halloween and the Day of the Dead. They are, however, two very distinct celebrations with different histories and different purposes.

In Mexico, Day of the Dead celebrations, especially in Oaxaca and Michoacan, see families spending the night in cemeteries as they await the return of the spirits of their beloved family members to return to earth for one night. The celebrations include lighting candles to guide

Figure 37—Day of the Dead celebrant as la Calavera Catrina. In Mexican culture, catrinas are fashionably dressed skeleton figures, inspired by the work of José Guadalupe Posada, that appear during Day of the Dead celebrations in Mexico.

the way of the souls of the dead. Grave sites are decorated with cempasuchil flowers (marigold flowers). The flowers represent the "flowers of the dead," and their fragrance helps guide the souls of the dead to their grave site, where relatives await them. The celebrations also include food and beverages to feed the souls of the departed as well as the family members present at the grave site. It is a deeply meaningful celebration for the souls of the departed.

In the southwestern states, Day of the Dead has grown into festive community celebrations with parades, music, and extravagant costumes with wonderfully stylized facial makeup and masks. It has joined Cinco de Mayo as an important Hispanic cultural celebration celebrated by Hispanos and non-Hispanos alike.

The Ofrenda

Making the *ofrenda*, the altar, is one of the best family activities of the Day of the Dead celebration. The constructing of the altar is an activity every family member can participate in. Making an ofrenda is a family commitment; it is a time for families to remember the strengths and love in a family and to celebrate the people who have lived in the family. In many aspects, making an ofrenda is as much for the living members of the family as it is for the departed. The ofrenda is an especially good activity for younger children because it allows them to participate at an appropriate level and still feel as if they contributed something important to the ofrenda.

There are no rules on how to make your ofrenda. Take your time, be thoughtful, plan ahead, let everyone participate. Every ofrenda is different, and every ofrenda is personal. Some are plain; some are ornate. Some are sparse; some are filled up. Some look like professional artists made them; some have a homemade quality. Some are traditional and look like they were imported from Mexico; some are modern and speak to an urban American life. The most important ingredient is the love you have for your family.

Figure 38—The making of the ofrenda can be a wonderful family activity.

La Iglesia: Religious Celebrations

Tiene más Dios que darnos que nosotros que pedirle.
God can give more than we could ever ask for.

Dios amanece para todos.
God brings the dawn for all. God's graces are for everyone.

Religious life is one of the fundamental experiences of the Hispanic culture. It is often said that one cannot enter Hispanic culture without passing through the doors of the Catholic church. When the *conquistadores* came to the New World in search of gold and personal glory, they were soon followed by Catholic missionaries on the holy mission of bringing Catholic Christianity to the New World. Along with the cultural practices of language and folklore, these early explorers and settlers firmly established their religion in the New World.

A simple recalling of the names of settlements established by these early missionaries and settlers scattered throughout the American Southwest illustrates the importance of religious life for these pioneers of the New World: San Francisco, San Diego, Los Angeles, San Antonio, San Jose, Santa Barbara, Santa Fe. The common practice for the founding missionaries was to give religious names to the early settlements, names which continue to this day.

From the earliest instances of Spanish settlement in the New World, the Catholic church was central to the lives of Hispanic people. With such a long heritage of religious activity, the Hispanic culture has innumerable opportunities for its people to practice and celebrate their faith. The Christmas season is an especially important time of religious observations. The season begins with the Feast of Our Lady of Guadalupe. The Christmas season features two community-wide celebrations: the performance of two religious plays, *Los Pastores* and *Las Posadas*.

The Feast of Our Lady of Guadalupe

Our Lady of Guadalupe and the image of her surrounded by a wreath of roses and enveloped by the sun's rays is one of the most powerful and artistic religious and cultural icons in Hispanic culture. Her story and her image are widely dispersed and believed among all levels of Hispanic culture. In 1754, the Pope recognized the Virgin of Guadalupe as patroness of New Spain. She became the patroness of Latin America in 1910. In 1959, she was named the Mother of the Americas. For many Hispanics, December 12, the Feast Day of Our Lady of Guadalupe, is the beginning of the Christmas season.

The Feast of Our Lady of Guadalupe celebrates the miracle given to a humble Indian, Juan Diego, on a hill in Mexico on December 9–12, 1531. After the conquest of the Aztecs in 1521, the Spanish missionaries began their mission to convert Aztec society to the Catholic religion. One successful strategy the missionaries practiced was to combine Catholic beliefs with Indigenous practices to facilitate the Aztec conversion to Catholicism. The legend of the Virgin of Guadalupe is a clear example of this successful practice. The legend of the Virgin quickly became very powerful in Mexico and spread throughout the territory of New Spain. Today, the legend is a Hispanic truth representing the possibility of apparition and the miraculous for true believers of the Catholic faith.

The legend of the Virgin of Guadalupe takes place on a hill named Tepeyac. Tepeyac was the site of an Aztec shrine to the Aztec Mother Goddess Tonantzín, the protector of earth and corn. The Aztecs came to the shrine of Tonantzín to pray. After the conquest, the Spanish missionaries built a shrine to the Virgin on the site of the shrine to Tonantzín. After the legend of the Virgin came into existence, the missionaries facilitated the Aztec conversion to Catholicism and the worshipping of the Virgin by painting pictures of the Virgin in which she looked like an Aztec princess and by having her speak in Nahuatl, the Aztec language.

Figure 39—When Juan Diego saw the roses on that cold winter day, he knew it was a miracle, and he knelt down to pray.

Nuestra Señora de Guadalupe

The Story of Our Lady of Guadalupe

Traditional story adapted by Angel Vigil

On one cold winter morning in December 1531, an Aztec Indian man named Juan Diego was walking to church. It had been ten years since the mighty battles with the men of Cortés had ended. The soldiers and warriors had put down their weapons, and now peace had returned to his land. Juan himself had recently converted to Christianity. It was his habit to go to the church for religious instruction.

His church was not in his village but in Tlatelolco, a village just outside of Mexico City. His usual path took him by the houses in the village, but this morning for some reason he decided to walk over the Hill of Tepeyac.

As he neared the top of the hill, he heard voices singing. Now, he had heard the voices of people singing the holy praises to the Lord in church, but he had never heard such beautiful music as this in all his life. He heard the tinkling of bells, and the voices moved around him like the wind itself. He thought that this must be what the voices of heavenly angels sounded like.

As he reached the top of the hill, the beautiful singing voices and music stopped. Everything became very still, and Juan no longer even felt the coldness. He heard his name being called: "Juan, Juan."

Suddenly, he saw a bright cloud with the shafts of a colorful rainbow coming out of it. The cloud came to a stop before him, and when the cloud split in two, there was a woman standing there. The woman looked like a beautiful Aztec princess. Her clothes shone like the sun, and she was surrounded by the heavenly light. When she spoke, Juan heard the heavenly music he had heard before. He knew it was a miracle, so he fell to his knees to pray.

"Juan," the heavenly woman said, "I have chosen you to deliver a message to the bishop at the cathedral."

"But beautiful woman," answered Juan, "I am a poor Indian. I am not worthy to deliver a message to the bishop. Why have I been chosen?"

With a soothing kindness in her voice, the woman answered, "I am the Blessed Virgin Mary, the mother of the Lord Jesus Christ. Just know that I have chosen you to be my messenger on this earth. Go to the bishop and tell him that he is to build a church for me here on the top of this hill. The church is to be a shrine that will show my love for all my people. Go, give the bishop my message."

Juan ran faster than ever to the cathedral to give the Virgin's message to the bishop. When he arrived at the cathedral, he knocked on the door to the bishop's quarters. The bishop's helpers opened the door and asked Juan what he wanted. He told them, "I have a message for the bishop from the Virgin Mary, the Mother of God."

When they heard his report, they could not help but laugh to hear a poor Indian tell such a story. But Juan was persistent, and eventually they let him in to see the bishop. The bishop listened to Juan's story but did not believe him. He told him, "Juan, your story is incredible. Imagine the Virgin appearing to you on a hill with a message for me to build a church! Go for now and I will think about it."

Juan left feeling like a failure. He knew the bishop's helpers had laughed at him and that the bishop had not believed his story. He felt that he had let the Blessed Virgin down. When he returned to Tepeyac he once again saw the Virgin. She floated on air as if nothing were holding her up except her heavenly powers.

"O Holy Mother. I have failed you. The bishop did not believe me. I knew I was not worthy."

"Juan, do you not know that now you are within my graces? I have chosen you, and I will make it be as it should. Go back to the bishop and give him my message again. A church must be built in my name on this hill."

Juan returned to the bishop a second time. Again, the bishop did not believe Juan. He said, "Juan, if you have truly seen the Blessed Virgin Mary, bring back a sign that the miracle is real. If not, then never come to me with this story again."

On his way back to tell the Virgin that he needed a sign, Juan received the news that his uncle was dying of typhoid fever. Juan immediately rushed to the side of his uncle, but when he arrived, he found out that it was almost too late. His uncle asked him to bring the priest because he knew he would not last for another day.

Juan rushed to the Virgin to tell her what the bishop had said and to ask forgiveness for not coming right back. "O, Blessed Virgin. I was late because my uncle is dying and is not expected to last another day. Also, the bishop requires a sign that you really spoke to me. Please help, Blessed Mother."

"Juan, do you not know that I am here to help you?" she replied. "I have already cured your uncle. He will live. Now go to the top of the hill where only the cactus grows. There you will find a rosebush in bloom. Take those roses to the bishop, and he will believe."

Juan went to the top of the hill, and there was a beautiful rosebush in full bloom. When Juan saw the roses on that cold winter day, he knew it was a miracle, and he knelt down to pray. He knew that when the bishop saw the roses that had bloomed in the middle of winter and smelled their beautiful fragrance, he would believe his story. Juan gathered the roses in his *tilma*, which is a kind of poncho. He showed the roses to the Virgin, and she said, "Now take these to the bishop and tell him to build the church in my honor."

When Juan arrived at the cathedral for the third time, the bishop's helpers refused to let him see the bishop. Juan told them that he had the sign the bishop had asked for. They said, "If you have the sign, let us see it. Let us see the sign of a miracle. Then you will see the bishop."

Juan opened his tilma and roses tumbled onto the floor. Roses fell out of the tilma like snow falling to the ground. Beautiful, fresh roses lined the inside of the tilma. In their astonishment, the bishop's helpers reached out to touch the roses and felt their soft, smooth petals. They knew that it was indeed a miracle.

When Juan showed the bishop the roses, the bishop also knew that it was a holy sign from heaven. As Juan opened his tilma, more roses fell to the ground. Even more miraculously, inside Juan's tilma was the image of the Holy Mother as Juan had seen her on the hill of Tepeyac. The bishop and his helpers fell to their knees at the sight of the holy image and prayed to the Virgin.

The bishop built a church on the site Juan showed them on the Hill of Tepeyac. Now the site is called Guadalupe. To this day, Juan's tilma with the image of the Holy Mother is inside the shrine to the Blessed Virgin. Prayerful worshippers can look at the tilma and be reminded of the love the Holy Mother has for her people. For all eternity, the shrine to Our Lady of Guadalupe is a reminder of the miraculous apparition that appeared to Juan Diego many years ago.

Las Posadas *and* Los Pastores

Las Posadas and *Los Pastores* are two traditional plays dramatizing the journey of Mary and Joseph searching for lodging in Bethlehem and the birth of the Christ Child. *Las Posadas*, translated "the inns," originally was part of an annual cycle of plays used to teach Christian values in Spain during the Middle Ages. The play is a community celebration lasting nine nights during which the community dramatizes Mary and Joseph's search for lodging. The dramatization of Las Posadas was a community event with participants celebrating the Christmas season with food and good cheer in all the houses at which they stop.

Costumed as Mary and Joseph, and accompanied by a legion of children playing angels and shepherds, community members proceed nightly from house to house seeking lodging. Olibama Lopez Tushar, in her book *The People of El Valle: A History of the Spanish Colonials in the San Luis Valley*, describes a traditional Las Posadas in which a community member playing Lucifer goes from house to house for eight nights and persuades the owners of the house not to give lodging to Mary and Joseph. A typical refrain had the owners of the house refusing to grant lodging because they had been warned, by Lucifer, that Mary and Joseph were thieves come to rob them. On the ninth night, Christmas Eve, Mary and Joseph finally receive lodging.

Mexican legend tells that the practice of Las Posadas began in the New World when Fray Diego de Soria received permission from the Pope to celebrate nine Misas de Aguinaldo, or Gift Masses, from December 16 to 24. These masses celebrated the Holy Nativity and occurred at the convent of San Aguatín de Acolmán near Mexico City.

Los Pastores, the Shepherds' Play, is the most well-known and popular nativity play in the Hispanic Southwest. It is a dramatization of the biblical account of the birth of Christ, telling the story of the journey of the shepherds following the heavenly star to the manger in Bethlehem. The play is a descendant of the Medieval European religious plays. Liturgical dramas have existed in Europe since the ninth century, and the nativity play was an established part of Spain's dramatic literature during Spain's Golden Age. Lope de Vega's *Los Pastores de Belén* is one of the primary examples of the well-developed genre of Spanish nativity plays. Franciscan missionaries probably wrote versions of the play in

Mexico, based upon European models, and carried these plays from the interior of Mexico to the northern provinces.

Los Pastores presents the biblical events of Christ's birth. It also depicts the eternal struggle between good and evil and mankind's effort to resist temptation. The final victory of Archangel Michael over Lucifer heralds the birth of the Christ Child.

While its themes are serious and religious, its great popularity is because it also has comedy, fun, and irreverence woven into the story. In this manner, it is similar to the Second Shepherd's Play of the Wakefield cycle in Britain. Several of the play's characters are buffoons tricked by temptation, and several of its scenes are almost slapstick in nature. Traditional performances featured ad-libs poking fun at community members and playfully exaggerated characterizations of Lucifer and the comic characters.

One of the lines of the play, spoken by a lazy buffoon named Bartolo, has entered the common language as a dicho, a folk proverb.

The line is "*Si quiere la gloria verme, que venga la gloria acá.*" "If glory wants to see me, let glory come to me."

The line is spoken in response to a plea for the lazy shepherd to get up and travel with his companions to witness "la Gloria," the Christ child. Today, people use the dicho to refer to a lazy person who does not want to do something.

Traditional performances of these plays often combined the two. A performance of Las Posadas would typically precede a performance of Los Pastores. Communities and churches, however, when performing the two together, would condense them into a one-day event. The celebration would end with Christmas Eve midnight mass, *La Misa del Gallo*. The community referred to this mass as "the mass of the rooster" because they often came home so late they would hear the rooster crowing. Another legend about La Misa del Gallo is that the name comes from the rooster that crowed over the stable in Bethlehem at the birth of Christ.

The parts of both of these traditional plays were greatly desired by adult and children alike, especially the part of Lucifer in Los Pastores. Lucifer was more of a trickster than an embodiment of evil and allowed for much playful exaggeration. Often parts were passed down through families, and scripts were handwritten legacies passed down from one generation to the next.

Additional Christmas Season Traditions

As a season of celebration, the Christmas season included many other traditional customs. These included the giving of aguinaldos, little gifts, the lighting of luminarias and farolitos, and the poinsettia.

Aguinaldos

The term *aguinaldos* comes from the Misa de Aguinaldos, the original Mexican masses celebrating Mary and Joseph's journey to Bethlehem. The masses included the giving of gifts to the native populations to entice them to attend the masses. In traditional Posadas, the hosts of the homes along the procession would give small gifts to guests. Children participating in Posadas would recite a verse requesting aguinaldos, little gifts.

Olibama Lopez Tushar, in her book *The People of El Valle*, presents a typical verse that sounds very much like the modern "trick or treat" on Halloween.

De nos aguinaldos, si nos han de dar,
Porque la noche es larga y tenemos que andar.
Oremos, oremos, que angelitos somos
Del cielo venimos a pedir oremos.
Y si no nos dan, puertas y ventanas quebraremos.

Give us gifts, if you will
Because the night is long and we have to go.
Let us pray, let us pray, for we are little angels
We come from heaven to ask for prayers.
If you don't give, we will break your doors and windows.
(1992, 120)

Farolitos/Luminarias

Farolitos or *luminarias* are one of the most common Christmas holiday decorations in the Southwest, especially in New Mexico. Simple to make, they add a light-filled festive element to any house, building, or driveway.

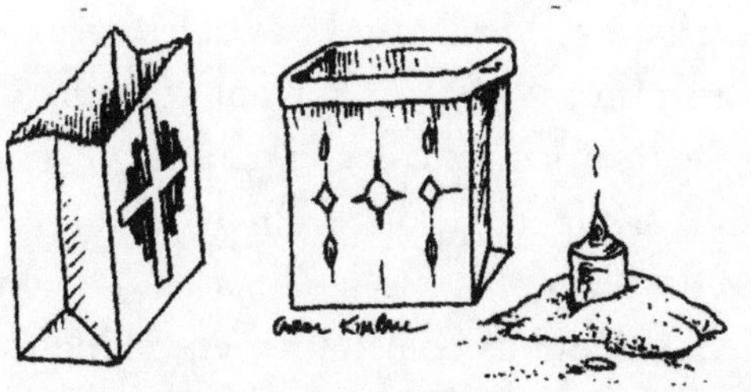

Figure 40—Farolitos/luminarias

In New Mexico the tradition of lighting *luminarias* and *farolitos* is to this day a widely observed practice for the Christmas season as well as other festive occasions. Its origins are in the folk practice of lighting small fires outside the home to light the way for the Christ Child to homes on Christmas Eve. Since the homes were built of adobe—bricks of dried mud and straw—and had flat roofs, another tradition evolved of building a fire on the roof.

Traditionally, luminarias are small fires built outside homes and farolitos are candle-lit paper bags. *Farolito* is Spanish for "small lantern." Over time, however, the two terms have become interchangeable as families began to concentrate on decorating with votive candles set in sand in paper bags and not build the small fires anymore. It is common now to hear the candle lit paper bags referred to as luminarias.

The Chinese use of festival lanterns came to Mexico from the Philippines. Tissue paper or *papel de china* was the first material these lamps were made of. The tissue paper, however, was too fragile, and soon after World War I, paper bags were used for the farolitos. Today homes, driveways, walkways, and even businesses are lined with the small paper bags with candles in them lighting the crisp Christmas air.

La Flor de la Noche Buena

The poinsettia, the favorite decorative plant of the Christmas season, is the central image in the miracle legend "La Flor de la Noche Buena."

The literal translation is "The Flower of the Good Night," with *la Noche Buena* being Christmas Eve.

The plant is native to Mexico and was called *cuetlaxochitl*, the flower of purity. The Spanish associated the plant with the Christmas season because that is the plant's most colorful period.

The US ambassador to Mexico from 1825 to 1830, Joel R. Poinsett, introduced the plant to the United States. A botanist, Poinsett was attracted to the plant and its colorful leaves, calling the plant "painted leaves." He took cuttings of the plant to his plantation in South Carolina, and eventually the plant became known as the poinsettia, after Poinsett. Its association with the Christmas season continued because of its colorful leaves during the season, with the green leaves symbolizing the continuation of life and the red leaves the blood shed by Christ.

The legend of la Flor de la Noche Buena tells the miracle story of a poor child with no gifts for the Christ Child. Deeply wanting to give the Christ Child a gift, in desperation on the way to the church, she grabs the common Mexican plant from the fields as a gift. Because the child's gift was a pure and true gift of love to the Christ Child, the plant's green leaves miraculously turned red before all gathered at the church for midnight

Figure 41—La Flor de la Noche Buena, the poinsettia

mass. Families remember the story of la Flor de la Noche Buena and tell it to children as a lesson about the true meaning of the Christmas season. From that time on, the poinsettia has given us its red leaves on la Noche Buena to remind us that the best gift of all is a heart full of love.

El Santuario de Chimayo

It is only proper to close out this section on the religious traditions of Southwestern Hispanics with a description of the most important religious pilgrimage site in America. *El Santuario de Chimayo* is another example of the powerful role of faith in Hispanic culture.

The Santuario, located in the northern New Mexico village of Chimayo, is considered the most important Catholic pilgrimage center in the United States. It is often referred to as the Lourdes of America. It receives almost 300,000 visitors a year. The site is a National Historic Landmark. Any traveler in northern New Mexico should visit the site and experience firsthand its historic importance in the faith of devout Hispanic Catholics.

The church features centures-old altar wall paintings that are historic examples of religious devotion art. A side room, *el pocito*,

Figure 42—El Santuario de Chimayo

Historical Coda #16

My childhood was filled with visits to the Santuario. We would reverentially enter the church, kneel in the pews for a few moments of silent prayer, light some votive candles, and then enter the room with the holy dirt. My childhood eyes would marvel at the walls filled with crutches and other signs of miraculous healing. I would read as many of the testimonials as time allowed.

The most important part of the visit was when my mother would take me into the sacred room and rub the holy dirt on my back at the same time saying a blessing in Spanish. We also always took few spoonfuls of the holy dirt with us for use in our home.

I had aunts who would finish their yearly pilgrimage to the Santuario during Holy Week crawling on their knees the last few steps into the church as a sign of their penance and faith.

I have always had some of the holy dirt in my own home. Sometimes I used it for silly reasons. Once, when my team was in the Super Bowl, I placed a vial of it on the top of the TV screen to help bless the team's efforts. Everyone made fun of my belief in the powers of the holy dirt, but my team did win the Super Bowl that year.

Another more profound instance of my use of the holy dirt was at the death of my brother. I helped my brother die by having him in hospice care in my own home. After he died, I took some of the Santuario holy dirt and anointed his body by making the sign of the cross with it on his forehead to ensure his safe passage into the other world, La Gloria, heaven itself.

This ritual was in response to the Greek myth that Charon, the ferryman of the Underworld, would not take a person across the River Styx to the other side unless they had had funeral rites. A person who had not had funeral rites would be doomed to walk the banks of the River Styx for one hundred years before Charon would ferry his soul across. By anointing his body with the holy dirt from the Santuario, I ensured that my brother would not walk the banks of the River Styx for one hundred years.

the little well, contains a small pit that is the source of the holy, healing dirt.

Several legends exist telling the story of the site's miraculous dirt and its healing properties. Another back room of the church is filled with discarded crutches, wheelchairs, and testimonials to miracles experienced at the church.

The church is especially known for the pilgrimages people make during Holy Week, especially on the days leading up to Easter Sunday. Faithful pilgrims will walk to Chimayo as a sign of their dedication to their faith and their belief in the healing powers of the miraculous dirt.

Remedios: The Healing Arts

Al enfermo que es de vida, hasta 'l agua le es medicina.
For the sick person who is destined to live, even water is medicine.
Medicine sometimes works in unknown ways.

The word *curandero* comes from the Spanish word *curar*, which means "to cure." In traditional Hispanic culture, the curandero, or *curandera* if a woman, was a folk healer who had the gift of healing. With knowledge and skill in the healing arts, the curandero was a health resource to communities that, because of their rural isolation, had little access to health care professionals.

The curandero practiced a form of healing that was remarkably similar to the modern system of holistic medicine. Health for the curandero was a state of balance, a life in harmony. The curandero treated the social, psychological, and physical health of the sick and infirm. By combining the knowledge of herbal, natural treatments with the attention given to the patient's psychological health, the curandero affected a physical and mental healing that contributed to both an individual's and a community's health. In its most positive aspects, *curanderismo* represented a self-reliant practice that was grounded in the strengths and support of family and community.

Today the practice of curanderismo is still a part of many Hispanic communities. The system of curanderismo is evolving new forms of practice that allow it to contribute to a health care system with modern medicine. The traditional successes of the curandero in physical health were based upon the folk knowledge of herbal remedies. Today the work of the curandero in mental health treatment is also a continuing aspect of mental health care in Hispanic communities.

The role of curanderos, healers, and their art of herbal healing was widespread throughout the Hispanic Southwest. Their knowledge of the uses of natural herbs as *remedios* (remedies) allowed them to practice a folk medicine that was a hybrid of two cultures, Hispanic and Native American. The herbal knowledge of these folk practitioners was based upon the accumulated learning of generations of healers who had passed on the knowledge of the curative powers of herbs. The Spanish brought to the New World their knowledge of such traditional herbs as *rosa de castilla* (rose), *manzanilla* (chamomile), and *alhucema* (lavender). From the Native Americans, they learned about *inmortal* (antelope horns) and *oshá* (porter's lovage, wild celery).

The use of remedios usually relied upon the plants that grew wild and were native to the local region. The use of herbs from other regions, however, was possible since almanacs existed that featured advertisements

Figure 43—Manzanilla, or chamomile, was used as a tea for fever.

for folk medicines and herbs, and herb traders traveled the Southwest dispensing herbs to restock family cupboards.

Even though herb traders conjure up images of the Wild West and the snake oil peddler and huckster, traditional folk healers were an integral and important part of the community fabric. While the traveling herb trader could possibly be seen in the same light as the unscrupulous traveling salesman, the traditional healer was a part of the community.

Being a curandero was a calling taken very seriously in Hispanic culture. The knowledge of remedios was usually passed down through families, usually in an apprentice fashion between an elder curandero and a younger student of remedios. Also, any person misusing the knowledge of remedios was quickly suspected of being a *bruja*, a witch. Most importantly, in the days when medical doctors were not readily available, the knowledge and services of the curandero were indispensable to the health of a community.

Most herbal remedies have uses for more than one ailment and in various preparations depending upon the ailment being treated. They are used in pastes as poultices, salves, and compresses. Another common practice is for the curandero to use the natural herbs in special brews.

Figure 44—Zábila, *aloe vera, was used to soothe and heal burns.*

The following table presents examples of common plants and their primary uses. The chart is for illustrative purposes only and in no way is meant to be a prescription for ailments.

Plants and Their Medicinal Uses in the Hispanic Southwest

Spanish Name	English Name	Use
ajo	garlic	constipation, cough
ajenjibre	ginger	unsettled stomach
álamo sauco	poplar	bark used for fever
albácar	basil	menstrual and labor pains
alcanfor	camphor	external use as a liniment for rheumatism
alfalfa	alfalfa	stomach pains
alhucema	lavender	colic, gas, and indigestion
amole	yucca root	hair shampoo
anís	anise	coughs, anxiety
barba de maiz	corn silk	urinary tract infections
canela	cinnamon	nausea
cebolla	onion	coughs, burns, sores
capulín	wild cherry	viral infections
cilantro	coriander	inflamed gums
clavo	clove	toothache
flor de Santa Rita	Indian paintbrush	water retention
inmortal	antelope horns	asthma
lecheros	milkweed	skin infections
manzanilla	chamomile	colds and fevers, colic
nuez moscada	nutmeg	indigestion
nopal	cactus	rash
oshá	root of wild celery	antiseptic
orégano	oregano	cough, sore throat
romero	rosemary	indigestion, baldness
ruda	rue	earache
salvia	sage	diarrhea in babies
toloache	jimson weed	external analgesic
yerba buena	mint	stomach ills
zábila	aloe vera	wounds and burns

Las Artes: The Arts

Quien bien baila, de boda en boda anda.
The good dancer goes from wedding to wedding.
The artist is welcome everywhere.

Traditional Arts

The traditional folk arts of the Hispanic people have been a source of cultural pride and artistry for centuries. Artisans and craftspersons have used the materials, techniques, and knowledge passed down through generations to provide beautiful secular and religious objects for families and communities. These artistic objects fulfilled both utilitarian and spiritual needs for Hispanic people.

As in so many other areas of Hispanic culture, folk arts contribute abundant examples of the influence of Indigenous and Spanish colonial culture in the work of Hispanic artists. This area of folk culture also has many examples of the effect and influence of American culture on the evolution of Hispanic traditional practices. With stores often a far distance away and visits from the clergy infrequent, the geographic isolation of the Southwestern Hispanic people was a further influence on the path their artistic practices followed.

As a rural, agricultural, and religious people, traditional artisans had the task of creating both utilitarian objects for everyday use and spiritual objects for religious practices. As part of a proudly self-reliant culture, the traditional Hispanic people used the conditions of their lives to create a strong tradition of expressive arts that has persevered for centuries through four distinct periods: cultural establishment, cultural expansion, cultural decline, and cultural renaissance.

As has been the experience for all traditional cultures in the world, the Southwestern Hispanic cultural arts prospered for centuries before they experienced a period of decline. Cultural decline in this sense has several clear indicators:

- a period of time in which people lose touch with traditional practices
- the advent of manufactured products replacing formerly handcrafted products

- society evolving from an agricultural to an industrial economy
- families moving from rural to urban settings
- work shifting from a trade and barter system to a wage and cash economy
- decreased market demand for traditional handcrafted products
- assimilation becoming a painful process of cultural loss

Each of these changes places inevitable stress on the cultural fabric to the extent that generations drift away from the traditional practices of their heritage.

Hispanic culture has not been immune to these societal forces. The recent experience of Southwestern Hispanic culture, however, has seen a renaissance and rebirth of cultural awareness, cultural pride, and traditional practices. Led by its artists, teachers, and scholars, Hispanic culture is in the process of rediscovering its traditional heritage. As families reaffirm the activities of the past, they build a stronger foundation for the future. Throughout the Southwest, people are painting murals, producing plays, carving santos, forming dance companies, opening art galleries, and baking traditional foods. A new generation has realized the importance of traditional artistic practices in maintaining and preserving culture for future generations. The traditional arts are the foundation of the next period of cultural development in the Hispanic Southwest, the cultural renaissance.

The arts described in this section are meant to be representative and not definitive. Many different folk arts are practiced by Hispanics throughout the Southwest. Modern and traditional artists work in many different art forms, all with their own artistic heritage and vision. Hispanics, however, recognize the folk arts presented below as primary folk arts because of their strong traditional origins, wide prevalence in artistic practice, and continuing influence in the renaissance of Hispanic culture in the Southwest.

Weaving

Weaving has long been one of the essential folk arts in the Southwest. It was a basic necessity of Hispanic settlers because of their need to make their own cloth for clothing, blankets, and rugs.

The cultural traditions of both the Native Americans and the Spanish contributed to the development of weaving as a textile art in the Southwest. When the Spanish arrived in the Southwest, the Pueblo Native Americans had a long-established and advanced technical ability in weaving. The Pueblo weavers grew cotton and used cotton yarn in their weaving. For their weaving, they also used the vertical loom. The vertical loom consisted of two poles set in the ground with horizontal poles at the top and bottom of the loom structure, forming a rectangle. The Pueblo weavers strung the cotton yarn warp vertically and worked the weft yarn horizontally. The Spanish called the Native American weaving *mantas*, which was a general term for cotton cloth. In the early period of Spanish colonization, weaving remained an important activity in Native American pueblos.

The Spanish changed the nature of southwestern weaving when they introduced sheep, and with these animals, wool as a material for weaving. Sheep raising became a major occupation, and wool became an abundant material for weaving. By the seventeenth century, wool had

Figure 45—Chimayo weaver at his loom.

replaced cotton as the source of the yarn used in weaving. The Spanish also brought the horizontal or treadle loom from Europe and introduced it to the New World. Because of their massive size, the looms themselves were not imported from Spain, but rather were constructed new in the New World.

During the Spanish colonial period, it was common for Spanish families to have *criados*, Native American servants. These servants, many of them children, assisted with the family's weaving. The criados usually performed the tedious tasks of washing, carding, and spinning the wool. A clear example of cultural cross-fertilization occurred when these criados returned to their tribes after living with a Spanish family. They took with them the skills of Spanish weaving with wool and transferred this knowledge to their native vertical loom.

The Pueblo weavers in turn influenced the Navajo. The Navajo became adept at sheep raising and wool processing, eventually developing their highly prized woolen blankets.

The Spanish, however, were little influenced by Native American weaving. The Hispanic weavers were more influenced by Mexican designs. The rugs Spanish merchants brought to Mexico from Turkey and the Orient also were a greater influence on the design of Hispanic weavings.

The three most common types of weaving were the *jerga*, the *sarape*, and the *sabanilla*. The jerga was a coarse woolen cloth with many domestic uses, two being horse blankets and rugs. The word *jerga* derives from the Arabic *xerca*, the word for a sack cloth, which reflects the material's rough and humble uses. The jerga usually had a simpler design, often a

Figure 46—Jerga weaving with traditional checkerboard design.

checkerboard or striped weave. It was woven in strips about two feet wide with a thick yarn and then sewn together to fit the area to be covered.

The sarape was a finer weaving used for blankets and poncho-like jackets. Its design was more colorful, striking, and intricate than the jerga. The traditional Mexican sarape is a poncho with a slit in the middle for the wearer's head to go through.

The sabanilla was a light woolen cloth used for clothes, mattress ticking, and sheets, and as the backing for another prevalent folk art, colcha embroidery. The word *sabanilla* derives from the Spanish *savana*, meaning sheet or plains. A sabanilla was a loosely woven white material with a plain weave. The activity guide for colcha embroidery lists a source for handwoven, traditional sabanilla cloth.

Traditional weavings were the result of a laborious process of hand spinning and dyeing. The dyeing of the yarn was a multistep process using vegetable and plant dyes. The Spanish brought a knowledge of wool treatment and dyeing from Europe. They also learned from the Native American traditions, which reflected centuries' worth of knowledge in developing and using natural dyes native to the New World to color their fabrics, basketry, and paints.

Examples of vegetable and plant natural dyes are abundant. Flowers, barks, plants, and roots all contributed to the coloring of woolen yarns. The golden flowers of the rabbit bush made yellow dye. Wild plum roots made rust red. Mountain mahogany made red. *Canaigra*, the roots of a desert plant, produced yellows and tans. Apple bark gave reddish yellow. Sumac was part of a process producing black. Dahlia blossoms made yellow-orange.

Cochineal, brazilwood, and indigo were imported natural dyes. Cochineal, a red dye ground from an insect living on the prickly pear cactus the Mexicans call *nopal*, came from Mexico and Central America. *Brasil*, or brazilwood, producing a beautiful rose and red color, came from the tropical hardwood that gave Brazil its name. Indigo, a deep blue dye derived from a plant known as anil, came from the West Indies.

The centuries-old and sophisticated knowledge of the gathering, preparation, and use of natural dyes eventually fell victim to the advances of science and industry. The introduction of commercial, synthetic aniline dyes in the 1860s, with their bright range of colors and ease of use, led to the decline of the use of natural dyes. These commercial dyes eliminated the work of gathering and preparing dyes. The introduction of commercial, machine-made yarn ended the tedious labors of washing, carding, and spinning wool. While the production of wool textiles continued, the late nineteenth century saw the abandonment of the traditional methods for the ease of use and ready availability of commercial fabrics used for weaving.

Three primary styles identify the designs of Hispanic weaving: (1) *saltillo*, (2) *Rio Grande*, and (3) *Chimayó*. The saltillo design originated in Saltillo, Mexico, and was brought to New Mexico in the 1830s. This design was probably influenced by the rugs imported to Mexico from the Orient. The saltillo design features a large diamond shape in the center of the weaving with interlocking, radiating diamond patterns repeated inside it. Diamonds and zigzag designs form a complex background design, with stripes at the top and bottom of the weaving.

The Rio Grande pattern is a variation of the saltillo design. It consists of detailed geometric patterns. The pattern is named after the region of the Upper Rio Grande River in New Mexico. One version is a zigzag striped pattern. A simpler version consists of bands or stripes.

The Chimayó weaving is a very identifiable version of the Rio Grande blanket. The pine cone design is characteristic of Chimayó weavings.

The coming of the railroad and the influx of Anglo settlers changed the sheep used for producing wool. This influx of new settlers to the Southwest also changed the market from one using sheep as wool produc-

Figure 47—Saltillo weaving with zigzag and diamond patterns

ers to one needing sheep as meat producers. The Spanish had introduced the Churro sheep, the common sheep of southern Spain, whose wool made a long, fine, strong, silky yarn allowing for a high-quality weaving product. The new settlers introduced the Rambouillet sheep to meet the increased need of sheep for meat. The Rambouillet eventually became

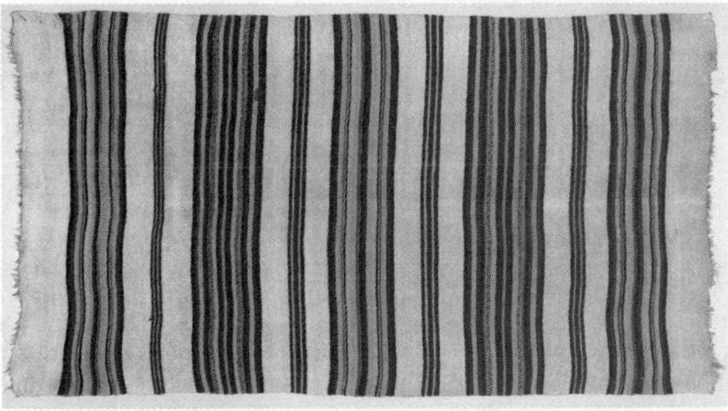

Figure 48—Hispanic weaving Rio Grande Blanket, New Mexico, around 1860. Wool worked in weft-faced plain weave; 98 x 51 in. Neusteter Textile Collection at the Denver Art Museum: Gift of Charles Winfred Douglas, 1934.11. Photograph © Denver Art Museum.

Figure 49—The pine cone design of Chimayó weaving on a vest from Ortega weavers, Chimayó, New Mexico, an eight-generation weaving family dating to the early 1700s in Chimayó. Photograph by Angel Vigil.

the major sheep strain in the Southwest. The Rambouillet was preferred because its shorter hair suited the grazing of sheep better. But its short, oily wool, with its harsher texture, produced a decline in the quality of wool textiles.

Despite these changes in the traditions of Hispanic weaving, the production of weaving textiles continues to be part of the Hispanic experience. The weaving of traditional products using modern methods and the development of new markets have resulted in a renaissance and revival of Hispanic weaving in the Southwest.

Santos

The worshipping of religious images has long been part of the Hispanic experience in the Southwest. The act of supplicant prayer has always been aided by physical representations of Catholic religious personages, especially the saints of the church. These religious images were valued as powerful mediators between God and humans. The deeply devout people of the Hispanic Southwest, and their religious practices, created a large demand for religious images for their churches, chapels, and homes. The folk art of painted and carved Catholic religious icons to meet this need follows a well-recognized path beginning with the Indigenous people of ancient Mexico.

The Aztecs had a highly developed cosmology and a profoundly religious society. They had developed the art of religious representation to a high degree, the most striking being intricately detailed stone-carved images of their gods.

After the conquest of the Aztec people, the Spanish immediately began the process of converting the Aztecs and other Indigenous tribes to Christianity and Catholicism. One of their first tasks was the replacement of the Indigenous gods with Catholic religious personages. The Spanish had brought to the New World their Catholic practices and its images of God, Christ, the Holy Family, and the church's numerous saints. The Spanish transplanted their Catholic images on the Aztec's existing image-worshipping traditions to facilitate the work of conversion from pagan practices to Christian religion.

The success of the Spanish in establishing the Catholic religion in the New World reached as far as its northern frontiers. In the three hundred years of New Spain, the Spanish settlers of the northern frontiers placed the Catholic religion at the center of their life.

The geographic isolation of the northern frontiers resulted in the development of a folk art of *santos*, carved and painted religious images. As they settled new regions, the Spanish colonists brought with them religious statues, canvas and tin paintings, and missals with engraved prints. The religious images new settlers brought with them, however, were not sufficient in numbers to fill the religious needs of the Hispanic populace. Also, since it was difficult for the Hispanics in the northern frontiers of New Spain to acquire new religious images from traders, they began to create their own images for their religious practices. Because it was also difficult to acquire basic materials, the Hispanics of the northern regions learned to utilize locally available materials in the creation of their religious images.

The name *santo* means "holy" and is an appropriate description of the purposes of the *santero*, or religious artist, in creating religious or devotional art. The santo art consists of three primary forms: *retablos*, *bultos*, and *reredos*. Retablos are devotional icons of saints and biblical scenes painted on pine boards. The bulto is a carved statue of saints or Christ figures. The reredos is a large, freestanding altar screen, placed behind the altar and containing multiple images of saints painted on pine board. They are used to decorate church altars. Smaller reredos are used to decorate family devotional shrines. The reredos had the appearance of an arrangement of retablos grouped together to form a large multipaneled religious backdrop.

The retablo ranged in size from large four- to six-foot images used for church decoration to small four- to six-inch images for home and personal use. The retablo from the Spanish colonial period was painted on wood or canvas. With the introduction of tin in the 1800s, the Mexican santero began to paint his retablos on this durable and inexpensive metal. Since tin was scarce in Mexico's northern frontiers, however, the artisans of the Hispanic Southwest painted retablos on locally available wood, usually pine or cottonwood.

The subject matter for the retablo consisted of images of the Holy Family: Jesus, Mary, and Joseph; the Holy Trinity: God, Christ, the Holy Ghost; biblical figures; the Christ figure; and saints of the

Catholic church. An especially popular saint in both the traditional and modern retablo is *el Niño de Atocha*, the patron saint of travelers and prisoners.

The santero would begin the creation of the retablo by selecting and carving a flat piece of wood. The retablo was predominantly rectangular in shape. The santero would then prepare the surface with a gesso mixture made from animal-hide glue and gypsum rock, ground and mixed with water. The next stage consisted of outlining the figures. The final stage was the painting of the religious image.

For paint, the santero used powdered natural materials mixed in egg yolk to make a tempera paint. The santero also used charcoal for black, clay for creams and reds, and ground minerals and earth materials for other colors. Examples of other natural sources of color were walnut hulls for brown; charred bones, honey, and water for black; beetle larva skins for red; rabbit brush for yellow; and azarite for light blue. Piñon sap mixed with grain alcohol provided a varnish. For a brush, the santero would use a yucca fiber chewed on the end to produce a frayed brush-like tip.

Figure 50—A modern santo wooden carving with a frame border. Sacred Heart religious image by Judy Miranda. Photograph by Angel Vigil.

A typical design for a retablo featured a semicircular "lunette" resembling a fluted shell or a scalloped half-wheel carved on the top of the wood panel. The santero often carved a frame into the wood to border the central religious image.

The second type of santo, the bulto, was a three-dimensional statue of saints and holy personages. The santero would use the same materials as for making a retablo: pine or cottonwood for the body and powdered minerals for the coloring. Bultos range in size from small figures for a home shrine to life-size figures with attached and movable arms and legs, used in religious processions and altars. Bultos are painted and frequently clothed to increase realism.

The subject matter of the bulto was as varied as the saints of the Catholic church. Santeros also created group sculptures of the Holy Family. A popular group sculpture depicted Joseph leading a horse carrying Mary seated on it holding the Christ child. Another had Saint Ysidro de Labrador leading his cattle, with an angel hovering nearby.

The traditional art of the santero flourished during the early to middle part of the 1800s. As with other traditional arts, the art fell into decline with the arrival of manufactured products. Lithographs and commercial paintings replaced retablos. Commercial ceramic and plaster of paris statues replaced bultos.

Today, however, as with other traditional arts, Hispanic artists are leading a revival of the work of the santero. Modern artisans are studying and learning the traditional arts, often dedicating themselves to using traditional materials as well. Throughout the Southwest, Hispanic artists are creating santos for personal and religious uses, museums, and art centers as well as for the tourist market. These artists are also dedicated to passing on their knowledge and skills to a younger generation in schools and community centers.

Santeros are usually self-taught. They approach their work as a santero from its traditional religious purpose and believe the carving of santos is a charismatic gift of the Holy Spirit. They also believe that santeros are folk teachers who teach religion without words.

Most modern santeros call their style "traditional/devotional" and claim as their inspiration the classic santos era. They believe in living in the spirit of the images and doing their part to continue the tradition. Most of all, they dedicate themselves to the holy work of carving religious images to help people realize the beauty of the religious spirit on this earth.

Folk Crafts

Folk crafts are enjoyed by people the world over. Because of their simple techniques, children as well as adults can enjoy these craft activities. Also, because of their low skill needs and material requirements, they are quickly learned and readily affordable. Folk crafts are as varied as the cultures of the world, for every culture has an abundance of these crafts in their folk traditions. The people of the Hispanic Southwest have three of these folk craft traditions that can provide hours of creative activity as well as beautiful folk objects to add to many cultural and family celebrations.

La Piñata

The *piñata* is one of the most delightful and playful Hispanic traditions. Enjoyed by Hispanics and non-Hispanics alike, the piñata typically includes a gaily decorated papier-mâché sculpture in the shape of an animal or some fanciful shape suspended from a tree limb or the ceiling by a rope. The piñata is filled with candy or other special treats. An adult controls the piñata while blindfolded children strike at the piñata with a stick, trying to break it. When one child succeeds and breaks the piñata, a mad scramble occurs as children try to fill their hands with the piñata's treats.

The origins of the piñata are lost in legend. Some say Marco Polo brought it from China to Italy in the twelfth century. The Chinese used a piñata-like object in their spring agricultural ceremonies to scatter seeds for planting. Others point to an old Roman game played at the end of the harvest, with blindfolded workers breaking a clay pot hanging over a branch and filled with nuts and fruits. The armies of Julius Caesar later spread this game to the Iberian Peninsula.

In sixteenth-century Italy, the Italians played a game called *pignatta*, which means cone-shaped. The pignatta was a cone-shaped clay pot used in games played by the nobility. These wealthy Italians would try to break the jewel-filled pignatta while blindfolded.

The Spanish borrowed this Italian game, decorated the clay pot with bright colors, and transformed it into a Lenten season activity. The Spanish designated the first Sunday of Lent as Piñata Sunday, on which they would break clay pots filled with candies. They called the game piñata.

The Spanish brought the piñata game to the New World, where it continued to evolve. As was their practice to use everything for a religious purpose, the Spanish missionaries used the piñata to teach the tenets of Christianity. The piñata symbolized the devil dressed in his finest attire to trick humanity. The blindfold represented the human difficulty of recognizing sin. Breaking the pot symbolized the triumph of good over evil. The treats were God's blessings falling on the earth.

Over the years, the piñata game evolved away from such religious purposes to its present purpose as a party game, especially enjoyed by children at birthday parties.

During the hitting of the piñata, children often encourage the hitter with shouts of "¡Dale! ¡Dale!" (Hit it! Hit it!). No matter the occasion, it can always be enhanced with a joyful game of piñata.

Figure 51—"¡Dale! ¡Dale!" (Hit it! Hit it!)"

Papel Picado

Papel picado, meaning perforated paper, are colorful paper cutouts. In some parts of the Spanish-speaking world, they are called *papel de seda*, paper silk, because of their delicate nature. In Mexico they are called *papel de china*, Chinese paper, because the practice of decoratively cutting images into paper originated in China. Traders brought tissue paper from Asia to Mexico in the 1500s.

Figure 52—Decorative papel picado

These tissue paper cutouts are used to decorate many different celebrations. They can be seen decorating rooms in homes and hallways in churches as well as city streets. One particular use of them is to decorate the *ofrenda*, the altar, for the Day of the Dead celebration. The pictures on them can be seasonal motifs, such as Christmas angels or Easter eggs. The cut images also can be simple geometric or floral designs and can decorate any festive occasion.

Usually they are draped over string and hung in the air to create a large, decorative banner of papel picado.

Ojos de Dios

Ojos de dios, gods' eyes, is a ritual object made by the Huichol people of Mexico. The Huichol Indians of the state of Jalisco live in the rugged and inaccessible mountains of the western Sierra Madre. They were one of the last native tribes to fall under Spanish rule, and they never completely adopted the Spanish ways. Of all the Mexican native people, they most closely live the indigenous life of preconquest Mexico. They still live in their traditional ways and practice their own religion.

The Huichol use ojos de dios as revered religious objects in their prayer ceremonies. Their yarn and bamboo creations symbolize the eyes of the gods invoked in their prayers. These eyes of their gods allow the gods to view human life and thereby grant people health and a good life.

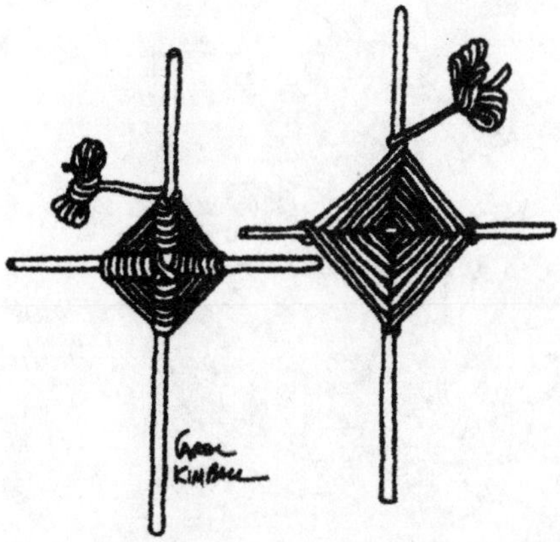

Figure 53—A simple ojos de dios, *gods' eye*

They call their gods' eyes *tsikuri* and their shaman holy men weave them to use in their religious prayers.

The Huichol symbolism of the gods' eyes is primarily associated with their prayers for their children—prayers for a good and long life. They pray that the gods' eyes look down with favor on their children. For their prayers, they place their gods' eyes on their altars, attach them to their prayer arrows, or have their children wear them.

Fathers dedicate gods' eyes to their children, with one gods' eye for each year of the child's life, up to age five. After age five, children are responsible for their own religious obligations and must make their own gods' eyes.

The Huichol also place gods' eyes in the frameworks of new houses and in their mountain shrines for protection of people and to ensure abundant crops and a long life.

Cascarones

In New Mexico, Hispanics would save eggshells during the Lenten season. Since religious Catholics often would give up meat during Lent, the period of sacrifice before Easter, eggs were a meat substitute providing an abundance of available shells. By carefully blowing the egg out of the shell, they were able to preserve the shell for decoration. The eggshells were decorated and used at dances after Lent was over.

Figure 54—
Traditional cascarones

Oral Traditions

Buenos Cuentos, Buenos Amigos
Good stories, good friends.

The origins of the oral traditions of the Hispanic Southwest are found in history and cultural memory. When the Spanish came to the New World, they brought with them the rich oral traditions of sixteenth-century Spain. Spanish culture at this time was a mosaic of varied influences. The Iberian Peninsula had experienced the Greek, Roman, Arab, and Jewish cultures over centuries. The Oriental and Indian cultures had also passed on their influences to the Spanish people. In addition, the Catholic church was a primary and powerful influence on Spanish life, thought, and cultural practices. This fertile cultural environment produced oral traditions with an immense scope in style and subject.

Folklorists have traced the roots of traditional *cuentos*, or stories, as far back as the magical tales of the Thousand and One Arabian Nights and the fables of medieval Europe. Juan B. Rael, in the introduction to his two-volume collection *Cuentos Españoles Colorado y de Nuevo Méjico*, describes similarities between stories he collected and the fabliaux of medieval French literature as well as the work of Giovanni Boccaccio and Marguerite de Navarre. In *The Folklore of Spain in the American*

Southwest, Aurelio Espinosa reports that 90 percent of the folk literature of the Hispanic Southwest can be traced to Spain. In this book, he tells several anecdotes about a research trip to Spain during which he finds exact versions of stories he had collected in the Hispanic Southwest. Many folklorists consider the Hispanic Southwest to be the richest store of folktales in the United States.

The oral traditions of the Hispanic Southwest composed a literary heritage for Hispanic families. The stories they told were their way of passing their culture from one generation to the next. The stories allowed older generations to pass on their wisdom. The stories allowed communities to share and sustain their religious faith between the infrequent visits from the clergy. And finally, the stories provided a way for families to pass the time after the work of the day was finished.

The stories were alive with the traditions of the family. The stories' natural context was family gatherings: weddings, birthdays, funerals, harvest celebrations, or the simple gathering of the family around the winter fire. The traditional storytellers were not in any way similar to the professional storytellers we know today. They were farmers, miners, sheepherders, weavers, cooks, brothers, uncles, aunts, and grandparents. They were family members who loved telling a good story and who held a special reputation in the family as a *cuentista*, a storyteller.

Traditional Hispanic culture has a vast variety of stories. Folklorists have categorized these stories with detailed indicators of story type and origin. But most of the stories can be categorized under several general headings.

Moral and religious tales were important to the Hispanic people as aid in maintaining their Catholic religion. During the Spanish colonial years, it took weeks and months for priests to make their infrequent visits from the interior of Mexico to the northern frontiers. Isolated geographically, the Hispanic people used moral and religious cuentos to sustain their religious beliefs. The stories centered on struggles with temptation and the search for the moral life on earth. The stories had God, the devil, death, and the saints as major characters. And each story contained a strong moral teaching from the Catholic church.

Chistes were short, anecdotal tales, usually with a comic twist at the end. The Hispanic people greatly enjoyed chistes. Over time, the cuento tradition has changed from favoring long, fully developed, detailed narratives to favoring shorter stories, especially chistes.

The *dos compadre* story is a unique story category. A *compadre* in Hispanic culture is technically the godparent of one's child. In common experience, however, a compadre is a good and close friend. These stories always pit two close but contrasting friends against each other. The stories about these opposite character types usually are for comic effect and reveal a moral teaching as an outcome of the characters' dramatic dilemma.

Animal stories are especially common. As in Aesop's fables of western culture, Hispanic stories often feature animals who speak and act as humans. The stories always have a subtle moral lesson as part of the story.

A final general category are stories of transformation, wonder, and wisdom. These stories are descendants of the great European folktales, especially those collected by the Brothers Grimm. They involve giants, princesses, magical transformations and objects, evil witches, and faraway lands. These are the well-known "Once Upon a Time" stories.

Traditional stories existed within the context of a larger oral tradition. Along with cuentos, the Hispanic people enjoyed a large repertoire of *dichos*, folk proverbs, and *adivinanzas*, riddles.

Following are two examples of traditional cuentos. For further study, the bibliography lists several excellent collections of traditional stories.

La Llorona: The Weeping Woman

The Most Well Known of Hispanic Folktales

Traditional story adapted by Angel Vigil

The story of La Llorona is the most well known of all Hispanic folktales. She has often been called "the Mexican Medea."

The origins of La Llorona have been traced back to the times of the Aztecs, who had stories about Cihuacoatl, a pre-Columbian goddess ruling childbirth and death. This powerful goddess, also known as Snake Skirt, was the virgin mother of a god/son who killed his own siblings. The Aztec Indians told of nightly hearing the screams of Cihuacoatl as her children were being killed.

Another version of the origin of La Llorona is the story of La Malinche, or Doña Marina, the Aztec Indian woman who was the mistress/interpreter for Cortés. The story is told about how Cortés wanted to keep their son because he had Spanish blood but abandoned La Malinche because she was only a mistress and Indian. In despair she killed the son, and as the spirit left his body, she cried out, *"¡Ay, mi hijo!"* (Alas, my son.)

The La Llorona story appears in many forms, and there are villages throughout the Spanish-speaking world that claim the La Llorona legend as their own. This one story has been elevated to the category of legend because of the personal narratives existing describing actual encounters with La Llorona. Reported encounters with La Llorona range from being chased by her on a dark country road to actually being captured by her and barely escaping with one's life.

There are many different versions of the La Llorona story. The story changes according to the storyteller and the folklore of the region. In some versions, the children die accidentally. In others, she has many illegitimate children whom she kills, and her divine punishment is to look throughout the world for children to replace her own. In others, she loses them instead of killing them. The version told here is the most common told in the Southwest.

The legend of La Llorona was often used to scare children into proper behavior. For generations, parents have admonished their children to correct their ways or else "La Llorona will get you!"

~~~

Once in a poor Indian village there lived a young girl. As she grew into womanhood, all the young men of the village asked for her hand in marriage. Hers was the greatest beauty of all the maidens in the village.

But she was a very proud young woman, and no man in the village was to her liking. She told all of them no, and she remained firm in her resolve to wait for the right man to marry.

One day a Spanish soldier, an officer, came to the village. He was the commander of a group of soldiers sent from Mexico City to assist the settlers in that region. As he rode into the village sitting high upon his shiny black horse, he appeared like a god to the people. He was a man of the world and easily commanded the respect of all the people in the
~~~

village. To the young women in the village, he was the most handsome and noble man they had ever seen.

The Spanish officer was immediately drawn to the young Indian woman. Her beauty and proud manners intrigued him. He made it clear to all the maidens in the village that she was the one for him. He courted her, and over time the Indian maiden and the Spanish soldier fell in love. They were soon blessed with two children. The children were the most precious things in the world to the Indian woman.

The soldier often was away for long periods. While he was away, his children would long for his return. Their mother would reassure them that their father was away doing important work for the people of their village and that he would soon return to them. He would always return with stories of his great adventures.

One day, after an especially long journey, he returned to the village riding in a carriage. In the carriage beside him was a Spanish *señorita*, a young Spanish woman. His Indian wife ran up to the carriage and asked who was the woman by his side. The Spanish soldier said she was the woman he was soon to marry.

The Indian woman asked how he could marry another when he was already married to her. The Spanish soldier said a marriage between an Indian woman and a Spanish soldier was not a true marriage and that he intended to marry the Spanish señorita. When the Indian woman asked how he could do this to his children, he told her that they were illegitimate children and that no child of an Indian woman could ever be the heir of a Spanish gentleman.

The Indian woman was overcome with anger and grief. She thought of the cruelest way that she could get back at the Spanish soldier. In a moment of rage and madness, she took the two children of the Spanish soldier and blindly hurled them into the river.

As soon as she had thrown them into the river she realized her terrible mistake. She jumped into the river and tried to save her two children. But it was too late. Both children had drowned.

Overwhelmed with sadness, she began to cry and wail for her two lost children. For days and nights, she walked along the banks of the river, crying for her children to return to her. Her mournful and anguished wailing could be heard throughout the village. The people of the village took their own children into their houses when they heard the cries of La Llorona, the crying woman, because they feared that she would take their children to replace her two tragically drowned children.

For all eternity, La Llorona is doomed to walk by the banks of the river, searching for her children to return to her. On many a cold and dark night, you can hear her crying and calling for her children. Her long, loud, mourning cry of grief often comes disguised as the sound of the wind by the river.

So all of you children who hear this story, take care. Mind your parents and be good boys and girls. Because, if you are not careful, La Llorona, the weeping woman, will take you to take the place of her two beloved but lost children.

Historical Coda #17

I have been honored to be designated the Colorado Heritage Artist for Hispanic Storytelling. The Spanish term is that I am a *cuentista*, the teller of traditional tales. In this capacity, I travel extensively to many different communities sharing the traditional tales of my culture. My favorite audience is middle-aged to elder Hispanic people. They always respond so warmly to the stories of their own childhood. Frequently an elderly woman will approach me after I tell the La Llorona story, and she will say, "Señor Vigil, I enjoyed your La Llorona so much, and you told it so well. But you got it all wrong!" Then she will tell me her family's version of the tale. I just love it every time that happens. It is a direct connection to the old-time ways of my people.

Doña Sebastiana—A Moral Story

A traditional story adapted by Angel Vigil

The fascinating story of Doña Sebastiana has been well documented in New Mexico and Colorado. In addition, the carved wooden figure of Doña Sebastiana riding her death cart and drawing her bow and arrow is very common throughout the region. Often, the figure was pulled in religious processions during Holy Week as a reminder of the power of death. An exceptionally fine example of this wooden sculpture is on display at the Denver Museum of Art in its Spanish Colonial section.

~ ~ ~

Once, in the high mountains of northern New Mexico, there lived a poor farmer with his family. Those of us who have lived in this area know that in a year when the rain is plentiful, the ground gives forth its abundance, and there is food for everyone. In a year of drought, however, the ground is barren, and the people struggle to make their living. It just so happened that this year had been a year of drought. The ground was rocky and barren, and there was little food.

As the farmer tucked his children into bed, he looked into their eyes and saw that they were hungry. They tried to be brave little girls and boys and said they weren't hungry, but he knew the truth. They had not eaten for days. The thought of his children going hungry gave him great pain.

Finally, he made up his mind to do something that was not in his character but which was in his will. He would be a man of action. He decided to become a thief. That night he would steal food, and tomorrow his children would eat.

In the still darkness of the night, he crept to his neighbor's chicken coop. Carefully stepping around the sleeping guard dog, who was doing a better job of sleeping than guarding, he stepped into the chicken coop. He grabbed one chicken. "If I am a thief once, I might as well be a thief twice," he said as he grabbed a second chicken. He then carefully crept out of the chicken coop, past the sleeping guard dog, and began the long walk back to his farm.

As he was walking home, he was happy that his children would eat tomorrow. He held up one chicken and said, "Tomorrow my children will eat!" But then he remembered that he had not eaten either for several days. Looking at the second chicken he said, "And tonight I will eat!" He took out his pocket knife and cut off the chicken's head. He then plucked it, and after making a fire with stone sparks and dry grass, he began to cook it on a makeshift wooden spit he constructed from sticks on the ground.

Figure 55—Doña Sebastina, José Inez Herrera, Death Cart, 1890-1910. Wood, leather, hair, feather, metal, silk; 48 × 21½ in. Denver Art Museum Collection: General acquisition funds, 1948.22A-C. Photograph © Denver Art Museum.

The farmer then heard a sound from the darkness he had never heard before. He heard the sound of someone pulling a heavy wooden cart across the barren and rocky ground of northern New Mexico. As a person came out of the darkness into the light of the moon, the farmer felt a chill go down his spine. He was frightened by the strange, dark figure. As the light of the moon shone beneath her hood, he could see the skeleton shape of an old woman.

In a raspy voice the woman said, "Good evening. I am tired from my long nightly journey. Will you share your meal with me?"

In a shaking, frightened voice the farmer asked, "Who are you?'

The woman answered, "You know who I am. I am Doña Sebastiana, *La Muerte*, Death herself. I am on my nightly journey collecting souls in my *carreta de la muerte* for their long journey into eternity. But do not worry, farmer. Tonight is not your night. Will you share your meal with me?"

The farmer thought for a moment and said, "Yes, I will share my meal with you. You above all people treat all people equally. At the moment of your touch, all people, rich, poor, young, old, beautiful, ugly—all people must answer your call. For this reason, I will share my meal with you."

Doña Sebastiana was pleased with the farmer's words. After they had eaten the chicken, in order to reward his generosity and courage, she offered him a reward. She said, "Because you have been brave and wise, I will give you a reward. Ask and you shall receive."

The still-frightened farmer answered, "Doña Sebastiana, I am but a poor and humble farmer. I am not worthy to ask for a gift from you. Give and I shall receive."

"Farmer," she said, "tonight I will give you the power over life and death. I will give you the power of the *curandero*. You shall enter a house of sickness and you shall take the dirt of the earth, the plants of the mountainside, and the water of the river, and with the power I give you tonight, you shall lay your hands on that sick and dying person, and life will return to that person. However, *curandero*, remember the agreement we make tonight. If you ever enter a house of sickness and see me at the head of the bed, you are to tell that person there is nothing you can do, and he is to say his prayers and prepare his soul for the long journey into eternity. If, however, you enter that room and I am at the foot of the bed, then know that I am but passing through, and you can use the powers I give you tonight to heal that sick and dying person. Remember this agreement, *curandero*. Your own life depends upon it."

As the years passed, the healing powers of the farmer became known throughout the valley. Many times he entered a house of sickness and saw Doña Sebastiana at the foot of the bed, and he used his powers to save the sick person. On the few occasions he had seen Doña Sebastiana at the head of the bed, he had said there was nothing to be done, for the soul of the sick person now belonged to Doña Sebastiana.

One night he was called to the house of the richest rancher in the valley. The rancher lay with the sickness of death. As the curandero entered the house of sickness, the rancher called to him with the eternal human cry, "Curandero, save me. Give me one more day to live. I am too young to die. Save me, curandero!"

As the farmer entered the sick rancher's room, he saw Doña Sebastiana at the head of the bed. He told the rancher, "There is nothing I can do. Say your prayers and prepare your soul for the long journey into eternity."

The rancher struggled to raise himself and desperately told the curandero, "Curandero, save me. I know it is within your powers. If you bring life back to me, I will give you all my wealth. Give me one more day to live!"

At the thought of all that wealth and in a moment of human weakness, the farmer was overcome with greed and the promise of the rancher's great wealth. For the second time in his life he decided to be a man of action.

He reached for the bed and turned it around so that now Doña Sebastiana was at the foot of the bed. He then used his powers and took the dirt of the earth, the plants of the mountainside, and the waters of the river, and he placed his hands on the sick and dying man, and life returned to the man.

As he was returning home that night, the farmer heard a sound he had not heard for many years. It was the sound of someone dragging a heavy wooden cart across the barren and rocky ground of northern New Mexico.

Out of the darkness of the forest came the skeletal figure of Doña Sebastiana. She said, "Curandero, tonight you made a grave mistake." She then pointed to her carreta de la muerte. On her death cart were two candles. One was tall, burning brightly, with hours left to burn. The other was short with a weak, flickering flame, about to be extinguished by the slightest breeze.

"Curandero, but a few moments ago the tall candle was your soul, brightly burning with a long life ahead. The short candle was the soul of the wealthy man, about to lose the bright energy of life. But now the tall candle is the soul of the wealthy man, with many more years to burn. And the short candle is your own weak and fragile soul."

She then took out one of her arrows and shot it through the flame of the short candle, extinguishing it.

At the moment the flame went out on the short candle, the soul of the farmer left his body and joined the other souls Doña Sebastiana had gathered that night in her carreta de la muerte for their long journey into eternity.

Historical Coda #18

As part of my work documenting the practices of Hispano elders, I received several grants to travel throughout the Upper Rio Grande Valley to interview and record the memories of Hispano elders in northern New Mexico and the San Luis Valley in Colorado. One memorable interview was with New Mexico's National Heritage storyteller Cleofes Vigil (no relation). Señor Vigil was renowned for his singing of the Penitente traditional sacred songs, the *alabados*, Spanish Catholic hymns that have been preserved by the Penitente Brothers of northern New Mexico. He also was a *pito* (flute) player in the traditional manner of his Spanish ancestors. He recited a version of Doña Sebastina that was remarkably similar to the others, but with the embellishment and changing of detail that marked the story as his own. One striking difference in his version was that the person in the story was not a farmer but a coal miner. Doña Sebastina is a story I remember from my own childhood in New Mexico. At the end of the interview, I asked him who he tells his stories to nowadays. With a sad lament in his voice he said, "Only white people from the university."

Dichos, *Folk Proverbs*

Para todo hay dicho.
There is a dicho for everything.

Dichos were part of the everyday experience of the Spanish settlers. Their wide familiarity with dichos was in large part grounded in their Spanish heritage. Spain in the sixteenth century had a well-developed tradition of folk proverbs. The greatest Spanish novel, *Don Quixote* by Don Miguel de Cervantes, with its ample expression of folk proverbs, is the most significant literary example of the extent and importance of dichos in Spanish culture.

Dichos are an expression of personal philosophy and folk wisdom. They serve as guidelines for moral values and social behavior. They often illustrate a clever insight to a person's character. The older generation often uses them to help younger people understand the subtleties of a situation or conflict. And often, they end a conversation with a pithy, final observation. There are literally hundreds of recorded dichos. Many have an untranslatable, idiomatic quality. And they vary family to family, region to region.

There is even a dicho about dichos: *Para todo hay dicho*: There is a *dicho* for everything.

A buey viejo, cencerro nuevo.
An old ox, a new cowbell.
(An old man with a young woman.)

Adonde va el violin, va la bolsa.
Wherever the violin goes, the case goes.
(Said about mothers who always chaperone their daughters.)

Cada cabeza es un mundo.
Each head is a world.
(To each his own.)

Cada oveja con su pareja.
Each sheep with its own kind.
(Birds of a feather flock together.)

Como es la vida, así es la muerte.
As life is, so is death.

Cuando el gato no está, el ratón se pasea.
When the cat is gone, the rat takes a walk.
(When the cat's away, the mice will play.)

El que al pobre le cierra la puerta, la del cielo no halla abierta.
He who closes the door to the poor will find the door of heaven closed.

En boca cerrada no entran moscas.
Flies do not fly into a closed mouth.
(Keep quiet and mind your own business.)

Gato llorón no caza ratón.
A crying cat does not catch a mouse.
(Complaining will get you nowhere.)

Hazte el tonto y come con dos manos.
Act the fool and eat with both hands.
(Live life to the fullest.)

Hoy anda en sus mulas prietas.
Today he is riding his black mules.
(He is in a bad mood.)

La verdad es como el maíz, solita sale.
Truth is like corn; it comes out by itself.

Los dichos de los viejos son evangelios chiquitos.
The sayings of old people are little gospels.

Panza llena, corazón contento.
Full stomach, contented heart.

Una de cal y otra de arena.
One of lime, one of sand.
(Variety is the spice of life.)

Una vez me llevo el coyote, dos no.
The coyote took me once, not twice.
(Trick me once, it's your fault. Trick me twice, it's mine.)

Vale más tarde que nunca.
It is better late than never.

Vale más hoy que mañana
Better today than tomorrow.
(A bird in the hand is worth two in the bush.)

Ya va otra vez la burra al maíz.
The burro is in the corn again.
(There he goes again.)

Adivinanzas, *Riddles*

Adivinanzas, or riddles, are also part of the oral tradition in Hispanic families. As with dichos, there are hundreds of collected adivinanzas giving testimony to the widespread practice of families sharing riddles with each other.

Adivinanzas vary from the simple question with a clever answer to the complex challenge requiring a knowledge of or familiarity with Hispanic culture and religion. Some are in poetical form. Some are brain teasers requiring thoughtful analysis. And some are simple children's ditties. Many traditional stories have adivinanzas as part of the plot and the hero's quest. But all are part of the family experience and a common social pastime.

Anda y no tiene pies
Habla y no tiene boca
¿Qué es?
(Una carta)

It travels, but has no feet.
It talks, but has no mouth.
What is it?
(A letter)

Arca monarca de buen parecer
ningún carpintero le puede hacer.
¿Qué es?
(La caja del cuerpo)

A royal box so beautiful looking
no carpenter could ever make it.
What is it?
(The human body)

Cajita de Dios bendita
que se abre y se Cierra
y no se marchita
¿Qué es?
(El ojo)

A little box, blessed by God,
that opens and shuts
but never wears out.
What is it?
(An eye)

¿Cual es la santa mas olorosa?
(Santa Rosa)

What is the saint that smells the best?
(Saint Rose)

Que cosa nunca puedes alcanzar
y siempre anda contigo?
(Tu sombra)

What thing can you never grab
But always walks with you?
(Your shadow)

¿Qué es que te lo tragas
y no lo ves?
(Aire)

What is it you can swallow
but cannot see?
(Air)

Sube el cerro y baja
y siempre está
en el mismo lugar
¿Qué es?
(El camino)

It goes up the hill
and comes down the hill
but is always in the same place.
What is it?
(The road)

Una vieja
con un solo diente
recoge a toda su gente
¿Qué es?
(Una campana)

An old woman
with only one tooth
gathers all her people.
What is it?
(A bell)

¿Qué es
Lo que hacemos todos
Con el tiempo?
(Envejecer)

What is it
That we all do
In time?
(Grow old)

¿Qué es
Que entre mas le quitas
Mas grande es?
(El poso)

What is it
The more you take away from it
The larger it gets?
(A hole in the ground)

Me acuesto blanca
Me levanto pinta
¿Qué es?
(La tortilla)

I lie down white
I get up spotted
What is it?
(A tortilla)

Music

Music is one of the most accessible paths into the heart of a culture. The songs a people sing spring from their deepest emotional centers. Songs pass from generation to generation, creating powerful cultural bonds and lasting cultural memory. Within the family, one generation passes musical talent, knowledge, and skills to another generation. The music people play to entertain themselves gives meaning to their life, for their songs help celebrate the greatest joys and bring comfort to the deepest grief. The instruments people play are their tools of cultural expression. Most importantly, the occasions of traditional music are centered in the experiences of family life—weddings, funerals, birthdays, celebrations, and reunions. Many of the events that mark a full and rich life on this earth are accompanied by music.

One of the most enduring characteristics of the Hispanic people is their great love of music. Just as with other cultural traditions, the Hispanic people have evolved forms of music that are widely varied and particular to each region of the Southwest. For the Hispanic people, their music is a constant reminder of the riches that result from the infusion of musical culture into all aspects of daily life, both secular and religious.

The music of the Hispanic Southwest is the result of centuries of cultural evolution, beginning with the historically momentous collision of Spanish and Aztec cultures. The history of the Spanish colonization of the New World, beginning with the conquest of the Aztec empire, includes the supplanting of Aztec musical traditions with those of the Spanish.

At the time of the Spanish arrival in the New World, the Aztecs had developed a sophisticated ceremonial and religious system that fully dominated their life. During the time of their consolidation of power and the establishment of their dominance in central Mexico, the Aztec people had also developed sophisticated literary, artistic, and musical traditions. Music especially was a central part of their cultural practices.

Music, singing, and Indigenous instruments were part of Aztec religious and ceremonial rituals. The Aztec instruments included drums, reed or clay flutes, shells, bones, gourd rattles, wooden rasps, and stringed instruments made with animal shells.

The *conquistadores,* and the missionaries who followed them, brought the instruments and the musical traditions of the Golden

Age of Spain to the New World. The Spanish soon used their musical traditions in their efforts to convert the Indigenous natives to Spanish culture. During the early period of colonization, the missionaries were intent on replacing all aspects of Aztec life, including the music and instruments of the Aztec people, with Spanish cultural practices. Soon Spanish violins, harps, and guitars replaced the Aztec drums and flutes. Aztec musical repertory eventually gave way to European musical forms.

The native musical traditions and instruments, however, were never completely eradicated. The Indigenous populations were successful in maintaining many aspects of their culture. The Deer Dance of the Yaqui Indians, with its characteristic sound of gourd rattles and wooden rasps, is one of the most famous indigenous dances performed by modern Mexican dance companies. Another example of the continuing influence of Native culture is the common sight of fabulously costumed *conchero* dancers performing the traditional and sacred Aztec dances at community festivals throughout the Southwest.

The people of the Hispanic Southwest have a varied and wide-ranging repertory of songs and musical styles. Many of the songs are directly descended from the traditions of Spain, while many evolved in the fertile mix of Indigenous and Spanish cultures in the New World. *Romances, rancheras, sones, corridos, inditas*, and *boleros* are a few of the primary musical styles heard in the Hispanic Southwest.

The *romance* is a narrative ballad of Spanish origin, with songs dating from the late Medieval and Renaissance Spain. They are the oldest type of folk song known in the Southwest. The songs tell the common and eternal stories of love, betrayal, desire, and honor. Romances often tell the stories of nobility and the upper class. The romances found in the Hispanic Southwest often share text, titles, and subject matter with the *cancioneros* of Spain, the songs of the Spanish Renaissance court.

The *ranchera* is the rural "ranch" folk music of Mexico. Like romances, rancheras often sing about lost love and powerful emotions. They also have lyrics telling of personal and regional pride. Its musical style can vary from the 3/4 meter of the waltz to the fast 2/4 of the polka. Well-known rancheras are "El Rancho Grande," "La Cucaracha," "De Colores," the anthem of the United Farm Workers, and the all-time great Mexican love song, categorized as a ranchera romantica, "Volver, Volver." Another is the lovely birthday song "Las Mañanitas."

The *son* is a characteristic musical style played by mariachis. It is a basic Mexican dance form with many regional variations. It is associated with the Mexican dance style *zapateado*, a heel-toe dance step known for its complex rhythms. The distinctive sounds of the zapateado are made by the stamping of the foot and clicking of the heels on the floor. The basic son is characterized by its rhythmic variations and its development of theme and variations. The son form appears in regional variations throughout Mexico. One of the most well-known examples is the song "La Bamba," a *son jarocho* from Veracruz.

Corridos are one of the most popular Hispanic musical styles. They are narrative ballads that tell the story of ordinary people and their adventures. Often corridos tell a very dramatic story and have death or some tragic event as their primary theme. A corrido often was a quickly improvised song reporting the facts of a dramatic event. Originating in Mexico, corridos have spread throughout the Hispanic Southwest. Corridos have generally been written in the last century and a half, as opposed to the romances, many of which are centuries old.

Corridos consist of the most common Hispanic verse form, the *copla*, the rhymed four-line verse, with eight syllables to a line. Two main features of the corrido are the opening verses, which present a detailed description of the time and place of the narrative, and the closing verses, the *despedida*, or farewell, in which the singer bids a farewell to the song. The despedida often begins with the line "Fly, fly, little dove," and can add a light ending or a moral to a tragic tale. Many corridos came from the events of the Mexican Revolution in 1910. "Adelita" is one of the most famous from this period, telling the story of a revolutionary heroine.

The *indita* is a folk song similar to the corrido in that it tells a narrative story, usually describing events that took place in a particular area. The indita differs from the corrido in its melody, which contains influences from southwestern Indian music. The indita also reflects the influence of native rhythms and is a obvious example of the cross-fertilization of Spanish and Native cultures.

Boleros are another form common to mariachi music. The form originated in Cuba and migrated to Mexico. The music is common throughout Latin America and is often heard in strolling duos and trios. Boleros are more sophisticated than rancheras, and they often sing of an idealized romantic love.

It is impossible to identify one dominant Hispanic musical tradition, for the musical map of the Hispanic Southwest is a combination of many musical traditions. Three musical forms, however, are especially prevalent in the Southwest: Mexican mariachi, northern New Mexican and southern Colorado colonial music, and Texas-Mexican *conjunto*.

Each of these forms represents the cross-fertilization of European and Mexican musical influences. As the colonial population spread throughout the frontiers of northern Mexico, the land that would eventually become the American Southwest, they established the musical traditions that are expressed in these three dominant musical forms.

Mexican Mariachi

Mariachi music is the most recognizable and popular Mexican musical style. In fact, as experienced in the southwestern United States, mariachi music has become the national music of Mexico. A broader perspective, however, recognizes that as little as fifty years ago, mariachi music was no more popular than a dozen or so other regional Mexican musical styles. Many states in Mexico had their own regional music, and the state of Jalisco, with its mariachi music, was one of these.

In a development similar to that with Texas-Mexican conjunto music, mariachi music began to rise to prominence in the 1930s with the commercialization of Mexican music away from folk music and into popular mass-media entertainment. The professionalization of folk music and musicians was a result of the national exposure radio gave to regional folk musicians. Mariachi music soon separated itself from being one of many regional folk music styles to being recognized as a commercial success. Gaspar Vargas, who founded the famed Mariachi Vargas de Tecalitlán, and his son Silvestre were two mariachi musicians who brought the music of Jalisco to the forefront of Mexican culture. By the 1930s and 1940s, mariachi music had moved beyond just being one of many regional music styles and was becoming the musical style representing Mexico as a whole.

There are several theories about the origin of the word *mariachi*. One finds the word *maria* at the heart of the word *mariachi*. One theory cites the origin of the word to be in the Catholic veneration of the Blessed Virgin Mary. This theory has little support in the academic world beyond a recognition of the coincidental similarity of the words. A second, and widely believed popular legend about the word, is that it is derived from the French word for marriage, *mariage*. It was common practice during the French occupation of Mexico under Maximilian, from 1864 to 1867, that the French would hire Mexican bands, including many Jalisco folk musicians, to play at social events, especially their weddings. According to this theory, the Spanish soon adapted the French word *mariage* into the term *mariachi*. The French phrase *C'est un mariage* (It is a wedding) became the Spanish phrase *Es un mariachi* (It is a mariachi). This theory, however, does not recognize the great resentment the Mexicans had for the French. A recognition of the antagonism Mexicans had for the establishment of French culture in Mexico weakens the likelihood of this explanation.

Another theory gives the word an Indigenous origin from the Nahautl language of the Coca, a native group from the area of Cocula, near Guadalajara, in what is now southern Jalisco. The supporters of this theory see the origins of the mariachi in Indigenous music, which, as in so many other aspects of the merging of Native and Spanish cultural elements in Mexico, later adopted and evolved the traits of Spanish culture, in this

Figure 56—Mariachi in Mexico City. Photograph by Dorotea Kraatz.

instance Spanish musical culture. Further support for this theory is the occurrence of the word *mariachitos*, which used to describe modern Indigenous performers who are Nahautl speakers in a region close to Jalisco.

The modern mariachi group consists of violins, the *vihuela* (a small, rounded-back, five-string guitar), a *guitarrón* (a six-string bass guitar), the regular six-string guitar, and, of course, the trumpet. The trumpet is the most recent instrument to join the mariachi sound, but it has quickly become a dominant part of mariachi music. The size of mariachi groups can vary from as few as four to as many as eight. One of the most identifying aspects of a mariachi group is their *traje de charro* outfits, adopted from the *charro*, or rural landowner-horseman in Jalisco: wide sombrero, boots, and silver-plated decoration on the jackets and pants.

Traditional mariachi music consisted of sones and jarabes. The musical repertory of the modern mariachi has expanded to include rancheras, corridos, and other popular Mexican musical styles.

Mariachi music has become so widespread throughout Hispanic culture that mariachi music can be heard at weddings, birthdays, political functions, and community celebrations. Mariachi music's great popularity is even evidenced in the mariachi mass that is becoming a common event at Catholic churches in the Southwest with large Mexican congregations.

Northern New Mexico and Southern Colorado Spanish Colonial Music

The Hispanic people of northern New Mexico and southern Colorado have retained aspects of Spanish colonial culture longer than others in the Hispanic Southwest. It is the one area of the Hispanic Southwest in which people still proudly refer to themselves as "Spanish."

The first Spanish settlement in the northern reaches of New Spain was in 1598, under the leadership of Don Juan de Oñate. Soon after his expedition came clergy and military, further settling the northern frontier of New Spain. In 1610, Santa Fe was established as the administrative outpost of this area.

These communities were far from the centers of culture, population, and political power of New Spain, which were one thousand miles to the south across a vast and barren frontier. This geographical isolation produced an exemplary self-reliance in the Hispanic people of these early southwestern villages. One aspect of this self-reliance was their development of their own independent artistic traditions. Left to themselves for generations, they sustained the original Spanish culture of the first settlers. Their musical traditions especially continued to reflect their Spanish colonial heritage. To this day, it is common to find centuries-old Spanish romances and the Spanish colonial *entriega de novios* existing along with a Mexican corrido.

The primary instruments of this area's Spanish colonial music are the violin and guitar, which were imported to Mexico and the Southwest from Spain. Musical duos will have the violin playing the melody line and the guitar playing the bass or rhythm line. It is also traditional to have one or both of the musicians sing as they play such Spanish colonial favorites as romances, rancheras, and valses.

A particularly unique song to this area is the *alabado*. A religious hymn, the alabado was sung by the religious brotherhood of Los Hermanos, or Penitentes. The songs resemble the chanting of the plain song or Gregorian chants of the medieval church. Sung in unison, alabados had simple accompaniment, usually the *pito* (reed flute) or *matraca* (rattle). They were deeply religious songs and helped the Hispanic people of this area maintain their Spanish Catholic religious practices, since visits from the clergy to this distant and isolated area were infrequent.

Texas-Mexican Conjunto

Conjunto, or as it is also known, *norteño* music, is a very popular form of music among the Hispanic people of Texas. Its joyful polka dance rhythms and bright accordion sound are its primary musical characteristics. Throughout southern Texas, one hears this most identifiable sound at family and community celebrations.

Conjunto music emerged as a dominant form of music in the region during the early part of the twentieth century. During the last quarter of the nineteenth century, the violin was the primary instrument for dance bands. In the 1860s, however, German immigrants introduced a new instrument, the accordion, into Mexican-Texan culture. In addition to the accordion, German musicians popularized dances such as the polka and the schottische. Bands that played this type of music were called *conjunto norteño. Conjunto* means "ensemble" when referring to musical groups, and *norteño* refers to the northern parts of Mexico as the source of the music. By the end of the nineteenth century, conjunto bands were popular and in demand at weddings and other Mexican-Texan celebrations.

One theory on the source of this German influence on Mexican music is that German settlers in and around Central Texas, San Antonio specifically, were the musicians who influenced the music of the Rio Grande Valley. Manuel Peña, in his book *The Texas-Mexican Conjunto*, however, presents a better case for the argument that German brewery workers in Monterrey, Mexico, were the musicians who introduced the accordion and the polka to northern Mexico around the 1860s. He supports his argument by describing the strong commercial link that existed between Monterrey and Mexican Texas up until the 1920s. Another point he makes is that the path of cultural influence historically was from south to north, from Mexico to the American Southwest. It is this cultural influence from northern Mexico, specifically Monterrey, and *El Norte*, Mexican Texas, that resulted in the development of what is now known as conjunto music.

The commercialization of northern Mexican music in the 1920s and 1930s resulted in the popularization of conjunto music in *tejano*, or Mexican Texas, culture. The godfather of conjunto music, accordionist Narciso Martínez, began to record during this time and greatly influenced the acceptance of conjunto music by the tejano working class. During this time, the instruments of early conjunto music were the accordion, the twelve-string *bajo sexto*, and the *tololoche*, or stand-up string bass.

From the 1920s to the 1960s, conjunto music became more established in tejano culture. The instrumentation evolved to include drum sets and the electric bass. In addition, its repertory expanded to include many popular Mexican song types, while the central musical characteristic of conjunto music continued to be its dance-oriented polka rhythm.

Today conjunto music is an established part of tejano culture. On the radio, in dance halls, at family celebrations, and at community events, it is common to find a conjunto band entertaining dancing crowds. Successful bands of all types include conjunto music as part of their repertory. While hard to find, the notable film *Chulas Fronteras* is a remarkable documentary of the importance of conjunto music in tejano culture. Modern musicians including the Mexican Los Tigres del Norte, the legendary accordionist Flaco Jiménez, and the Texas Tornados continue to infuse creative energy into conjunto music and truly make it a music of the tejano people.

Three Traditional Hispanic Songs

Here are three examples of classic traditional Hispanic songs the casual listener might encounter. Each are well known throughout Southwestern Hispanic culture and are considered standards. Many varied musical artists, both Hispanic and non-Hispanic, have recorded the songs. The Spanish lyrics are standard versions, and the loose English translations are my own.

Las Mañanitas

"Las Mañanitas" (a morning song) is a ranchera with a beautiful and romantic Mexican tradition. The romantic tradition has it sung at the beginning of daybreak, when young men serenade their girlfriends as an expression of love and admiration. The singer can be accompanied by his friends or musicians to add harmonies to the occasion.

Another popular tradition is for "Las Mañanitas" to be sung on special days: saints' days and especially birthdays. "Las Mañanitas" is one of the most well-known songs in the Hispanic Southwest. It is sung at birthdays, parties, and family reunions. Many varieties and translations of verses exist, and often communities and families have their own version. The loose translation that follows is my own adaptation.

An especially beautiful version of the song, with its own variation in lyrics, is by legendary Mexican singer Pedro Infante and can be viewed on YouTube. Listen to it to understand why "Las Mañanitas" is such an important part of Hispanic culture. While you are on the YouTube page for Pedro Infante, listen to his mournful and heartbreaking song "Cucurrucucú Paloma," the black-and-white version. Watch him perform these two songs, and you'll understand why acclaimed author Denise Chávez titled one of her novels *Loving Pedro Infante*.

Estas son la mañanitas	These are the morning songs
Que cantaba el rey David.	That King David sang.
Hoy por ser día de tu santo	Because today is your saint's day
Te las cantamos a tí.	We sing them to you.
Despierta, mi bien, despierta,	Wake up, my love, wake up,
Mira que ya amaneció,	See that the day has dawned,
Ya los pajarillos cantan,	The little birds are singing
La luna ya se metió.	And the moon is gone.
Qué linda está la mañana	How beautiful is the morning
En que vengo a saludarte	When I come to greet you.
Venimos todos con gusto	We all come with joy
Y placer a felicitarte.	And happiness to congratulate you.
Ya viene amaneciendo,	Here comes the dawn,
Ya la luz del día nos dio.	The light of day is here.
Levántate de mañana,	Get up in the morning,
Mira que ya amaneció.	And see what has dawned.
El dia que tu naciste	The day you were born
Nacieron todas las flores,	All the flowers were born,
Y en la pila del bautizmo	At your baptism
Cantaron las ruiseñores.	The nightingales sang.
De las estrellas del Cielo	Of the stars in heaven
Tengo que bajarte dos.	I want to give you two.
Una para saludarte,	One to greet you,
Y otra para decirte adiós.	And the other to tell you goodbye.

De Colores

"De Colores," a traditional Mexican ranchera sung on special occasions and celebrations, has its origins in sixteenth-century Spain. In the United States, it is a Chicano favorite and is well known as the anthem of the United Farm Workers of America, the farmworkers' union founded by Cesar Chavez. As with many traditional folk songs, there are variations in both verses and translations. This loose translation is my own adaptation.

There are many spirited versions of the song on YouTube. Listen to it to understand why it became part of a national movement. Its melody is easy to sing; its message is eternal; it is a great song to sing in unison in a group.

Dr. Juana Bordas, in her discussion in chapter 5, Giving Witness, describes how she always ends her talks by having the audience sing "De Colores."

De colores,
de colores se visten los campos
en la primavera.
De colores,
de colores son los pajaritos que
vienen
de afuera.
De colores,
de colores es al arco iris que
vemos lucir.

In many colors,
in many colors the fields
dress up in the springtime
In many colors,
in many colors are all the little
birds
which come from far away.
In many colors,
in many colors is the rainbow
we see shining.

Coro
Y por eso los grandes amores
de muchos colores me gustan
a mí. (cantar dos veces)

Chorus
And that's why I love the many
colors.
(sing twice)

Canta el gallo,
canta el gallo con el quiri, quiri,
quiri, quiri.
La gallina,
La gallina con el cara, cara, cara,
cara.
Los pollitos,
los pollitos con el pío, pío, pío, pí.

The rooster sings,
the rooster sings quiri, quiri,
quiri, quiri.
The hen,
the hen sings cara, cara, cara,
cara.
The little chicks,
the little chicks sing pío, pío, pío, pí.

Coro
Y por eso . . .

Chorus
And that's why . . .

La Llorona

There is even a traditional song to accompany the La Llorona story that was presented in the preceding section on oral traditions. The story is the most well known of all Mexican traditional tales. There are many versions and translations of the song, and its origins are obscure. This loose translation is my own adaptation. It has a haunting, mournful, and melancholy melody. There are many beautiful versions of the song on YouTube. Two recommendations are versions by Victoria Arcos for its melancholy simplicity, and the other by Angela Aguilar for its cinematic and dramatic visuals.

Todos me dicen el negro, llorona	They call me the dark one, weeping woman,
negro pero cariñoso	dark but full of love.
Yo soy como el chile verde, llorona,	I am like the green chile, weeping woman,
picante, pero sabroso.	hot, but full of flavor.
¡Ay de mí! llorona,	Woe is me, weeping woman,
llorona de ayer y hoy,	weeping woman of yesterday and today,
Ayer era maravilla, llorona,	Yesterday I was a marvel, weeping woman,
y ahora ni somba soy.	and now I am not even a shadow of myself.

Dance

One of the most immediate and most enjoyable experiences in Hispanic culture is the movements and rhythms of its dances. Just as with music, the people of the Hispanic Southwest have an old and joyous tradition of dance as part of their living heritage. There is not a wedding, a quinceañera, or a community celebration without that exuberant moment when families and individuals express their great shared happiness by dancing.

The dances can range from the free-spirited modern movements of the young to the traditional dances of the elder generation. The dances can be as spontaneous as family members joining in a wedding march, as informal as observing Aztec *conchero* dancers at a community fair, or as formal as a professional dance troupe presenting an evening concert of Mexican dance. But no matter what the style, the meaning is the same—dance is a central expression of joy and pride for Hispanic people throughout the Southwest.

The dances of the Hispanic Southwest, as with so many other cultural practices, have their roots in the dances of the Indigenous people of Mexico and the Spanish colonialists who settled the New World. This discussion of Hispanic dance will examine these roots and present the origins of the dances enjoyed throughout the Hispanic Southwest today. It will also describe several representative dances from both Mexican and Southwest Hispanic traditions. The purpose of this section is to introduce the reader to the background and traditions of the dances, as well as to place the dances in their proper social context. Its educational purpose is to give the reader an appreciation of the history of traditional dances and an ability to recognize and understand several of the primary dances that might be encountered in the Hispanic Southwest. Any occasion providing the opportunity to witness or participate in any of the described dances will give the reader a heartfelt and fun experience of the beauty of Mexican and Southwestern Hispanic dance.

Aztec, Spanish, and Mexican Roots

The Aztecs of ancient Mexico had a highly developed ritual and ceremonial life. Their calendar was marked by festivals called *veintenas*, which were festivals in honor of their gods. Singing, music, and dance were important parts of their ceremonial life. The demands of a strict and rigorous religious cosmology dictated that all aspects of their life reflect their profound religious practices. Dance was one aspect of this ceremonial life that served the Aztecs in both their religious and secular practices.

The Aztecs had houses of song and dance called *cuicalli* near their temples. These houses were schools for students who began their dance studies at the age of twelve. Both men and women danced in Aztec ceremonies, usually separately. Large-scale dances were performed in the temples or main plazas for major religious observances. Smaller dances were for private occasions for nobles, such as a wedding. Their instruments were the simple instruments derived from the natural world: the drum, the clay ocarina, the gourd rattle, the wooden flute, the scored bone scraped with a stick.

The most common Aztec dances were both religious and military in function. As a warrior society, the Aztecs used dance to celebrate their warriors, to prepare warriors for battle, and to fortify the spirits of young recruits. The strong, percussive beat of the drum was a perfect sound for the dances of this warrior society.

In contrast to this warrior aspect of their society, the Aztecs had a deep appreciation of beauty and the natural world. Many of their festivals were dedicated to the beautiful flowers and feathers that decorated their world. Their dances to Xochiquetzal, the Flower Goddess, and Macuilxochitl, also known as Five Flowers, the god of music, were two of their more popular festivals. As an agricultural society, they also had dances to the gods to ensure a good harvest and to give thanks for a bountiful year.

The Spanish had a profound effect on the religious and ceremonial life of Aztec society. Of course, the primary effort of the Spanish was to destroy all cultural aspects of Aztec society and supplant it with Hispanic religious and secular practices. While they were successful in their efforts in almost all areas of Aztec life, the Spanish recognized that the ceremonial and dance traditions of the Aztecs would be next to impossible to totally extinguish. The Spanish, therefore, took the tactic of encouraging music, dance, and fiestas among the Aztec population, but with the substitution of Christian symbols and the Christian God for pagan motifs and gods.

The Spanish also introduced European music and instruments, especially the guitar and other stringed instruments. In time, the guitar became a popular folk instrument, and a mestizo folk music evolved, containing elements of both Aztec and Spanish musical traditions. Accompanying this musical evolution was a similar transformation in dance, for the Spanish also brought to the New World the dances of Spain and Europe. By the 1800s, both the waltz and the polka had become very popular in Mexican society.

In time, Mexican dance traditions became a rich mix of dances reflecting both its Indigenous and Spanish roots. Dancers today refer to the traditional folk dances of Mexico with the generic term *folklórico.* This term has come to represent the dances of Mexico, which are the result of the centuries of evolution of dance as both a popular and traditional art form in Mexican and Southwestern Hispanic culture.

Los Concheros

Los conchero dancers are the most dramatically and brightly costumed dancers of the folklórico tradition. Conchero dances are ancient Aztec dances that reflect the dancers' pride in their Aztec heritage. An important purpose of modern conchero dancers is to keep alive the Aztec dance traditions. An additional purpose is to educate communities about the wisdom of the traditional ceremonies and to maintain a spiritual life based on ancient practices.

In Mexico, the dancers are also called Chichimecas, after a tribe from the region of Querétaro. After the conquest, the Chichimecas originated the dances that are the heritage of the conchero dancers today. The dances are characterized by theatrically dramatic costumes, percussive and rhythmic drumbeats, and fancy footwork.

Figure 57—Aztec dancer at Juana de Asbaje Park in Tlalpan, Mexico City. Photograph by Alejandro Linares Garcia.

Conchero dances have a ritual and religious symbolism as part of their purpose. Many dancers consider their dances to be sacred prayers, much as the Aztecs used dance to honor their gods. The dance ceremony begins with a blessing to the four corners of th earth with the *incensario* burning *copal.* The incensario remains at the center of the dance with the pungent fumes of the copal enveloping the dancers as they dance. Usually the dances follow a circular pattern on the floor.

Another aspect of the conchero tradition is its embrace of the family as an important part of its dance practices. It is common to see children dancing along with adults in conchero dances. Often, children too young to dance will be sitting at the feet of the drummer, mesmerized by the sound of the drums or wandering through the dancers dressed in miniature costumes.

One of the most recognizable aspects of the conchero costume is the immense feathered headdresses worn by the dancers. The dancers pattern their costumes after ancient native dress and decorate them with long, colored feathers, bright fabric, beads, mirrors, and shells. The shells around the knees and ankles serve as rhythm instruments complementing the persistent percussive sound of the drums.

El Danza del Venado

One of the most famous Mexican dances reflecting its indigenous origins is *el Danza del Venado,* the Deer Dance of the Yaqui tribe of northern Mexico. El Danza del Venado is one of the best-preserved native dances in Mexico. The dance depicts the chase, hunt, and capture of a wild animal, in this instance a deer. The dance is an example of the Native use of dance to address their experiences in the natural world. For the Yaqui, the dance is a sacred ritual dance.

In the dance, the dancer wears only a loincloth. He carries two gourd rattles in his hands and wears shells tied around his legs and ankles. The most identifying element of the costume, and most famously recognized, is the stuffed deer head with antlers the dancer wears on top of his head, very much like a headdress.

Figure 58—El Danza del Venado, *the Deer Dancer*

The music for the dance is a high-pitched flute, accompanied by the beating of a small drum. A bone rasp completes the sound of the dance. Of course, the dancer contributes his own rhythmic emphasis to the dance with his gourd rattles and shell leggings. The music is a haunting melody that gains in intensity as the chase quickens and the hunt reaches its inevitable climax with the capture and killing of the deer.

The dance begins by portraying the grace of the deer in the natural world. The dance then continues to the chase of the deer by hunters. As the hunters close in on the deer, the music quickens and builds in intensity. Finally, with a climatic crescendo of percussive and rhythmic accent, the deer is captured and dies.

The dance is an opportunity for strong virtuoso dancing, with its opening graceful movements, followed by quick, nervous darts and desperate leaps about the stage, and ending with a poignant stage death that rivals the dying swan of classical ballet in dramatic intensity. The dance ends with a melancholy recognition of the triumph of humans over nature and the lament that such a noble animal as the deer has to die at humanity's hands.

Los Viejitos

Los Viejitos is a comical dance from the state of Michoacán, especially in the villages around Lake Pátzcuaro in the southwestern region of Mexico. The title literally means "little old men," but the dance typically is danced by the agile and athletic young men in the village. The dance is an example of the hybrid nature of many Mexican dances. The dance appears to be of native origin because of its style and its common performance at village fiestas, but its use of *zapateado* steps is clearly Spanish derived.

Zapateado is a characteristic rhythmic heel-and-foot brushing and stamping in Mexican dances. The emphasis in zapateado is on the rhythmic sound of the feet during the dance. While zapateado's similarity to Spanish flamenco suggests its common origins, the two dance styles are very different in body carriage, musical style, and footwork rhythms. The classic zapateado for the los Viejitos dance is an alternating series of right-left-right-left-right step rhythms.

The dance begins with the "old men" entering the stage, feeble and tottering on their canes. The tapping of the canes on the stage adds an additional rhythm to the dance. The beginning of the dance is punctuated by the leader tapping his cane at each dancer to see if he is ready to dance. After this start, the leader then taps his cane for the music to begin. The music is played on a guitar-like stringed instrument called a *jarana.*

Figure 59—Los Viejitos

During the dance, the men remain hunched over their canes, but their steps are transformed into agile, athletic, and startling step variations as youth temporarily returns to the old men. This comic transformation is the heart of the dance, and it is the part audiences most anticipate and appreciate. At the end of the dance, the dancers return to their weary and feeble condition and hobble off the stage.

The dancers' costumes add to the dance's comic portrayal. The dancers wear wide-brimmed palm hats with brightly colored ribbons streaming down from the brim. A white wig usually completes the headpiece. The costume includes a red handkerchief at the collar, a bright poncho, white peon pants, and usually a Mexican blanket draped over the shoulders. The dancers wear shoes with pronounced heels, which are used to accent the sound of the zapateado.

The most identifying image of the dance is the masks worn by the dancers. The masks have snaggle-toothed grins, rosy but wrinkled cheeks, and a bright, cheery disposition. The masks complete the comic look of the costumes, and they enhance the comic nature of the dance.

El Jarabe Tapatío

El Jarabe Tapatío, also known as the Mexican Hat Dance, is the best-known and most popular of Mexican dances. Also recognized as the national dance of Mexico, the dance originated in Guadalajara, the capital city of the Mexican state of Jalisco. There are many different jarabes, but the word *tapatío* identifies this jarabe as from Jalisco. *Tapatío* is the adjective used to describe dances, as well as other cultural items, from Jalisco.

The *jarabe* is a generic name for a collection of popular dance forms. Mariachi musical groups typically play *jalisciense*, the *son* music from Jalisco, which forms the basis of traditional mariachi repertory. The son is the musical form most often associated with zapateado dances.

The steps of el Jarabe Tapatío involve the zapateado—the brushing and stamping of the heel and toe characteristic to many Mexican dances. The Mexican jarabe has been traced to the *seguidillas manchegas*, the step dances of the La Mancha region of southern Spain. There are over seventy jarabe steps and combinations, which vary in the dance according to the skill and talent of the dancer.

El Jarabe Tapatío has had an interesting history in Mexico. It was first danced in Mexico City in 1790. The dance quickly became popular in general Mexican culture. In the early 1800s, the viceroy Don Felix Berenguer banned the dance and music because of the perceived indecent words in the song. Another theory about the banning of the dance and song is that the Mexican government banned the jarabe in an effort to repudiate anything Spanish in the country, as Mexico was desiring to be an independent country. The court of Maximilian and Carlota during the period of the French occupation of Mexico revived el Jarabe Tapatío, and the dance regained its popularity.

El Jarabe Tapatío is a dance representing the courtship of a young maiden by a gallant young man. The young man, the *charro*, a horseman from Jalisco, courts the maiden, the *china poblana*, a Chinese girl from Puebla, through the dance. At the beginning of the dance, the charro attempts to gain the attention of the china poblana, who is flirtatious and coquettish. In order to impress her with his love, the charro throws his hat on the floor between them. The charro dances with his hands behind his back. In traditional versions of el Jarabe Tapatío, the charro holds his pistol behind his back as a gesture of respect for the china poblana. The two dance around the brim of the hat until the china poblana accepts his love by reaching down and putting on his hat. The two then joyously dance together facing the audience while a *diana* plays to end the dance. A diana is a triumphant musical flourish played at the end of el Jarabe Tapatío.

The costumes of el Jarabe Tapatío are beautiful in their splendor and folk identification. The charro wears a riding costume consisting of tight-fitting trousers decorated with silver buttons or braid down the sides of the legs. The costume also includes a short jacket matching the pants, also trimmed with silver buttons or braid. The shirt is made of embroidered silk. A wide-brimmed hat, also decorated with silver or gold braid, completes the costume. The charro also wears boots and spurs. If a jacket is not worn, then a Saltillo *sarape*, a brightly woven blanket draped over the shoulder, is the final touch to the charro costume.

The costume for the china poblana consists of a full red skirt richly embroidered with sequins in designs of flowers and fanciful geometric patterns, and a white embroidered blouse. She also wears a *rebozo*, a silk shawl worn by the majority of Mexican women. The rebozo is crossed around her waist, over her back, and draped over her shoulders in front. Traditionally, the china poblana wears her hair in braids down her back decorated with bright ribbons.

A charming legend exists about the origins of the china poblana costume. In one version of this legend, a Chinese princess was brought to Acapulco as a slave. She was then sold to a wealthy family in Puebla, who adopted her as a daughter. She had a gentle disposition and became known for her virtue and charity. When she died, all the young women of Puebla wished to be like her, and so they adopted her style of dress—a simple red skirt, white blouse, and rebozo. In her memory, they named this style of dress after her: *china* for Chinese and *poblana* for Puebla.

Figure 60—El Jarabe Tapatio

As with all legends, there are scholars who dismiss this. Mela Sedillo, in *Mexican and New Mexican Folkdances*, refers to Andalucía and its Arabian influence as the origin of the china poblana costume. But the legend is much more engaging and is the popularly believed origin of the costume.

Los Matachines

Los Matachines is one of the oldest and most unique dances in the Hispanic Southwest. It is unique in that folklorists and musicologists consider it both a dance and folk drama. Also, it is still performed throughout the Southwest and northern Mexico. The word *matachine* has several obscure meanings, one of which is "masked sword dance." Los Matachines performances can be found in New Mexico in both Hispanic communities and Native American pueblos. In northern and central Mexico, one of the traditional native ceremonial dances is *los Matlanchines*, a dance related to los Matachines of the Hispanic Southwest. As with all folklore, each community has its own variation of the dance, but they all share identifiable common characteristics.

The dance/drama traditionally was performed in association with the feast of the Virgin of Guadalupe on December 12. In modern practice, the dance is also performed on other church holidays and community celebrations.

A performance of los Matachines is a dance/drama presenting the eternal battle between good and evil. It is descendant from sixteenth- and seventeenth-century Spanish pageants and dramas that were used to teach Catholic ideology. Aurelio Espinosa, in *The Folklore of Spain in the American Southwest*, describes several of these Spanish plays, which were dramatic representations of the battles between the Moors and the Christians. The Spanish brought these plays to the New World, and eventually the plays were well known throughout Spain and New Spain. In the New World, the dance/drama evolved to contain two distinct elements, the matachines dance and a mock battle between the forces of good and evil.

Espinosa also describes a seventeenth-century Spanish dance of los Matachines, which was a mock battle with musical accompaniment. It was performed during carnival season and has a comic and burlesque quality to its performance. The common elements in its New World versions are the dance of the matachines and the mock battle within the ceremonial dance. The Indio-Hispanic version performed in New

Mexico appears to be a descendant variant of the Spanish dance with Native elements incorporated into it.

In the New World, the Spanish Franciscan missionaries introduced and developed los Matachines in both Hispanic and Native communities, retaining its primarily Spanish elements. The dance served one of the missionaries' purposes of converting Indigenous populations to Christianity by telling the story of the Spanish conquistadors' quest to bring Christian beliefs to the Aztec people.

The dance exists with variations wide enough to include interpretations as diverse as the conversion of the Aztecs to Christianity, the conquest legends of the Aztecs and Spanish, its dedication to the Virgin of Guadalupe, and its celebration of the birth of Christ during the Christmas season.

The costumes of the dancers are especially unique and theatrical. Most notable are the masked headdresses worn by the dancers. The masked headdress is called a *cupil* and resembles a bishop's miter at the top. The masks cover the faces of the dancers and are decorated with beads, jewels, and ribbons and are topped with crownlike headdresses. A six-inch fringe of beads or fabric hangs in the front of the headdress,

Figure 61—Matachine dancers, Ohkay Owingeh Pueblo, New Mexico. Photograph by Larry Lamsa.

covering the face of the dancer. The dancer's costumes are bright and festive, also heavily decorated with ribbons, beads, and jewels. Long drapings of ribbons or fabric, called *listones*, hang from the back of the costume from the headdress to the knees. Another unique part of the costume is silk bandannas worn across the face, covering the mouth in the style of the wild West bandit. The girl playing *la Malinche* wears a white communion dress with a lace veil on her head.

As in all folk dance and drama, the messages of los Matachines are cloaked in the symbolism of its various elements. Los Matachines remains a wonderful example of how the Hispanic people of the Southwest use their cultural traditions to maintain and preserve their history and beliefs.

Los Bailes de los Manitos

The land of southern Colorado and northern New Mexico was the first area in the northern frontiers of New Spain colonized by the Spanish when they began their fabled explorations for gold, honor, and glory in the sixteenth century. For the following centuries, this area, because of its geographic and cultural isolation, retained its Spanish colonial traditions more than other areas of the Hispanic Southwest. The term *manito* describes the descendants of the Spanish colonials of southern Colorado and northern New Mexico. *Manito* is the diminutive form of the Spanish word for brother, *hermano*, and it expresses a tender caring and warm brotherhood.

Manito culture has maintained many aspects of Spanish colonial society. The Hispanic dances of southern Colorado and northern New Mexico especially reflect the area's Spanish heritage. The folk dances of this area are from the Spanish colonial period and are mostly of European origins, evolving from the European court dances brought to Mexico during the brief rule of Emperor Maximilian. In social gatherings called *bailes*, it is common to find the polka, the schottische, the waltz, and the *varsoviana*.

The varsoviana, also known as the Spanish Two-Step, is a dance introduced to Mexico by Polish nobility during the time of Emperor Maximilian. It is similar to the American "Put your little foot, put your little foot" folk dance. *El Chote* is the New Mexican version of the

Figure 62—Valse de la Escoba, *Waltz of the Broom.*

American barn dance the schottishe. *La Cuna* (the cradle) is a dance of four couples similar to a square dance in which a cradle is formed by linked and rocking arm movements.

The *valse de la escoba* (the broom dance) is another popular dance game with similarities to musical chairs. In this version of the game, the dancers use a broom to determine who is left over after the music stops.

The *marcha* is the traditional introductory dance at wedding bailes. It follows the pattern of a march through the dance hall, ending in the dancers forming an arch with their arms. The dancers and the bride and groom march under the arch, and they then begin the wedding dancing.

An especially enjoyable dance is *el baile de cascarones*, in which dancers break confetti-filled eggshells over each other's heads during the dance. *Cascarones* are another Mexican tradition appearing in the customs of the Hispanic Southwest.

To prepare for the dance, the dancers drain eggs through small pinholes and then fill the eggshells with cologne-sprinkled confetti. The dancers then paint the eggs with designs ranging from simple to artistic. At the *baile*, the dancers break the eggshells over the head of the person they want to dance with.

Dr. Lorenzo Trujillo, in his article "Hispanic Tradition, Folkloric Music and Dance," listed in the bibliography, describes the symbolism of one of the best examples of Spanish tradition surviving in the popular manito traditions of Colorado and New Mexico.

> The valse de los paños means the waltz of the scarves. During the dark ages and early renaissance in Spain it was forbidden for physical contact to occur between a man and a woman.

> Therefore, an acceptable way for a man to dance with a woman without touching her was to have a material scarf bond the dancers together. The scarf of a woman was symbolic of her honor. (1992, 9)[5]

During the valse de los paños, a man and two women dance, with the man between the two women. One man and one woman can also dance the valse. Instead of holding hands, the dancers hold scarves in their hands between them. The dance consists of waltz steps and arches formed by the dancers' linked arms and the scarves, under which other dancers waltz. The dance is visually beautiful and graceful and is a reminder of the beauty of Spanish colonial culture.

Figure 63—Valse de los Paños, *Waltz of the Scarves*

Theater

The Hispanic Southwest has a long tradition of folk drama dating back to the establishment of a Spanish colonial culture in the New World. Hispanic theater in the Southwest can be categorized in four historical periods:

- The folk drama of the Spanish colonial period. Religious and secular plays performed for entertainment and education in the frontiers of New Spain. These plays originated in Spain.
- The popular professional and amateur Spanish-language productions of the late nineteenth and early to middle twentieth centuries. A little-known history of touring and resident Mexican theater companies in America. These plays were Mexican plays originating in Mexico.

- The farmworkers theater beginning in the 1960s. The establishment of a politically active Chicano theater.
- Modern Hispanic theater. Individual voices and dramatic visions.

Spanish Colonial Folk Drama

The Spanish brought to the New World a rich dramatic tradition dating back to Spain's Golden Age. The first theatrical presentation in the New World was performed in 1598. Written by Marcos Farfán de los Godos, a capitan with Don Juan de Oñate, the play was in honor of Oñate claiming the new land for the Kingdom of New Spain.

Oñate's men also performed the heroic tale of *Los Moros y Cristianos*, the story of the Spanish defeat of the Moors and their expulsion from the Iberian Peninsula.

The folk plays of the Spanish colonial period fell into two categories: religious and secular. The religious plays came directly from Spain or were written by Spanish missionaries in the New World. The secular plays were mostly historical plays recounting the battles between the Moors and Christians as well as plays depicting the encounters with the established Native American cultures. They often presented the history of early colonization and the battles for European cultural supremacy in the New Spanish Empire.

The religious plays had their sources in the mystery, miracle, and morality plays of medieval Spain. The Spanish missionaries brought the traditions of these plays with them to aid in their task of establishing Christianity in the New World. The plays served the dual functions of entertainment and education. Their most important role was to teach the tenets of Christianity to the Indigenous populations and to aid colonial settlers in the maintenance of their own religious practices.

The Christmas season was especially marked by plays celebrating the biblical accounts of the birth of Christ. *Las Posadas* was a community reenactment of the nine-day journey of Joseph and Mary to Bethlehem and their search for shelter. The play centers on the refusal of villagers to provide shelter until the last night, La Noche Buena, Christmas Eve.

Las Posadas was often a preface play for *Los Pastores*, a play telling of the journey of the shepherds to Bethlehem to honor the newborn Christ child. The play featured several stock comic characters, which greatly endeared the play to Spanish settlers.

Secular plays also were varied and instructive. *Los Moros y Cristianos* told the historical account of the epic battles between the Moors and the Christians. In this drama, the Moors deceive the Christians and steal their holy cross. At the end of the play, the Spanish recapture their cross, defeat the Moors, return Christianity to their land, and convert the Moors to Christianity.

The dance-drama *Los Matachines*, described in the section on dance, evolved in the New World from fifteenth-century Spanish sword dances depicting battles between the Moors and the Christians. The New World version, performed in both Hispanic and Native American communities, has as one of its themes the conversion of the Aztec emperor Moctezuma to Chritianity.

Los Comanches was another historical play presenting the struggles of the Spanish settlers against the Indigenous tribes. It is the first-known Spanish language play with a distinct southwestern United States (Colorado and New Mexico) theme. This play was enacted in the open air with the players riding horses as they played out the dramatic events of the defeat of the Comanche braves by the Spanish settlers. The action of this fierce horse battle centers on the pursuit and defeat of the great Comanche chief Cuerno Verde.

The theater of the Spanish colonial period was not studied, professional theater. It was folk theater, performed by members of the Hispanic community. The secular plays were dramatic battles between good and evil serving to indoctrinate Native tribes into Spanish culture and to reaffirm that culture for Spanish colonists. The religious plays had a greater task: the establishment and maintenance of Christianity in the New World.

Today, Hispanic communities throughout the Southwest are reestablishing these folk plays as part of their efforts to preserve traditional Hispanic culture.

Spanish-Language Theater

California during the 1850s provided the first home of professional theater in the Hispanic Southwest. Prior to this time, Hispanic theater consisted of folk drama performed in rural communities by amateur community members. When Mexico became independent in 1821, a distinctly Mexican culture began to form in the southwesten United States. Mexican Spanish-language plays were part of this Mexican cultural development.

The California port cities of Los Angeles and San Francisco provided available access, via steamship travel, to the touring companies from Mexico. The professional Hispanic theater of Texas and New Mexico developed after California's.

By the 1860s, California had developed such a strong Hispanic theatrical environment that touring companies from Mexico would establish residence in Los Angeles. Nicolás Kanellos, in his book *Mexican American Theater: Legacy and Reality*, states that by the turn of the century, Spanish-language theater companies were performing all along the Mexican–United States border, following a circuit that extended from Laredo to San Antonio to El Paso, through New Mexico and Arizona and on to California.

These touring companies consisted of both Mexican and Spanish performers. The theatrical entertainment presented by these troupes resembled a variety show composed of Mexican and Spanish plays and Mexican melodramas interspersed with song, dance, and comic dialogue. The repertory of these companies was diverse and large. A typical company would be able to stage serious drama, *zarzuelas* (Spanish operettas), and comedies. Larger cities had established theaters featuring major dramas and repertory companies. Smaller cities had tent theaters and makeshift performance spaces. The Mexican Revolution of 1910 further enhanced the Spanish-language theater in the Southwest as Mexican theater artists came to the United States. When vaudeville circuits developed in the 1920s, Mexican performers toured in both the Hispanic and American circuits.

Also during this time, Mexican *carpa*, or tent plays, toured the southwestern United States. These carpa plays prefaced the Chicano theater movement of the 1960s through the use of stock comic character such as the *pelado*, the use of English and Spanish languages, and skits that commented on social events. The pelado (literally bare-skinned or penniless) character was a comic underdog, a combination Mexican hero-victim-trickster. This style of theater would provide a theatrical antecedent and cultural context for Chicano theater artists of later generations.

These Hispanic theater companies and artists served a dual function in their communities. Of course, they primarily provided theatrical entertainment. But another important function of these theaters during this time was the cultural connection they provided for the Hispanic and Mexican immigrants who were struggling to find a place in America.

By the 1930s, the golden age of Spanish-language theater was diminishing. The forces causing this decline were the advent of the Great Depression, which affected all aspects of life in America; the forced and voluntary repatriation of Mexicans back to Mexico; and the development of film as a form of public entertainment. Hispanic theater did not disappear after this time, but it existed in a greatly reduced form. Hispanic artists continued to bring their plays to their communities, but Hispanic theater would not become a strong social force again until the 1960s.

The Farmworkers Theater/Chicano Theater

The 1960s saw the development of a pioneering style of Chicano *teatro* with its origins in the social activism of Cesar Chavez and the struggles of the United Farm Workers Union. In the fall of 1965, Luis Valdez, a young Chicano from Delano, California, the son of migrant farmworkers himself, began the work of El Teatro Campesino. His teatro was dedicated to the cause of the migrant farmworkers who toiled in the fields of agricultural California. The song "De Colores" presented in the music section on page 199 is considered the anthem of the farmworkers union.

In the beginning, the farmworkers theater grew out of simple dramatic improvisations Valdez would do with the farmworkers about the conditions of their work and lives. These improvisations evolved into a true farmworkers theater—theater by farmworkers, about farmworkers, and for farmworkers. Valdez quickly developed a form of agitprop theater using humor, political awareness and commitment, and a broad *commedia dell'arte* theater style based in folklore and popular culture to dramatize the efforts of the farmworkers to gain unionization.

These early skits developed in the rich cultural context of Mexican theater influences. They were influenced by the carpa Mexican tent shows with their distinct brand of Mexican humor and working-class sentiments. The carpa teatro established a precedent for comic skits presenting a satirical reflection of cultural conflict. The carpa had evolved in Mexico and performed in the United States until the 1950s.

Another influence was the archetype *pelado*, the comic underdog tradition of Mexican theater. The great Mexican film star Mario Moreno developed his film character Cantinflas from the pelado tradition in Mexican theater. Another influential Mexican character was El Bato Suave, a smooth, street-savvy dude who was from San Antonio, wore a zoot suit, and spoke *caló*, a Spanish-English urban border slang. These Mexican teatro characters became central stock figures in early Chicano teatro.

The work of the teatro featured *actos*, one-act plays based upon improvisations of political or social issues. These socially and politically aware actos addressed the many pressing issues of the Chicano community: the injustices of the farmworkers' plight, the struggles for quality education, the difficulties of racism, the tragedy of drugs and crime in Chicano communities, the need for cultural pride and knowledge, and the power of political action.

Humor and satire were the main dramatic tools used in the actos. They also used the dramatic elements of older cultural forms: cuentos from the folklore tradition, the Mexican carpa or tent play, and the popular corrido musical form. The performers in the actos further reached out to their audiences by performing the plays in both English and Spanish.

One of the greatest strengths of the early teatro movement was that it defined a Chicano aesthetic that was enormously appealing to young social activists in the 1960s and 1970s. The teatro was a grassroots theater movement speaking directly to the issues of Chicano communities throughout the Southwest. The cultural themes addressed by these numerous community-based teatros continued to reflect the experiences of the Chicano community: education, politics, poverty, war, cultural domination, cultural survival, ethnic pride, and personal accomplishment at the service of one's community.

The teatros created a public theater to serve as a platform and an opportunity for the public discussion of important community and national issues. The intentions of the first Chicano teatro artists were both political and spiritual—political because they saw teatro as their form of political activism to bring change and improvement to society; spiritual because they saw teatro bringing understanding, strength, and hope to their communities.

In addition to social and political issues, the teatro also presented a Chicano version of history. This Chicano historical perspective recognized the overlooked contributions of Hispanics to American society. It revealed forgotten heroes and corrected distorted history. It returned to Chicano communities and individuals their own proud history.

Led by the work of El Teatro Campesino, community activists and college students formed dozens of teatros in their own communities. Throughout the Southwest, Chicano activists and theater artists used Chicano theater as part of their political activism and cultural teaching. With this development, the teatro movement expanded beyond its origins as a farmworkers theater and became a true community theater movement.

Although El Teatro Campesino continued to be enormously influential, the Chicano theater movement developed other effective teatro companies. While many of these companies were community based, many others were college based. These college-based teatros were connected to the sociopolitical activism of Chicano students during the 1960s and 1970s.

As with other periods of Hispanic theater, the teatro period itself evolved as the times changed and Chicano communities changed. Formed in the glory days of 1960s social activism, the teatros changed as founding members dropped out of the teatro movement, continued the dream of a Chicano theater on their own, or moved on to professional theater. Luis Valdez himself moved on to Broadway and Hollywood, directing the successful "new American musical" *Zoot Suit*, a dramatization of an infamous Los Angeles race riot, and *La Bamba*, the film biography of the first Chicano rock star, Ritchie Valens. The Chicano theater movement of this period, however, was a central and critical part of the establishment of the Chicano movement throughout the Southwest.

Modern Teatro

Modern Hispanic theater artists are as diverse as the Hispanic people themselves. It is impossible to mention or describe the full range of theatrical activity in the Hispanic Southwest today, but two carefully chosen examples will illustrate the continuing vibrancy of Hispanic theater and the deep commitment of its theater artists to give a dramatic voice to their community.

Many theater artists in communities throughout the Southwest have persevered with the work of the Chicano teatro movement. One of the most successful and artistically respected teatro companies is Su Teatro, a fifty-two-year old teatro from Denver, Colorado. Headed by playwright and artistic director Anthony J. Garcia, Su Teatro is the third-oldest continuous Chicano theater company in the United States. Garcia has guided Su Teatro in its longstanding dedication to creating a Chicano theater voice that serves its community with plays that address the experiences of the Chicano community. From its beginnings as a grassroots teatro, it has become recognized for its original and well-produced plays dramatizing community issues.

Su Teatro has produced plays by such renowned artists as Luis Valdez, Rudolfo Anaya, Cherríe Moraga, and Evelina Fernandez. Two of their most significant original productions are *Intro to Chicano History 101* and *La Carpa Aztlán Presents: I Don't Speak English Only*. Its work is notable in that they have produced forty "homegrown" original plays, the largest contribution to Chicano theater by any teatro company. Su Teatro has recently expanded its work with the establishment of Su Teatro Cultural and Performing Arts Center, a Chicano-centric arts center, producing teatro, Chicano film and music events, artistic residencies by emerging and established Chicano theater artists, and community cultural events.

Su Teatro has persevered through the years and has maintained a careful balance between holding true to its founding commitment to be a people's theater and becoming a well-managed professional company recognized by funding agencies through significant grant support. One aspect of its success is the manner in which it maintains its community base with local productions in churches, arts festivals, and community centers. It has also achieved long-term organizational stability through the purchase and mortgage payoff of the theater and an additional facility in the Santa Fe Arts District outside downtown Denver.

Su Teatro is an example of the original vision of the teatro movement: a vision of a community-based theater using its talents to improve the lives of its community members. Through the years, the company has persevered with this vision, dedicated itself to its community and the Chicano experience, and grown as respected and accomplished theater artists.

Another significant example of the thriving nature of Chicano theater is the work of Dr. Carlos Morton, one of a few Chicano PhD professors in theater in the United States. Morton is one of the most successful examples of the transition Chicano artists made from the early teatro days to the main stage of American theater. Recognized by *Time* magazine as one of the most significant Chicano playwrights in the nation, he is honored with a Fulbright fellowship for study in Mexico, Poland, Greece, and Peru. A professor emeritus of theater and department chair at the University of California, where he taught playwriting, Morton is the son of second-generation Mexican American parents.

An amusing anecdote about the origins of his family name tells of his grandfather, whose name was Pérez, wanting to change his name in order to find work in Chicago after the Mexican Revolution ended in 1917. As Señor Pérez searched for work, he realized that employers were hiring Europeans but not Mexicans. As he walked through the streets of Chicago, he saw a billboard with a Morton salt advertisement and decided then and there to have a good American name: Morton.

At the beginning of his involvement in Chicano theater, Morton studied the techniques of El Teatro Campesino. He later joined the San Francisco Mime Troupe as a playwright and explored their process of collaborative political work. During this time, he was forming his voice as a playwright writing *El Jardín* (The Garden), a Chicano version of the Garden of Eden story, and *El Cuento de Pancho Diablo*, dedicating the play to El Teatro Campesino.

Morton has had many books of his works published. *The Many Deaths of Danny Rosales and Other Plays* and *Johnny Tenorio and Other Plays* are collections of his own plays. *The Fickle Finger of Lady Death and Other Plays* is a collection of plays of contemporary Mexican playwrights. Morton translated these plays into English for this collection in order to introduce American theater companies and audiences to the dramaturgy of Mexico's new generation of playwrights.

From his early beginning at the center of the Chicano teatro movement, Morton developed into a major Chicano playwright with productions at community teatros, university drama departments, regional theaters, and international festivals, as well as such esteemed national theaters as Joseph Papp's New York Public Theater. In his career as a theater artist, he has written over two dozen plays with nearly one hundred productions.

Morton is an amazingly diverse and prolific playwright. His plays easily move from historical drama to humorous musicals to social issues. His most constant characteristics as a playwright are sharp humor, the inventive use of well-known dramatic characters from Chicano culture, a penetrating analysis of cultural issues, and a deep commitment to creating a theater reflecting the truths of Chicano experience. Morton is an illustrative example of a Chicano artist remaining true to his roots in the Chicano teatro movement while realizing success in American theater.

His first major success, *The Many Deaths of Danny Rosales*, is a historical documentary about the death of a young Chicano man while in Texas police custody. *El Jardin* is a humorous, musical retelling of the Chicano Garden of Eden. *La Malinche*, a play that won first prize in the Arizona Theatre Company National Hispanic Playwriting Contest, is a reflective reconsideration of the native mistress and interpreter for Cortés. *The Child Diego* is a dramatization of the life of the great Mexican muralist Diego Rivera. Concerned about the crisis in schools and teenage culture, he has also written a cycle of teenage plays under the title *At Risk*.

Visionary Su Teatro founder Tony Garcia and playwright Dr. Carlos Morton are just two of the many examples of theater artists throughout the Hispanic Southwest who are writing and producing plays that tell the story of their communities and people. Given the dearth of opportunity for theater artists of color in the mainstream movie and theater business, Hispanic artists have chosen to create their own opportunities on their own terms. Working from a centuries-old theatrical legacy, modern Hispanic theater artists, in Chicano barrios, universities, and amateur and professional theaters, are the proud extension of their people's cultural vision.

Visual Arts—Muralists

Along with the development of the teatro movement, Chicano communities witnessed in the 1960s the blossoming creation of the Chicano mural movement. Throughout barrios, Chicano neighborhoods in the Southwest, as well as in other parts of the country, students and community activists painted large murals on the walls of schools, churches, stores, libraries, highways, and public buildings. Even today, the Chicano mural movement continues to be a significant artistic presence in the Chicano community. The most casual exploration of a Chicano community will reveal the continuing vibrancy and importance of this art form.

This mural movement had its community origins in the rise of social activism among Chicanos influenced by the Civil Rights Movement, the United Farm Workers movement in California, and the student activism of college campuses. Energized by the struggles and successes of other activists, Chicano artists recognized the enormous power of mural art to contribute to the awareness of Chicano issues.

The spirit of Chicano muralism reaches as far back as the preconquest era of ancient Mexico. The preconquest world of Mexico was a world characterized by the intense visual creations of ancient cultures. The Indigenous civilizations all utilized mural painting to express their mythic histories and spiritual cosmologies. At the great religious center Teotihuacán, near the Pyramid of the Sun, painted murals depict Tlaloc, the god of rain. At Tulum, the ancient Mayan citadel, murals cover the Temple of the Descending Deity. The Mayans also painted sacred murals on the interior walls of the Temple of Warriors at Chichen Itzá. The Aztec *codices*, folding multipanel paintings, were mural-like stories of their culture, history, and world. The Aztecs also painted the inner and outer walls of houses and temples of the City of Gods, their sacred city Teotihuacán.

These are just several examples of innumerable instances of mural painting from the preconquest era of Mexico's history. The rediscovery and affirmation of their Indigenous heritage by Chicano activists led them to include this artistic legacy in their own murals.

Early Chicano mural artists were also greatly influenced by the work of *Los Tres Grandes*, the three great ones, Mexican muralists Diego Rivera,

José Clemente Orozco, and David Alfaro Siqueiros. Los Tres Grandes were important models for Chicano activists on how an artist could use mural painting for social and political causes. Los Tres Grandes were pioneering leaders of the Mexican mural movement beginning in the 1920s. Diego Rivera was known for his magnificent murals illustrating the entire history of Mexico. José Orozco painted murals in a stark, dramatic style, lamenting the ravages of the modern industrial world on the human soul. His murals are famous for their depiction of the Mexican workers. David Siqueiros not only painted impressive murals of mankind's struggle for justice and well-being; he also dedicated his time to assisting those fighting for social causes. His murals, with their themes of the revolution, reflected his lifelong support of political activity in Mexico.

Each of Los Tres Grandes was central to leading a Mexican mural movement that became an important factor in the revolutionary fight for justice in Mexico. Their murals portrayed working peasants in their noble work. They elevated to mythic status the history, life, work, and aspirations of Mexico's working class. Each was a social activist as well as a powerful artist. They saw painting as the language of Mexico. They believed that mural painting, dating back to the preconquest era, was the natural form of expression for the Mexican people. Together they led mural painting to the center stage of Mexican artistic consciousness. Through their work, mural painting became the genuine expression of the Mexican spirit, a true national art form.

Chicano artists used the example of Los Tres Grandes as models of what Chicano murals could be for the Chicano movement. They worked to create a mural movement, a public art, that would express a collective vision of contemporary Chicano culture.

The Chicano mural movement was a public folk art. Its purposes were to illustrate Chicano history for ordinary people, demonstrate cultural pride and identity, reinforce community consciousness, and empower communities in their struggles for social justice. Chicano mural artists created murals in response to the needs of their communities. The public accessibility of mural art was critical to this movement because traditional artistic venues were closed to the Chicano experience. Another important aspect of the mural movement was the public

Figure 64—Historical mural in Delta, Colorado, by Emanuel Martinez.

ownership of the murals. The murals belonged to the community, not the artist, collector, or gallery owner.

Another factor contributing to the quick establishment of the Chicano mural movement was that the actual painting of the mural often was a communitywide event, a shared community experience. While an individual artist or group of artists often were commissioned to paint a mural and did the work themselves, it just as often was the case that the artists were coordinators for the work of community members, both adults and children, on the mural. An often-repeated but true bit of folk legend is the story of how a community would paint a mural and it would remain unmarked by graffiti because of the respect community members had for it. A legendary enhancement of this story has graffiti artists so filled with remorse for defacing a community mural that they repainted it themselves.

Chicano murals are powerful artistic statements presenting many themes. Murals literally cover the totality of Chicano experience: Aztec mythology, imagery, and heritage; the farmworkers' exploitation and efforts for unionization; the injustices of the judicial and police systems;

the failure of the education system; the devout sense of spirituality and Catholicism; the destructive evil of drugs; the awareness of ethnic pride; the veneration of cultural heroes; and community issues and history, as well as a catalog of other sociopolitical concerns. Artists create murals to educate their communities, to increase cultural sensitivity in observers, to express solidarity with the struggles of the community, and to give artistic voice to the heart and soul of their people.

Literary Arts

The four eras defining the evolution of the literary arts in Hispanic culture in the Southwest are Spanish colonial (1598–1821), Mexican (1821–1846), Mexican American (1846–1960s), and Chicano (1960s–present).

As has been discussed in previous sections, the Aztecs had a flourishing artistic culture at the time of the Spanish arrival in the New World. Their literary arts were especially developed. Aztec codices, a type of visual narrative recording history and cultural practices, were an important part of the Indigenous literary heritage collected by the Spanish. Aztec poetry was especially profound, reflecting their love of nature and their consciousness of their status as a chosen but doomed people. They also had a complex pantheon of gods and an oral tradition of stories about their gods. These codices, poems, and stories presented a literary legacy that, centuries later, would greatly influence Chicano literature.

The Spanish brought to the New World the literary heritage of Spain's sixteenth-century Golden Age. The *conquistadores*, missionaries, and later settlers had Cervantes and Lope de Vega as their literary legacy. This Spanish literary heritage would define the literary arts in the Spanish colonial New World for three centuries. One of the soldiers in Oñate's colonizing expedition in 1598, Gaspar Pérez de Villagrá, began the Spanish literary tradition in the Southwest with his epic poem "La Conquista de la Nueva México"—"The Conquest of New Mexico."

During the Spanish colonial era, the primary literary forms were historical, religious, and oral folk literature. Historical plays such as *Los Moros y Cristianos* recounted great historical Spanish victories. Religious plays such as *Los Pastores* originated in medieval Spain and supported the work of the Catholic church in establishing and maintaining its religion in the New World. The great oral literature of *cuentos, dichos,* and *adivinanzas* (stories, proverbs, and riddles) was firmly established in Spanish tradition and was widespread throughout the Southwest.

During the Mexican period, a short twenty-five years, the literature of the Spanish colonial period, both written and oral, continued. The plays, both historical and religious, and the cuentos continued to be active in the daily lives of the Mexicans of the northern frontier. These Spanish colonial traditions were extended by the introduction of corridos, narrative songs, and, because of the proliferation of the printing press, an increase in the publication of poetry and prose. The picaresque novel and autobiographical accounts were especially enjoyed prose forms.

The long period from 1848 to the 1960s was a time of great social, political, and cultural change for the Hispanic Southwest. The area became American in 1848 with the Treaty of Guadalupe Hidalgo. The Mexican Revolution in 1910 caused another cultural upheaval and further immigration of Mexicans into the United States. These two factors were critical in the development of the Chicano literary movement in the 1960s.

During the latter part of the 1800s, numerous Spanish-language newspapers began publishing throughout the Southwest. These newspapers published poetry, short stories, and serialized novels. In many ways, these newspapers were the literature of the common folk.

The great immigration of Mexican workers and educated professionals after 1910 caused another change in the literary habits of the Southwest. Publishing houses began producing novels, with many stories set in the context of the Mexican Revolution. After the Depression, the work of literary writers continued to expand their themes, exploring personal narrative, social history, and social commentary.

A major and significant literary development from the late 1800s into the twentieth century was that many authors began writing in English. This language change made the works of these authors available to a much larger English-speaking audience.

All the literary and historical events of more than 350 years came into focus in the Chicano movement of the 1960s. The writers of the Chicano movement gave literary voice to the realization that Chicanos had their own historical, cultural, and aesthetic heritage and identity. These writers, along with visual artists, theater artists, and community activists used the arts to explore the issues of Chicano communities.

Chicano poets Rodolfo "Corky" Gonzales, Alurista, and Abelardo Delgado created Chicano poetry that served as political, social, and artistic expressions. Novelists Tomás Rivera and Rudolfo Anaya wrote books that would set standards for later generations of Chicano writers. Publishing houses such as Arte Publico Press dedicated themselves to publish the works of Chicano writers.

Chicano writers used all of history as their sources and inspiration. The myths and legacy of the Aztecs created the artistic homeland of Aztlán for Chicano writers. Spanish and English both served as expressive languages for these writers, their works often reflecting the bilingual world they lived in. Their themes covered the full gamut of the Chicano experience: Aztec spiritualism, Mexican revolutionary pride, Catholic religious beliefs, oral folklore traditions, and political and social issues. They explored their complex history, traditions, religion, and culture. They used literature to create images and metaphors for Chicano social conditions and yearnings. The purpose of their work could not have been more noble—personal and community self-awareness and cultural pride.

Chapter 6 contains a selection of literary works of Hispanic writers. The list, of course, is by no means comprehensive or complete. But the list does include books representative of many of the best recognized writers. View these books as a quality introduction and foundation to Hispanic literature that will prepare you for your own discovery of other Hispano writers.

The recommended activity, of course, is to read as many of them as you can. These stories are intended for adults and mature teens. They each offer an important cultural, historical, and personal insight into the Hispanic experience in the United States.

"Low and Slow" Arts

The lowrider phenomenon is related to the Pachuco zoot suit experience in the 1940s. In both instances, Chicano youth and later adults developed exaggerated styles of personal expression. In the zoot suit era, the expression was one's fashion and clothing. In the present lowrider era, the object of expression is one's automobile.

Both of these forms of cultural expression experienced the scorn of the larger, more traditional culture while empowering Chicano youth with a source of cultural pride. This cultural pride then evolved into the larger Hispanic culture and became not only a source of cultural pride for all but also a source of cultural identification. What was once an outlier experience became an accepted part of the culture. Go to any Cinco de Mayo celebration, and lowriders will be cruising "low and slow" down the street, and some men—and women—will be sporting Pachuco zoot suit style.

"Low and slow"—the motto of lowriders throughout the Southwest. In Los Angeles, San Antonio, Houston, San Francisco, Phoenix, Denver, and the lowrider capital of the world, Española, New Mexico (this is one good way to start an argument, for many cities consider themselves to be the heart and capital of low rider culture), as well as many other cities throughout the Southwest, exotic custom cars cruise the streets in their full majesty.

As a folk art, the lowrider car symbolizes a cultural pride and identification that it shares with other more traditional objects of folk art. The lowrider car has become a unique part of the Chicano experience, a focal point of many aspects of Chicano life in the barrio.

Befitting its position as a modern folk art form, the origins of lowrider cars are clouded by legend and personal versions of lowrider history. One version of its origins has it beginning in the 1930s and later being part of the zoot suit cultural expressions of the 1940s. Another version states that it began in the 1950s when Chicano youth, too poor to build expensive custom cars, simply removed the front suspension coils and rear leaf springs, thereby creating a low-sitting car. These early car customizers were part of the hot rod era of the 1950s, which in their own words produced cars "chopped, channeled, and lowered."

In her essay, "Remapping: Los Angeles Lowriders," a chapter in her book *Looking High and Low*, Brenda Bright places the origins of the term *lowrider* in the 1960s. According to her version of lowrider history, the modern lowrider evolved from the low custom look of the 1950s, when the California State Vehicle Code outlawed car chassis bodies riding lower than the bottom of the wheel rim. In order to evade this limitation, lowriders began installing airplane and industrial hydraulic pumps to their suspension systems. These hydraulic systems allowed the lowriders to raise their cars when necessary.

An extremely important part of the lowrider experience and the clubs that form around them are their potential to be a positive alternative to the street and gang life afflicting Chicano communities and youth. In magazines dedicated to lowriders, articles and letters to the editor give testimony to the positive activity creating lowriders can be for Chicano youth, if led by older, more responsible men of the community.

The lowrider car is a highly developed artistic statement. The art of lowriders can be compared to the art of the Chicano mural movement. Lowrider artists paint their cars with highly detailed and colorful scenes. The images are similar in content to those in murals: Aztec warriors, fanciful geometric designs, personal images, and Catholic religious icons, Our Lady of Guadalupe being the most frequent. Indeed, because of their extraordinary paint jobs, the lowrider car can be seen as a moving mural.

The cars themselves are amazing artistic creations. Originally, the cars were American classics from the 1950s and 1960s. Recently, foreign cars and mini trucks have been customized into lowriders. Outfitted with expensive paint jobs, plush interiors, sound systems rivaling the best home stereo systems, special chromed wheels, and, of course, the unique hydraulic systems giving the cars their distinctive hopping ability, a lowrider car can be a very expensive expression of cultural and personal pride. Lowrider artists with low financial resources will build their cars from an inexpensive used car outfitted with a simple hydraulic system and a special set of inexpensive wheel rims.

Lowrider cars fall into three distinct categories: "Bombs" are classic American cars built between 1939 and 1958. "Traditional" cars are full-size American cars built between 1959 and 1996. "Euros" include sports cars, imports, and trucks.

At lowrider shows, cars are judged in three categories: "Street customs" are built without any sponsorship or professional assistance. "Mild" are cars built with some professional assistance. "Full custom" cars are elite, extraordinarily expensive show cars built by a professional customizing shop.

Figure 65—Lowrider car hopping. 1963 Chevrolet Impala convertible with hydraulics, Just Klownin Virginia Car Club. Photograph by Jarek Tuszyúski.

A central aspect of the lowrider experience is its reflection of Chicano pride. Lowrider magazines and car shows include expressions of Chicano issues and the importance of cultural awareness. Car owners speak to the pride they have in their cars and their culture.

A recent development in the lowrider world is the lowrider bicycle. By customizing a bicycle, Chicano youth, usually junior high and high school-age students, can participate in the lowrider experience before they are old enough or have the financial means to build a lowrider car.

The lowrider bicycle is also an amazing creation. Sitting so low to the ground that its pedals cannot turn, tricked out with elongated frames, chromed and painted just like their big brothers, the lowrider cars, the lowrider bicycle is a personal artistic statement. It is common to see lowrider bicycles displayed at Chicano community festivals. The young builders proudly present bicycles artistically positioned over engraved mirrors, pulling miniature trailers holding portable sound systems.

As modern folk art in Chicano communities, the lowrider car and lowrider bicycle are symbols of individual aspiration, expressions of artistic craft and skill, and an accepted part of the Chicano community experience. From their beginnings as a fringe experience of car customizers, lowriders have evolved into their present cultural acceptance to such an extent that community fairs and festivals advertise their lowrider car and bicycle shows as part of the festivities. Also, the lowrider

Figure 66—Lowrider bicycle in Victoria de Durango, Mexico. Photograph by Thelmadatter.

car show, with its cars, music, and festive atmosphere, has become a fiesta of Chicano cultural life in barrios throughout the Southwest.

La Cocina y La Comida—Traditional and Celebratory Foods

Panza llena, corazón contento.
Full stomach, contented heart.
El pan partido, Dios lo aumenta.
God blesses the bread that is shared.

In the Aztec creation legend of the Five Suns, Quetzalcoatl, one of the Aztec's supreme gods, transforms himself into an ant in order to enter a sacred mountain. Once in the mountain, he steals maíz, or corn, and like the Greek Prometheus bringing fire to humans, he introduces this staple of life to the Aztec people.

This legend and its description of how corn came into Aztec life illustrates the importance of corn to native life when the Spaniards arrived in the New World. Corn was a New World food, the most important food staple for Native culture. In time, corn became a central staple for the Spanish also. As with so many other aspects of Hispanic life in the American Southwest, the history of food is the history of the blending of Native American and Spanish customs and practices.

Even though the Spanish brought with them the tastes and traditions of European foods, they quickly adapted to the foods of the New World. The Indigenous cultures all had their own food practices and specialized knowledge of the land and its agricultural possibilities to produce Native foods. The Native Americans introduced the Spanish to corn, beans, tomatoes, potatoes, pumpkins, turkey, chocolate, and chile. Tortillas and atole are two of the Native foods adopted by the Spanish. A few of the foods the Spanish in turn introduced to New World cooking included pork, rice, wine, wheat, cinnamon, black pepper, garlic, lettuce, carrots, oranges, peaches, apricots, and milk and cheese, because of the cows and sheep they brought with them.

Over the centuries, Hispanic culture developed a cuisine integrating both Native foods and Spanish traditions. Present-day Hispanic foods are a combination of Native American, Mexican, and Spanish influences. Many traditional dishes are based upon Native foods: corn, beans, squash, and chiles. The ancestral Puebloans of Mesa Verde had a nickname for corn, beans, and squash: "the Three Sisters." *Chile con carne*, chile with meat, and *tamales*, meat and chile wrapped in steamed cornmeal dough, are two examples of the combination of New World and European foods.

It is important to remember that Hispanic foods developed in a culture that was rural and agricultural. Hispanic people, like all other people forging a life based on the land and self-reliance, got their food from the land they worked and the animals they raised. Food was planted, grown, and harvested. Animals were raised and slaughtered, with every part of the animals being utilized. The diet of the early Hispanic settlers was determined by how successfully they worked their farm. The food of present-day Southwestern Hispanic culture is easily recognized as food originating on the farm and based on the necessities of agricultural life without the conveniences of modern store-bought foods.

A folk saying states that a true Mexican eats only corn, rice, beans, and chile. While this statement has an element of truth to it, representing as it does the basic staples of Hispanic foods, it does not allow for the wide variety of foods found on Hispanic tables throughout the Southwest. Eating practices vary from family to family, region to region. Southwestern Hispanic cuisine is as varied as Hispanic people are.

While there are restaurants that advertise a specialty in Spanish or Hispanic foods, the most common practice is to categorize it all under "Mexican food." This is obviously a great simplification, for Mexico has its own varied and rich cuisine, often without any similarity to food found in the Hispanic Southwest. The foods of the Hispanic Southwest do, however, share a basic set of staples with the foods of Mexico.

The cultures of both regions share a culinary heritage with Native American foods. The *enchilada* is one ready example of this cultural cross-fertilization. The Spanish simply took the Aztec dish known as *chilaquiles*, added cheese, onions, and a fried tortilla, and created the enchilada.

There are many, many excellent books containing the recipes of the Hispanic Southwest. Many of these cookbooks feature recipes for delicious variations on traditional foods. These recipes have in their own practice introduced even more variety into Hispanic cuisine.

The traditional foods presented here are enjoyed in homes throughout the Hispanic Southwest. Several of the foods are particularly associated with seasonal celebrations.

A favorite joke among Hispanics is the answer to the question "What is the best Mexican restaurant in town?" Of course, there is only one answer: "My mom's house!" There is some truth to this joke, for the food of one's home is the food of one's warm childhood memories.

Chile

Comida sin chile, no es comida.
A meal without chile is not a meal.

We might as well start at the center of Hispanic cuisine. The heart and soul of Southwestern Hispanic food is the chile. The following poem by the esteemed Chicano poet Abelardo Delgado best presents the spirit of chile in the Hispanic soul.

Chile

by Abelardo Delgado

Symbols come, symbols go
but for those in the know
a chile
    best explains
the culture of my gente,
PICOSEO PERO SABROSO
Pico de gallo,
    salsa picante,
as well as jalapeños,
have carried on
an invasion of their very own
into gringolandia.
We can now say,
    As American as chile,
and I'll bet
    we are right.
Chile bola,
    chile serrano,
chile pasilla, chile piquín,
chile güero,
chile para rellenar
and chile all around.
As to why
    some think
chile best depicts
our gran cultura,
it's because it, like us,
gives life flavor.
Chile en el menudo

and chile in los frijoles,
chile con carne
and chile dogs.
Soon there will be
chile ice cream.
In football
    we'll have
our own chile bowl.
We hang in Aztlan
like chile ristras in the sun.
As Aztec myth has it,
it was a handful
of chile pods
that drove Quetzalcoatl away
to return that chile colored day.

Chile is more than a sauce, a condiment, a flavoring, an ethnic cooking ingredient, a hot pepper. Chile is more than just the most distinctive ingredient in Mexican and Southwestern Hispanic cooking.

Chile is a source of cultural pride. It is the pride of your mother's kitchen. It is the pride of learning how to skin the pods for the first time. It is the pride of knowing your chile is better than any other in the neighborhood. It is the pride of finally being able to sit at the table with the men and match them spoonful for spoonful. It is the pride of telling all within earshot that this year's batch is the hottest ever, wiping your brow and serving another helping. It is the pride of winning first prize in the best chile contest.

In many cities in the Southwest in the early fall, the streets are marked with chile stands where vendors sell chile by the sack and roast it on the spot for the customer. Then begins the family chore of peeling the chile, packaging it, and storing it for a future time.

Historical Coda #19

Two family anecdotes illustrate the importance chile plays in the life of a family's meals. When I was a child, we lived in Kansas City, and my mother and father both longed for true New Mexico chile. Each year when the chile harvest was happening in New Mexico, my uncle would dutifully pack a box of fresh-picked chile and send it by the bus overnight to Kansas City. As soon as we were notified by the bus station that the package had arrived, we, as a family, would trek to the station and claim the longed-for package. The Holy Grail itself would not be more welcomed. An especially funny memory of this scene is the pungent odor of fresh chile that filled the bus station when we entered.

Another childhood memory is of another uncle in a fancy restaurant taking a container out of his jacket pocket, opening it, and pouring homemade chile on his meal. He honestly and simply could not stand a meal, no matter how good or how expensive, without his own chile.

While there is no substitute for fresh chile, a cook has other choices if no fresh chile is available. Modern stores stock frozen and canned chile. Powdered chile is also readily available, as are chile sauces and salsas. Jalapeños, fresh or pickled, can serve as a green chile substitute. Each of these products has its own best use and will add its spicy flavoring to a meal.

There are many different types of chile. Each varies in look, size, texture, and, most importantly, hotness. The critical ingredient giving chile its hotness is an oily acid called capsaicin, and it is usually true that the smaller the chile, the hotter it is. The hottest chile is the *habanero*.

The standard cooking chile is the *poblano* chile. Two of the most common types are the Anaheim and New Mexico Green. Each is a bright green chile about six to seven inches long. Both chiles are usually roasted and used in green chile sauces and *rellenos*. Chile growers argue over which and whose chile is the superior chile. It is truly an argument that will never be settled.

There are as many recipes for chile as there are cooks. Some like their chile like a sauce. Some like it thick. Some fix it with meat; others make it vegetarian. Some add corn, potatoes, onion, and tomatoes. Some prefer green chile; others, red chile, which is really just green chile pods that have matured and aged into red pods. As the pod ripens, it becomes sweeter and more flavorful. A common sight in the Southwest is a wreath or string of red chile, called a *ristra*, hanging outside the home.

Before they can be used, chiles must be roasted and peeled. Roasting helps remove the bitter skin and brings out the chile's flavor. While there are many methods of roasting chiles, the easiest is to have the chile vendor roast them for you before you take them home. If you decide to roast them yourself, wear rubber gloves, and whatever you do, do not rub your face or eyes. Many a cook has regretted a simple gesture to the face while peeling chile!

One of the great pleasures of life is taking out a bag of frozen chile in the cold winter month of January, thawing it, and making a fresh batch of *chile verde*.

Frijoles—*Pinto Beans*

Beans, beautiful beans! No meal is complete without beans. Beans in burritos. Beans with chile. Beans with cheese. Beans with onions. Beans with *chicos* (corn). Beans with ham. Beans by themselves. Beans with everything. Beans freshly made, beans refried. Beans as a side dish or the main course itself. Beans are basic, nutritious food, and there is no end to their possibilities.

Many a parent, with the end of the month at hand and the paycheck still days away, has proudly announced, "Only beans for the rest of the month!"

Before beans can be cooked, they must be cleaned. Almost a ritual in itself, the cook must sort the beans, separating out the rocks and debris that accompany the beans on the journey from the farm to the kitchen. Individual opinion varies on how to best to prepare the beans. Some cooks put the beans right in the pot and start cooking them. Some swear by soaking them overnight. Some use a pressure cooker to speed the process. The modern cook throws them all in the Crock-Pot, adds water and ingredients according to the secret family recipe, puts the lid on, and walks away. Soon the house is filled with the unmistakable aroma of cooking beans.

Tortillas

Hecho a mano, hecho de harina, hecho con cariño.
Made by hand, made with flour, made with love.

Tortillas are another basic food of the Hispanic culture. Flat like a pancake, they are the bread staple enjoyed with every meal.

The original tortilla was made from corn in a long, arduous process. Women would first soak dried corn in lime water. The softened corn was then mashed in the *metate*, a concave grinding stone, with the *mano*, a handheld stone. This ground corn became the *masa*, which was patted by hand into little round pancakes and cooked over the fire or on a griddle.

Today, of course, cooks go to the store and buy packaged tortillas. But just like homemade chile, there is no better version than freshly made tortillas, hot off the griddle.

The perfect tortilla is round with light brown spots. A common joke is for cooks to dismiss their tortillas by saying, "My tortillas come out shaped like Texas."

Calabacitas—*Green Summer Squash*

Calabacitas is a delicious dish featuring green summer squash. Easy and fast to make, it is a great side to any meal. A tasty Mexican variation adds Monterey Jack cheese, red and green peppers, and picante sauce. Proportions of ingredients are to individual taste; this is basically a stir-fried vegetable dish.

Posole—*Hominy Stew*

The holiday season would not feel complete without *posole* at festive gatherings. Christmas would not be Christmas without a bowl of posole after midnight mass. And no New Year's Eve party can really herald in the new year without a large pot of posole simmering on the kitchen stove for the revelers to fill their bowls with as the evening proceeds toward midnight. Posole is especially good with red chile poured on top.

Posole is similar to hominy in that it is made from large white corn kernels. Some people make posole with canned hominy, but as is the case with changes to traditional recipes for the sake of ease, it does not taste as good. Any supermarket carrying a good supply of Mexican foods will have posole. Specialty Mexican delicatessens also will carry posole.

Menudo

Menudo is a traditional tripe soup served in homes and restaurants throughout the Southwest. Many consider it a specialty food with legendary medicinal and recuperative powers for anyone who has partied too long and too hard. Often, a Sunday morning after an especially late Saturday night will begin with a bowl of menudo. It is often referred to as the "breakfast of champions" because of its curative powers. As with many traditional recipes, each family has its own menudo recipe, that it swears is the real recipe.

Arroz a La Española—*Spanish Rice*

Rice is another basic staple of southwestern cuisine. Spanish rice is a common side dish, usually accompanying beans.

Sopaipillas—*Fried Bread*

Sopaipillas have become a dessert specialty at many Mexican restaurants. They are very easy to make and delicious eaten with honey, jam, or powdered sugar. Native American fry bread and even French *beignets* are similar variations on the same idea—fried puffed dough eaten with sweetening. Some cooks and restaurants put cinnamon in the batter before cooking to vary the taste. It does produce a good-tasting sopaipilla, but traditionalists view this practice as ruining them.

Empanaditas—*Mincemeat Fried Turnovers*

Empanaditas are a favorite of the Christmas season. A traditional empanadita is a sweet fried turnover filled with meat, nuts, spices, and mincemeat.

There are two ways to make empanaditas: quick and easy or the traditional way. The quick and easy version substitutes pie pastry for the *masa de empanaditas*. It simplifies the process because the pie pastry is simply cut, filled, rolled closed, and fried.

As with most changes to traditional recipes to accommodate easily available ingredients, the results are pleasing in themselves but do not compare with the traditional taste. A similar situation exists with the practice of restaurants making *chile rellenos* (cheese-stuffed chiles) with egg roll wrappers instead of the more laborious but much better-tasting process of dipping them in floured egg batter before frying.

Biscochitos—*Anise Cookies*

These licorice- and cinnamon-flavored cookies are another favorite treat of the Christmas season.

Puddings

Arroz Con Leche Dulce—*Rice Pudding;* Natillas—*Milk Pudding;* Capirotada—*Bread Pudding*

Mexican and Southwestern Hispanic cultures are recognized for their love of sweet foods. In addition to candies and sweet breads, these three traditional puddings continue to be served as dessert in Hispanic homes.

Flan Caramelisado—*Caramel Flan*

A great flan is the true mark of an excellent, skilled cook. This is a traditional dish enjoyed worldwide in many cultures.

Atole—*Blue Cornmeal Drink*

Food made with blue corn has recently become very trendy. Restaurants featuring new southwestern cuisines have begun offering blue corn enchiladas as a featured dish. A recent trip to the grocery store found blue cornflakes in the health food section!

The original use of blue corn in the New World was the Aztec drink *atolli.* When the Spanish arrived in the New World, they discovered this favorite Aztec drink. The Aztec mixed ground-up cornmeal into a light-flavored drink and greatly enjoyed it.

In the Spanish colonial years, *atole* was the drink of those who could not afford coffee or chocolate. It was made from the same *masa* used for making tortillas. This *atole blanco*—white atole—was the poor people's drink throughout New Spain and the Southwest.

Today this Aztec drink continues in the Southwest. People enjoy atole like the Aztecs did, as a light blue cornmeal drink sweetened with sugar or honey. When flavored with chocolate, it is called *champurrado.* Some people make it thick as a hot cereal in the winter months. Blue cornmeal can be found in any supermarket with a good supply of Mexican food.

New Traditions: *Cinco de Mayo*

An interesting recent cultural tradition is the celebration of *Cinco de Mayo*, May 5, in the southwestern United States, especially in the states in the Class of 1848. Along with Dia de los Muertos, a religious celebration with ancient Mexican roots that has become a popular United States community celebration, Cinco de Mayo is becoming an American tradition.

A side note is the confusion in the United States that Cinco de Mayo, May 5, is Mexican Independence Day. Cinco de Mayo is *not* Mexican Independence Day. This is a common mistake in the United States made by those who do not really know Mexican history.

Cinco de Mayo is a minor holiday in Mexico celebrating the victory of a ragtag group of Mexican patriots and soldiers over what was considered one of the strongest armies in the world in its time, the French army. Mexico's biggest celebration of the holiday is in the city of Puebla, the site of the battle. On May 5 in Puebla, historical reenactors dressed as both Mexican and French troops act out the battle to commemorate the Mexican victory.

The Mexican victory over the Second Empire of France at the Battle of Puebla in 1862, led by Mexican General Ignacio Zaragoza, was short-lived in that the French regrouped, came back and captured Mexico City, and took over the country. The battle's victory, however, became a symbol of Mexican pride and resistance to invading colonial powers.

After Mexico had finally gained its independence from Spain in 1821, the concentration of wealth remained in the hands of an elite class of government and church rulers. The life of the Mexican Indian remained as poor as it always had been under the *encomienda* system of the pre-Independence era.

Benito Juárez, a Zapotec Indian, realized the injustice of the political and social system and fought for equality for all Mexicans. Because of his efforts for equal justice for Mexican Indians, he has been referred to as the "Abraham Lincoln of Mexico."

Since its independence in 1821, Mexico had experienced great civil strife and economic struggle under a series of governments and leaders. It had also lost a disastrous war with the United States and ceded half of its land to the United States. When Juárez assumed leadership of Mexico, it was an economically bankrupt country torn apart by years of internal hostilities. Even the great silver mines had been allowed to stop production by former governments. In order to gain the time and resources necessary to rebuild the Mexican economy, one of Juárez's first acts as president was to suspend the interest payments on the country's foreign debts. He also acted to institute the Constitution of 1857, which established a republican form of government under which he was elected president. The constitution also ended special privileges and political power for the church and the ruling elite.

Mexico's refusal to pay the interest on its debts angered the European powers of England, Spain, and France. At the time, Mexican conservatives, who were not in agreement with the idea that a republican form of government was best for Mexico, created political unrest in the country and tried to change the government back to a conservative form with power in the hands of a ruling elite and the church. These conservatives also sought supporters in France to aid them in the overthrow of the elected Juárez government.

At the same time, France was seeking to establish an extension of its empire in the Americas. Even though one tenet of the Monroe Doctrine of the United States was that no European power would establish a governmental presence in the Americas, France knew that the United States was engulfed with its own civil war at the time. France seized the opportunity and sent an invading force to Mexico.

Juárez felt that he could assure the three countries that Mexico would honor its debts, but it needed time to establish a new government and rebuild its economy. Mexico owed the largest debt to England: 69 million pesos. It owed 10 million to Spain. The smallest amount owed was 2 million pesos to France. The Mexican Congress voted to support the debt moratorium, and both England and Spain eventually agreed to Mexico's request to delay debt payment. Only France denied the request and demanded payment of its debt.

Mexican conservatives, led by General Juan Almonte, the Mexican ambassador to France, had convinced Emperor Napoleon III to invade Mexico and establish a conservative government to rule in France's name. Napoleon agreed to send a French army of six thousand troops to invade Mexico, under the leadership of the famous French general Charles Latrille de Lorencez.

Even though the French forces were vastly superior, the Mexican forces were in a desperate battle for their country. Their valor and courage prepared the Mexicans for an astounding victory.

The French army was the greatest military force in the world at that time. Its soldiers were professional, well trained, well equipped, and experienced in battle. The Mexican army, in contrast, was a peasant army, ill equipped and gathered together just to fight the invading French army.

On May 5, 1862 the French army attacked the Mexican town of Puebla, intending to easily defeat the Mexican defenders and continue its march to Mexico City. Three times the French attacked the forts surrounding Puebla. And three times the Mexican army, under the leadership of General Ignacio Zaragoza, repelled the French army. Fighting valiantly, the Mexican army finally succeeded in defeating the vastly larger French army and forced its retreat. The French army was stunned by its defeat. The Mexican army had won one of the most astounding victories in military history.

Napoleon III was determined to conquer Mexico. In response to the defeat of his forces at Puebla, he sent an army of thirty thousand troops to restore France's efforts to conquer Mexico. Eventually the immense size of the French forces proved victorious, and a year later Napoleon III placed Emperor Maximilian in Mexico City and established a French monarchy in Mexico. Juárez fled Mexico City with the vow to never give up the fight for his country.

In 1867, Juárez and his followers of Mexican loyalists finally succeeded in defeating the French and once again established Mexico as an independent nation. Maximilian was executed, the French left Mexico, and Juárez resumed leadership of his country.

The victory at Puebla on May 5, 1862, came to symbolize the strength, determination, and national pride of the Mexican people. The victory of the Mexican army on that day was an important historical moment for the new country of Mexico. Benito Juárez's own words about the great victory at Puebla best represent the spirit of Cinco de Mayo: "Between two individuals as between nations, respect for another's rights is peace!"

Through the years, the holiday of Cinco de Mayo has evolved in the United States from just a memorial of an important Mexican historical event to a more encompassing celebration of cultural pride and accomplishment. Cinco de Mayo has become a major holiday celebrating Mexican culture and heritage.

Cynical observers have commented that beer companies created the enthusiasm for the American celebrations. Another criticism of the Cinco de Mayo celebrations in America is that its marketing perpetuates racial stereotypes.

Many cities and communities, however, have embraced the celebration as an opportunity for community building and racial pride. The celebration includes parades, mariachi musicians, *folklorico* dance companies, food and vendor booths, and lowriders and traditional artisans to display their pride in their cultural heritage.

With the documented growing population of Hispanos in the Class of 1848 states, the Cinco de Mayo celebrations in the United States will continue to serve an important cultural purpose. Few celebrants know the history of the holiday, but all can enjoy the fiesta and the celebration of Hispano culture.

CHAPTER 5

GIVING WITNESS

Latino/a Voices Speak Their Truth

A continued theme of this book has been whose story gets told and who gets to tell it. This chapter answers the question of who gets to tell the story of Hispanos in America: Hispanos get to tell their story. Here, seven Hispanic, Latino/a, Chicano/a leaders in the Hispano community share their thoughts about their histories and lives as a Hispanic person in America.

In many ways, this chapter is the heart of this book. The subtitle of this book is *Living in Two Worlds*, and this chapter gives living testimony of what it is to live in two worlds and how to successfully thrive in both.

These Hispanic leaders are the elders of our community. While each speaks only for herself or himself, collectively they speak for the generations of Hispanos who have lived in two worlds and who have given so much to America over the centuries.

They represent a wide range of roles in the Hispano community: educator, administrator, activist, publisher, author, writer, poet, musician, historian, academic, and parent. These modern-day Hispanic leaders and their stories are representative of all the Hispanic leaders who have risen to positions of leadership and influence.

As we listen to their stories, they tell us of their journey through America. They tell their own life story as both an American and as a proud Hispanic in America. Their stories reflect on the many themes of history's journey for Hispanos in America.

They are all greatly successful by the standards of American culture. They are highly educated. They all have PhDs or master's degrees. They have held top positions of leadership in many and varied institutions. They have founded service organizations. They have mentored others. They have been of service to their communities. They have received esteemed awards and recognition for their life work.

They have managed to live in two worlds: the world of accomplished American culture and the world of their traditional Hispanic culture. They have answered the question of whether it is possible to assimilate and be successful in the dominant culture and at the same time retain the heart and soul of your heritage. Their answer is a resounding yes.

Our leaders are no longer the unsung heroes of previous histories. They have received the deserved recognition of their significant contributions to American life in their own lifetime.

Their individual bios are descriptions of the accomplishments of their lives. Here, they speak in greater detail about their life and their journey. Each of them also shared their reflections on America's 250th anniversary in answer to the following questions:

Question 1: As we celebrate America's 250th, what does being an American mean to you?

Question 2: How does your culture make America better?

Question 3: What do you wish America knew about you?

Question 4: What is your dream for America?

Question 5: What are your memories of your family's cultural traditions?

Question 6: Of all the terms used to describe us, what term do you use and why?

Dr. Juana Bordas

Dr. Juana Bordas is recognized as an elder and icon in the world of leadership, diversity, and the advancement of Latinos and communities of color. The first Latina faculty at the Center for Creative Leadership (CCL), she taught in the Leadership Development Program—the most highly utilized executive program in the world. As a leader, teacher, activist, and author, Bordas continues sharing her wisdom and insights with people across the globe.

Bordas received an honorary doctorate from Union University and received the 2019 Lifetime Achievement Award from the International Leadership Association. She is the first Latina honored with this prestigious award.

Bordas is president of Mestiza Leadership International, a company focusing on leadership, diversity, and organizational change. Her many accomplishments and awards include:

- Founder and executive director of Denver's Mi Casa Women's Center
- Founding president/CEO of the National Hispana Leadership Institute
- Commended by *Latina Style* magazine for creating "a nation of Latina leaders."
- Her book *The Power of Latino Leadership* recognized by the International Latino Book Awards as best business/leadership book and by the Nautilus Book Awards as a prestigious Gold award winner in the area of Multicultural/Indigenous Literature
- Her book *Salsa, Soul, and Spirit: Leadership for a Multicultural Age* recognized by the International Latino Book Award as best leadership book
- Inducted into the Colorado Women's Hall of Fame
- Featured in the documentary *The Voice and Vision of Latina Leadership*

We Are All Mestizos: The De Colores People of the New World

My family left the Caribbean coast of Nicaragua because of a tsunami that wiped out Cabo Gracias a Dios, which was our ancestral lands. And so, like the immigrants before us, we came to America seeking a better life following the vision and the promise of America. When I was growing up, America was the promised land—the land of opportunity where my family could achieve and succeed.

We immigrated in the late 1940s—a time when an ordinary family like my family could educate their children, could buy a little house.

The way my family got here was that my father and my two older sisters came first to earn money to bring the rest of the *familia* to America. My mother and five of my brothers and sisters got on this big freighter in Nicaragua that had a bunch of bananas and coconuts in it. In the bottom of the boat was this little room with bunk beds. And that is how we came to America.

When we landed, my father was waiting with open arms, welcoming us to a new land, a new life, and the endless possibilities of America. The interesting thing is that if you look at my family now, we *are* the American dream. My mother, who had a fifth-grade education, now has a great-grandson with a PhD in nuclear physics, a granddaughter who's an architect, and another granddaughter who has a PhD in chemistry. My grandson is a lawyer. My daughter is a lawyer. My three daughters have advanced degrees. Where else could that happen except in America?

My mother and father were these humble people who had this vision for their children. I like to say we are the dreams deferred of our parents and our ancestors, because they believed that one day, one of their own would be able to take their place in the great American mainstream. And it actually happened.

As the youngest daughter, I had the most opportunity. My mother, my father, my brothers and sisters poured themselves into me. My mother helped me get a scholarship to a private girls high school, and so I was able to be the first to go to college.

This has given me a sense of responsibility to give back, because I stand on the shoulders of all these people who worked so hard. Our parents dreamed that someday the lives of their children would be better and sacrificed to make that happen. So, we're the dream deferred. And we are the American dream.

When my father got here with my two sisters, World War II was going on. My sister Rosemary, who is the oldest in the family, enlisted in the Waves. Here she is, this immigrant girl from Nicaragua, who worked in naval intelligence. They needed people who could speak Spanish because Argentina was on the other side of the war, so they sent her down to Miami, and she interpreted the documents in Spanish.

After the war, she took her GI Bill and bought our family a little home. Now this is very Latino, the oldest daughter, not thinking about herself, but thinking about her family. We got our little home for $10,000. The GI Bill was the way Latinos first got into the middle class—buying homes and getting college educations.

When you look at that kind of history for my family and for Latinos as a whole, and you look at what we were doing at that time to become who we are today, we were fulfilling the vision and promise of America.

To talk about my culture making America better, I think we need to talk about America from the perspective of the Latino community, or from the perspective of the *mestizo*, or the people who are Spanish and Indian and the mixed people of this hemisphere. Because really, that's what America is. It's not just the United States; it's the whole hemisphere—from Colorado all the way down through Central and South America.

And people of Latino descent are the dominant people. We are the root of the entire Western Hemisphere that was here before colonization, along with the Native people who were here first.

When I look at our culture, we are the bridge between the Old World and the New World—between the European and the Indigenous. We are the bridge between that which will come and that which has been. We are the new people, *La Raza Cosmica*, the mixed multicultural people of the future.

And this is not just the Latino culture. It's this incredible cauldron of people who came together to form a new humanity, a new race, a new people. Our culture is the prototype for that which will come in the future, for the multicultural age, the multicultural people. Half of the children in the United States today identify as multicultural.

The majority of people in this hemisphere are mestizos, which means "the mixed-race people." So, we are the culture of the future, but also the culture of the past.

What makes our culture so great is that we have kept those ancestral roots and values. Values such as generosity, like being a collective where we take care of each other, hard work, and where everybody contributes to advance collectively.

That sense of generosity is so evident in the saying *mi casa es su casa*, that we share what we have. This is a very old Indigenous root and the way humankind survived. We made it to the top of the evolutionary pile because we supported and helped one another.

Latinos are also not a materialistic culture. Sharing and caring is our wealth. Regardless of how successful we get, our job is to take care of people and to make sure those who come after have a better life. Latinos respect you not because of your success or how much money you have, but because you give back, you're part of the community, you help others.

When Anglos came here, they were urged to cut their roots, to change their names, to forget their language, their ancestors and grandparents. Sometimes they don't even remember their grandparents.

One of the gifts Latinos will make for America is that we are going to give people back their ancestors. We are going to say, "Remember your past." Dia de los Muertos is already becoming one of America's favorite celebrations, and it beckons people to connect to those who came before them. We're going to infuse America with very important values.

Latinos are the whole rainbow of humanity, all of the colors. We have our cultural core, the root that comes from our traditions and our history. But because we are a fusion culture, our *cultura* is alive. It's still changing. It's still growing. A good example is how Latinos have been able to become part of the American mainstream while retaining their identity.

The concept of La Raza Cosmica is that our culture is the merger of many cultures, races, and nationalities. We are hybrids. For instance, my father was French Nicaraguan. His family were Cajuns and French who went from New Orleans down to Nicaragua. Then my grandfather marries a Nicaraguan, and voilà, I'm French, Indian, Spanish, and American.

We are the mixed people of the New World, and our culture preserves the old culture that made humanity survive and thrive for all of these generations. At the same time, we love to change, to grow, to add, but never forgetting where we come from, never forgetting our root.

La Raza Cosmica is the next evolutionary step for humanity. It is what we all shall become—a mixed people that integrate and synthesize many cultures, taking the best of every culture forward. This is the Latino prototype.

The important thing that America needs to know about me personally, but also Latinos generally, is that we are an integral part of America today. I went through years and years of education in the mainstream culture. When we bought that little house, it was where all the White people were living. So, I walked into this White school at seven years old not speaking English. There's nobody else like me there. That is when I assimilated.

When I was young, in order to be successful, you had to assimilate, to learn the Anglo cultural context. I was able to do that and went to college in the 1960s. To my parents, this was the great gift of America—that their children could get educated.

When I finished college, I realized I was the first literate person in my ancestral stream. Not that I was more intelligent, but I had learned the Anglo way of being intelligent. I felt this huge sense of responsibility. What do I do with this great gift I've been given?

I was fortunate to see the great leader John F. Kennedy on my campus, and so I joined the Peace Corps, and I went to Chile. I wanted to serve—to give back. And actually, I was following the example of my parents and the Latino tradition of serving others. I think Anglos need to understand that we come from a different cultural paradigm. That when we have more, we are expected to give more.

But here was the thing that was so amazing. I had assimilated and was even ashamed of my family and being Latino. My mother had this thick accent. We were poor. I grew up an immigrant in the 1940s and '50s. And then I go to Chile, and I see this incredible culture, this incredible country, where Nobel Prize winner Pablo Neruda was the poet of the country. Gabriela Mistral had also received a Nobel Prize. Violeta Parra had written "Gracias a la Vida."

And I'm sitting there thinking, "Why didn't anybody ever tell me that my culture was so great?" I grew up never having a Latino teacher. Never having a Latino in a position of influence. Never even seeing a Latino driving a bus or as a businessperson.

What I want America to know about us and to know about me is that we come from this incredible cultural heritage and that we're here to contribute to America. Not to make America great again, but to fulfill the vision and promise of America. To bring our gifts to America—to add value. To show how working together, building community, and uplifting everyone makes us a great people. And this includes honoring our ancestors and those who came before us.

Latinos understand that we have been on a collective journey; we only survived because we worked together. And that is how we will move forward. I think that's a great gift that I bring, and that's what I wish people would see and acknowledge.

One thing I'd like to say about the American dream is that we are the great experiment that is still unfinished. And that it is our destiny to fulfill the vision and promise of America.

Family Traditions

I think a lot of my family's traditions arc spiritual, and thesc were a mixture of the Catholic church and our Indigenous faith. What really spoke to my soul was our love and devotion for the Blessed Mother, or *Tonatzin*, in the Indian tradition. My family really believed in the love, the comfort, the protection of the Holy Mother.

I didn't meet my *abuela* (grandmother) until I was thirteen, when she came from Nicaragua. She never cut her hair and had these long braids that wrapped around her head like a halo. I was a little embarrassed because I was trying to be an American, and my grandmother shows up, and she is an Indian. And yet she became my spiritual anchor.

What I learned from her was the deep faith that sustained my family and our people as a whole. My abuela would gather us every night to say the rosary in Spanish. Sometimes I would roll my eyes when we were saying the *Santa Maria Madre de Dios* because I knew forty-nine more were coming. Forty-nine more were coming! I was like, "Oh my God!

We have to go all the way around the rosary!" But I developed a deep sense that *Santa Maria*, the Holy Mother, would take care of me.

We had an altar with *santos* and candles. I learned to pray and to rely on God's guidance and providence. We really believed *estamos en los manos de Dios*: Spirituality is what I get from my family traditions.

My life has really been shaped by those experiences. I believe I am protected, loved, and guided. I get my courage, my sense of self, the belief that I am doing what I was sent here to do, my purpose out of that tradition.

I also knew that women were central to our families, our culture, and our community, and were the keepers of our spiritual traditions. The women in my family were very strong. In truth, we are a matriarchal culture. My *madre* Maria was so determined and dedicated to our future. She sacrificed her life for her children, and there is no greater gift than that. My mother got us scholarships to go to Catholic schools, and that's how I became an educated woman.

Now you tell me how an immigrant has that kind of vision. My mother was a strategic leader, a servant leader. She left a legacy, which is the highest form of leadership you can have. To develop the next generation, that's leadership. She planted this in me. If you want to talk about traditions, the tradition in my family is we help each other. This tradition of helping others has shaped my life.

I think that is why my life has been dedicated to the uplifting of Latinas and women. I think it comes from my abuela, mother, sisters, the nuns in the Catholic schools I attended, and the many, many women who have guided me and enriched my life.

When I came to Colorado in my twenties, I came to Pueblo. I was so happy because Pueblo is the heart of Colorado. My daughter, Carmen, my first child, was born there.

I started at a very young age working with women. First, in the Peace Corps. Then when I got to Pueblo, it's 1969, 1970, and we're doing the Vietnam moratoriums. I'm part of the Chicano Movement and the Vietnam moratorium. But the feminist movement is just beginning, and I get together with Betty Jo Tucker, who's the head of student affairs at the college. We started the first women's group in Pueblo in 1970. It's only a small group, but we're celebrating and empowering women.

In those days, colleges used to have this thing called a teach-in, when they would bring all incoming students together, and they would tell them about the Black Movement, the Chicano Movement, the Vietnam movement, and how to get involved.

I called the man heading it up and asked, "Who will be speaking about women's issues? He said, "Oh, Juana, you know there is the Black, Chicano, and antiwar movements going on." I said, "Okay, but you have to understand that there's going to be eight or ten women in the back with signs saying that this is a sexist thing going on here."

He paused and said, "What time do you want to speak, Juana?" That was the first time I gave a public speech in Colorado. I like to tell that story because women need to know we can't wait. We have to say, "No, it's our time."

I self-identify as *mestiza*. The reason is that, like I said, my grandmother was Indian. When I look at my own lineage, it's the mixture of Indigenous and Spanish, and with my father, French. And I am a proud American. So, I identify as a mixed person, but the mixed person of this hemisphere, of the merger of the Spanish and Indian, of the new race that's being born, of that which is the culmination of all the traditions of people who have come to this hemisphere from across the world.

I think it's a really important term because we are all mestizos. That's who we are now. Find me a thoroughbred. It's impossible. It doesn't exist. People have tried to create the thoroughbred race. It is such a mistake. Every time you have a race that thinks that they're better than someone else or that they're the chosen people, you have racism and ethnic cleansing.

I identify as the mestiza of the new world. If you look at the word *Latino*, that comes from Rome. If you look at the word *Hispano*, that's the old name of Spain, Hispania. I would say that I'm a Chicano at heart because I'm a political person, and I know that we have to change society, and that we have to be involved in social change in order to create this new world.

I wish that people would start using the term *mestizo*. My business is called Mestizo Leadership International, and I chose that in the 1990s because it was the only designation that worked for me and because we are all mestizos and we are all *De Colores*.

For the last thirty or forty years, when I end my speeches, I have people sing "De Colores." I've written in my books that "De Colores" should be the Latino national anthem because we are the "De Colores," the multicultural people of this new world that's coming. I think it is really important for us to have that sense of identity that we are the "De Colores." So, one legacy I would love to leave for my people is to have "De Colores" become our national anthem.

Dr. Ramon Del Castillo

Dr. Ramon Del Castillo is past chair and professor in the Chicana/o Studies department at Metropolitan State University of Denver (MSUD, 2006–2019) and a past faculty member at MSUD in the sociology and Chicana/Chicano Studies departments (1984–1996). He is an accomplished author, poet, freelance columnist, and journalist.

Del Castillo was a newspaper columnist for the *Rocky Mountain News* and *El Semanario: The Weekly Issue*. He has several chapters from his doctoral dissertation on *curanderismo*, or folk healing methods, published in textbooks and used in classrooms. He also edited a book with Dr. Lisa Grayshield titled *Indigenous Ways of Knowing in Counseling: Theory, Research, and Practice*, with an emphasis in indigenous epistemology.

His many publications include articles in the journal *Applied Anthropology*. Two titles include "Population Growth, Activism, Social Movements, Coalitions and the Future of African American and Latinas/os in Denver and Beyond" and "Culturally Competent Assessments with Immigrants, Mexicans and Mexican Americans: Transforming Misperception into Culturally Relevant Perspectives."

A short story he wrote entitled "Primos Hermanos" was published in *La Revista Almagre Review* (2019). His poetry collections include *Chicana/o Rhapsodic Rhythm and Blues* (2017), *Quetzales Are Not Extinct* (2016), *Tales from a Michoacano* (2002), *When the Owl Can't See at Night* (1995), *From the Corazon of a Bato Loco!* (1994), and *Broken Concrete* (1988).

Del Castillo also has poems published in various journals and collections, for example, "Human Rights" in *Yellow Medicine Review* and "My Journey to Michoacan" and "Flowers from the Same Garden" in *Cantos Al Sexto Sol: An Anthology of Aztlanahuac Writings* edited by Cecilio Garcia-Camarillo, Roberto Gonzales, and Patrisia Gonzales (Wings Press, 2002).

When Del Castillo became a columnist for the *Rocky Mountain News*, he was one of very few Chicano columnists for a major newspaper in Colorado at that time. In 1996 he began writing for *El Semanario*. His commentary covers a wide range of political, cultural, and social issues, usually pertaining to the Chicana/o community.

He has received more than forty awards for his leadership, activism, scholarship, and poetry. His awards include

- Cesar Chavez Leadership Hall of Fame, Denver Public Library (September 13, 2014)
- Cesar E. Chavez Award, Labor Council for Latin American Advancement (March 31, 2012)
- Rodolfo "Corky" Gonzales Civil Rights Award, Latin American Research and Service Agency (October 30, 2009)
- National Law Student Association Award, National Latino Student Association (2005)
- Martin Luther King Humanitarian Award, Colorado Civil Rights Division (January 1998)
- First Place: Statewide Chicano Theme Writing Contest, MSCD (1991)

The Pride of Being a Chicano in American Society

Yes, I am an American. I am the product of the beauty and magnificence of my Mexican heritage and culture, rooted in Native and Indigenous history. My ancestors struggled in this society to maintain cultural identity and passed the baton to the next generation—something I treasure and hold dearly in my heart as a second-generation immigrant Chicano in American society. My familial ancestors experienced what immigrants are experiencing in today's society, entering America through levels of social disempowerment, alienation, and cultural suppression, accused of wanting to take over Western civilization. They struggled to preserve and pass on the values necessary for our generation to endure and be victorious over the incessant dehumanization they experienced. My spirit will not allow me to succumb to being a victim of my ancestors' historical fate, but rather become the creator and agent of my own and my community's destinies.

On my mother's side, the Macias immigrated from La Piedad, Michoacan, Mexico, and on my father's side, the Del Castillos immigrated from El Distrito Federal, La Ciudad de Mexico. Both sides of my family settled in the United States, one in Newton, Kansas, and the other in Wichita, Kansas, during the 1910 Mexican Revolution. On my father's side, my grandfather Rosalio Lopez Del Castillo was part of the indigenous Zapotec people of Mexico, probably mixed with Azteca lineage. He shared stories about his involvement in the Mexican Revolution. He worked on the Santa Fe Railway in Newton. He was distinctive looking and always dressed to a T following a hard day's work. My grandfather Pancho Macias was from the Tarascan civilization also known as the Purepecha civilization. He was a hard-working ranchero, employed at the Cudahy Packing Company. His influence on the Mexican population that eventually settled in Wichita left an indelible mark on this community because of his demeanor and hard work ethic. We were taught to respect America but not lose our identity in the process.

A *dicho* in Mexican history that has impacted me was coined by Mexico's only Indigenous president, Benito Juárez: "Respect for the rights of others is peace." That motto stuck with me as I began to read and understand who I was and the role my ancestors played in history and its relationship to the United States of America.

The second creed that I have internalized is contained in the Constitution of the United States of America. It reads, "We hold these truths to be self-evident, that all men are created equal, and that they are endowed by their Creator with certain inalienable rights. Among those rights are life, liberty, and the pursuit of happiness."

Those precious words are implanted in my mind even though America's practice regarding Chicano fundamental rights has been challenging as they suffered against omnipresent negative forces in American society. I have not lost my faith that Americans can create a unified nation, living up to the creed that defines this nation.

Throughout my life, I've been disappointed at America. My resentment grew intensely after I started college. I was embittered because of the history of oppression that La Raza experienced in the United States. Those experiences, both personal and historical, were the impetus for why I studied Mexican American Studies at the University of Northern Colorado. My ambition was to learn my history and culture, which had been buried underneath Mother Earth, only to be revived during the Chicano Movement. La Raza's history, culture, and our contributions had not been shared in American educational institutions at the time I went to grade school. There were never any books with Spanish surnames in the curriculum. I worked arduously with several leaders and legislators in Colorado to pass HB19-1192, a piece of legislation that mandates that all public schools in K–12 teach the history, culture, and contributions of the four major ethic groups in American society.

Being an American means love of country, with all of its pitfalls, but with an intentionality of making things better for the next generation. Conversely, being an American from the outside looking in means being accepted for who you are and working collectively to make a better world for everyone.

Social justice is an important value in the Mexican and Chicano cultures. Activism is as American as apple pie. Mexican culture, like all cultures, has its unique beauty, with its food, music, poetry, language, values, and traditions. Chicano history is an integral element in the cultural beauty of Colorado. Colorado's roots can be traced back to indigeneity in Meso America, sprinkled with Spanish influence and eventual independence, French Intervention, the birth of Mexico, the Mexican-American War, and the birth of Chicano culture. One of the greatest challenges we face is the question of the oppressor/oppressed dichotomy. The Mexican/Chicano cultures add cultural depth, vibrancy, diversity, excellence, and struggle to our world. One has only to travel to Meso America and see its monumental pyramids, aqueducts, and social structures to realize that magnificent empires thrived on this land long before the White man arrived. This land was part of Mexico; what exists are the remanants of great civilizations that are an important part of Chicano history. Many Chicanos house the Indigenous persona as well as the Spanish oppressor. We are part of the colonizer and the colonized. We are *el mestizaje*.

America's Manifest Destiny did not include La Raza. Mexicans were stripped of their identities, and our gifts were hidden in the crevices of a monocultural curricula in educational institutions. Prior to the movement, instruction relative to Mexican history in American education institutions was based on racist stereotypes that had been developed by social scientists. Failure to include La Raza's narrative in America's history caused psychological and cultural damage to members of our group.

Sharing our experience with other groups will make America a better and stronger nation. We were a people in search of our identity. We dealt with macro issues that included cultural hegemony, colonization, racism, sexism, and xenophobia, and more concrete issues like educational equity, imigraphobia, adverse language policies, economic inequities, and lack of political representation in American society. During the Chicano Movement, La Raza struggled for cultural respect and autonomy. Writing about and struggling for space in American society and history to include these forgotten cultural elements was empowering.

We have a social responsibility to destroy the myths and stereotypes that have been created and replace them with our true selves, the protagonists of a play called life—we are not an existential threat to American culture. If we don't create cultural productions that reflect our realities, our culture will again be ignored, and our origins will again be left out of the Master Narrative.

The Chicano Movement catapulted us from invisibility to visibility as our collective forces took action. Chicanos have contributed significantly in this country to make America what it is. We have achieved some victories, just like our ancestors, but more development remains. Stories about Chicano heroes and heroines are beginning to be included in curricula across the nation. We have a social responsibility to build upon that knowledge base.

America is a stronger nation when it demonstrates respect for all groups and provides opportunities for all people to participate in the American way of life. The splendor of America is its diversity. If this country does not become educationally inclusive, then the stories and contributions of its beautiful people will be lost for another two generations. Being an American to me means creating pathways for full participation in the planning, development, construction, implementation, and management of democracy in America.

America's recognition of my humanity, with the right to be respected, walk in dignity, and practice my own agency as a human being, should be a prerequisite for all Americans. My participation in the Chicano Movement, often viewed as a cultural rebirth, was a worthy cause. There are Americans who didn't understand and embrace it—seeing the Movement as a bunch of radicals protesting without good reason. One of the goals achieved during the Movement was some semblance of social justice. We were actually fighting for the same ideals that our Mexican and American ancestors fought for—place and space.

During the Chicano Movement, I had the distinct honor and privilege of meeting and working with several nationally recognized leaders in this country. I spent time organizing the annual marches in concert with Nita and Rodolfo "Corky" Gonzales and the Crusade for Justice in 1980–1985, celebrating El Diez y Seis de Septiembre. While at the University of Northern Colorado, I chaired the Lettuce Boycott in northern Colorado (1972–1976) for Cesar Estrada Chavez and Dolores Huerta of the United Farm Workers. I am one of the founders of the Cesar Chavez Peace and Justice Committee of Denver (2001), an organization that celebrates and honors Chavez and Huerta with an annual march and celebration, and by giving out leadership awards to community residents. My activism included meeting and consulting with José Angel Gutiérrez, founder of La Raza Unida in Crystal City, Texas. As a member of the National Association of Chicana and Chicano Studies, I have collaborated with top scholars in this discipline, writing papers, organizing, and presenting at annual conferences.

What I would like for America to know about me is that amid all of the atrocities and suffering that my community experienced, a sense of loyalty to this nation remained in my consciousness. Finding the balance between my desire for autonomy and respect for legitimate authority was a grave challenge. During the movement, I studied and adopted the theory and philosophy of nonviolence, ideals I continue to embrace and practice in my activism in a peaceful and nonviolent manner.

In 1969, when I was drafted into the US Army, I reported to Fort Leonard Wood in Missouri. Military service was part of the tradition of La Raza, as they defended American democracy throughout history. American Democracy would not be where it's at today if La Raza had not participated in the many wars to defend it—often at the price of death. Even after participation in wars, Chicanos were seen as "foreigners," still not accepted by mainstream America.

The contradiction is that when Chicano soldiers returned home from the Vietnam War, they were alienated; like other veterans, they were abandoned. Chicano soldiers returned and suffered from post-traumatic stress disorder (PTSD). I treated a lot of them at El Centro de las Familias, and I wrote one of my master's theses on PTSD.

I am grateful for the gift of poetry that I have acquired and grown to love. My involvement in the field of Chicana and Chicano literature in juxtaposition to the Chicano Movement was an invaluable tool I used to connect with my community. The power of the written word is a liberating force. Its utilization included teaching poetry classes to K–12 students and at the universities.

I hope my poetry empowered my students in the classroom, community groups, associations, organizations, and gatherings while I was a professor at MSU Denver. Poetry also became a method for sharing the beauty of my culture, life, death, and struggle. The power of the pen was a magical tool to inspire others to write and become activists in their respective communities. Poetry, as the soul of the community, is one of those instruments that can be transformed into a tool for liberation, a tool for self-psychoanalysis. It provided me with insight into the psychology of human behavior and expanded my social conscience. The power of the word assists others in delving into the depths of their consciousness, uncovering dark shadows and unveiling hidden contradictions. It became a healing force for enlightening others regarding social justice. Poetry challenged oppressed communities to stand up, speak out, and take action—a glaring realization of how difficult social change can be.

My time as a columnist in the field of journalism allowed me to use the power of the pen to create critical consciousness in our community. I am enamored of this country for its Constitution with freedom of speech and freedom of press, two human rights that are essential elements of Democracy. As a columnist for the *Rocky Mountain News* and *El Semanario*, I found it challenging to investigate and present alternative perspectives on hot topics and controversial issues. Local newspapers like *El Semanario* are the poor man's way of fighting against oppression.

I spent thirty-six years at Metropolitan State University of Denver, entering in 1984 as affiliate faculty and retiring as a full professor and chair of the Chicana and Chicano Studies Department in 2020. Teaching and guiding students was the greatest challenge in my life. I developed a passion for teaching, assisting students in molding a passion for the true meaning of life.

Developing minds and hearts into critical thinkers and productive citizens, ready to take their place in a democratic society, is challenging. The transformative process with inherent internal emotional and psychological stressors was an opportunity for self-growth that includes a deeper love for humanity and hope for the future. A successful educator has to be willing to experience this with students in a dynamic process. I continue this journey with enthusiasm and love for the profession.

I was one of the scholars for the recent La Raza Report, commissioned by Dr. Alex Marrero, the superintendent of Denver Public Schools, titled "Latino Families and Denver Public Schools: At the Crossroads." My faith in social change came to life, knowing that our communities will overcome a century of negligence in the school system. This includes the idea that La Raza will receive an equitable education in this society. To accomplish this vision, there has to be a unified effort with a lot of determination. Recognizing and honoring my culture is on the top of the list of what America means to me. I do not long to be the gatekeeper of knowledge, but rather one of the constructors of knowledge who was omitted from participation because of who I am.

I have a dream that all Americans will feel proud to acknowledge Latino contributions to this society, providing Latinos pathways to fulfill their collective destiny in this country and the world. A society cannot take away the dignity of a human being and expect that person to be fulfilled in life. When humans experience dehumanization, they lose their souls and the will to participate in society.

As America continues its journey toward a multiculturalism in which our traditions are valorized and used to empower our people, I envision a world that includes respect for all human beings, with opportunities to share and learn from each other. However, I do not envision a form of multiculturalism that is watered down, further robbing people of their cultural identities. The question of multiculturalism cannot be tantamount to assimilation. It must be an authentic form of valuing, understanding, and acting upon the world in unity.

I have a dream that children of all colors will love and embrace each other as brothers and sisters. The vestiges of white supremacy will be shredded into particles that turn to dust as the final act of destroying racism will be completed.

I have a dream that oppression will be eradicated as the bells of freedom ring across the country to announce a new beginning, inviting all to participate. My dream includes the eradication of poverty that prohibits the physical, mental, and spiritual growth of children dying of malnutrition on the streets. My dream includes the dissolution of anachronistic schools, replaced with a constellation of institutions at all levels of education that share knowledge, insight, multicultural creativity, and love for each other.

For those groups that have been invisible in American society, my dream includes America hearing their cries for justice and providing them opportunities to become visible in American society. All of God's human creatures will participate in the further construction of a truly free nation where all human beings are respected. Until this happens, we will not have embraced our true humanity nor practiced true democracy. I believe and continue to struggle for what I think the American dream can become through struggle, love, and nonviolence.

This list of memories could be a novel, but only a smidgen of my cultural traditions will be shared. What I really loved as a child was my extended family and our love for each other. There were five branches in the Macias family that are included in my reminiscences. It was a matriarchal family, with one brother, my Tío Pancho.

I remember the many *jamaicas* and cultural and holiday celebrations held at the church. The church was the center of the community. The midnight masses on Christmas Eve were very sacred traditions. My Tía Concha lived across the street from Our Lady of Perpetual Help Church, located near the Catholic school that I attended. After midnight mass, there was a tradition wherein my tía would make tamales and piping hot chocolate for all of the families. These were precious gatherings for interacting with extended family members.

My tíos, my tías, and my mother loved their religion. They were devout Catholics working hard so that their children, including myself, could attend Catholic schools. Private Catholic schools in Wichita charged tuition—becoming a challenge for working-class families. My mother worked hard at her regular job, then took orders for the cuisine she had become known for in the community, selling it for reasonable prices to make extra money so that her four sons could attend Chaplain Kapaun Memorial High School, a Jesuit institution. Her dream was fulfilled.

Music was a major part of our family's cultural traditions. I remember my father's love for Mexican and Latino music. He played with Johnny Hahn and the Tropical Suns. I discovered later on in my life that the music they were playing was actually Afro Latin jazz. They also played Mexican classics as part of their repertoire. The group was ahead of its time. My father played the saxophone and the clarinet, and he was also a tap dancer. Johnny Hahn and the Tropical Suns would come to the house on Sunday afternoons. All of the furniture would be taken out of the living room in our home and put in the front yard. The band would set up, and they would practice. It didn't take long for neighbors to bring chairs out to the street, listening to this band playing beautiful Mexican and Latino music. This influenced me to become a *conguero*, playing with a few local bands.

Hard work was another value honored in our culture. Many of my family members worked at the packing house, El Pacador. Through hard work, families built our community, resulting in the development of the North End Barrio that exists today.

Instilling democracy and participating in the military were strong cultural values built into the family structure. Although struck by tragic deaths because of the wars, families supported each other, using their religion as a mechanism to survive the pain and suffering, through velorios and rituals, never losing faith in their God.

The following is a brief cultural vignette regarding the important role that religion played in the lives of our community. My father was an ex-Marine. We grew up in a very patriotic family, believing it was our duty to go to the military. I thought that going to Vietnam was my lot in life. During the Vietnam War, my brother and cousin enlisted into the Marine Corps on the "buddy plan." This plan included an agreement that my brother and cousin, Roger, would spend their tours together. I recollect my mom vowing to make a *manda*, which is a Catholic vow to visit a religious figure to pay homage in return for a favor/gift; in this case, the visit was to La Virgen de Guadalupe in Mexico. The request made was that my brother and cousin would return home after their tours of duty in Vietnam were completed. My mother and Tía promised to visit La Virgen after my brother and cousin returned.

Before the manda could be made, the local priest came to the home to do a *bendicion* (blessing). I remember his visit to my mother's home. There was a big supper with tamales, enchiladas, and fried chicken. Before the Padrecito left, everybody knelt down, and he gave the blessing to my brother and my cousin. They left for Vietnam soon thereafter.

My cousin was severely injured, stepping on a mine in the fields in Vietnam. He didn't return as a whole person. My tía's heart was broken. She had a hard time realizing why she should go fulfill her manda. In her mind, her son didn't come back the way that he left, and she felt that she did not need to honor her *promesa*.

The elders of the family interceded. My tía's sisters visited my tía at her home. "*¡Débes de ir! Su hijo está aquí con nosotros. Él no se murió.* He's alive." They had to convince her to fulfill her manda. I thought about it and what it really meant. You could not break a promise to Christ.

My brother was also injured in Vietnam, thirteen days after Roger had stepped on the mine. I remember a Marine sergeant coming to my mother's home. My mom was deathly afraid to answer the door. She thought that my brother had gotten killed. When my mother saw the sergent at the door, she screamed, "*Ay, Dios, no, Dios.*" When we opened the door, the sergeant was standing there. She was ready to faint. He told her, "Your son has been injured in Vietnam. He's in a naval hospital."

Unfortunately, my cousin Roger was later killed in a car accident after he had returned to the states for recovery. My brother participated in his ceremonial burial, per the buddy plan.

My cousin's funeral was large and the procession to the *pantion* was probably four blocks long. Taps were played at Roger's funeral. That sound is implanted in my mind, especially on Veterans Day.

I was drafted in 1969, went to basic training, and hurt myself while engaged in maneuvers. My injury turned out to be a preexisting condition. Company and platoon officials came to me when I was in the hospital and informed me, "You'll never have to go fight that war. You can stay in the military for two years if you want." But I had no desire to stay in the military. A lot of my buddies had been killed. I left and went back home.

Anti-war demonstrators were in deep conflict with the government during this time. I left and returned to Wichita, but I carried guilt about not going to Vietnam for a long time. As my life unfolded, I realized my destiny—to treat Vietnam veterans—was coming to fruition. I counseled veterans at Centro de las Familias and heard about the war from my clients—stories filled with pain, anxiety, and symptoms of PTSD.

El Día de los Muertos was a special holy day for our families. Different families practiced it differently, depending on where their ancestry originated. But there was always something sacred about setting up your altar with saints and praying to them. The centerpiece at our home was La Virgen de Guadalupe. Families pray to her because the belief in Mexican culture is that La Virgen will go directly to her Son and ask him for a favor. In our culture, sons do not refuse their mothers; therefore, Christ would never refuse La Virgencita.

In Wichita, we lived in what was termed a Mexican community and were referred to as Mexicans. After arriving in Colorado, I was influenced by students from throughout the Southwest and the Chicano Movement. I began to identify as a Chicano after taking classes in Mexican American Studies at the University of Northern Colorado, instructed by Chicanos, which was also a new phenomenon. I had rediscovered my identity, with a deeper understanding of how Mexican and Chicano history intertwine.

During my home visits from college, a lot of explanations to my friends about the significance and meaning of the interacting of Mexican and Chicano history occurred. The idea that part of my racial, ethnic, and cultural identity was rooted in Indigenous, Spanish, and Mexican experiences was exciting. How did this disappear? What forces deprived me of this knowledge? My political consciousness had been reframed, and part of this was an acknowledgment of my ethnic identity.

My father made periodic visits to my family in Greeley, Colorado. During one of his visits, an invitation from the University of Northern Colorado Education Department was extended to me to provide some lectures for current and future teachers relative to Chicano history and psychology. On the way back to Denver from Greeley, my father remarked to me, "I need to talk to you when we get to your *chante*. It's regarding this concept Chicano."

After we arrived at my home, he started our conversation by stating, "I'm confused about you." I asked him, "What are you confused about, Papi?" He stated, "You are a Mexicano. I don't know what this Chicano stuff is. So help me understand. We raised you as a Mexican, and don't ever forget that. *Tu eres Mexicano.*"

I said, "Papi, a Chicano *is* a Mexicano. I know who I am. The word *Chicano* has been around for a long time, Papi. We just didn't know it. So, I've not lost who I am. I'm very proud of the way you brought us up." And he stated, "Okay. By the way, you're really a good teacher."

My father and grandfather, Rosalio, envisioned their grandsons and granddaughters going to colleges or universities. I helped fulfill their dreams. I had the privilege of having my father see me teach at a university. That is a feeling that will always remain in my heart. *Yo soy Chicano!* I don't want the Chicano tribe to ever be forgotten.

Dr. Renee Fajardo

Dr. Renee Fajardo is a mother of seven, an author, an educator, and an activist in Denver, Colorado. She is the Director of the Journey through Our Heritage Program in Chicana/o Studies at Metropolitan State University of Denver. She is chair of the Chicano Humanities and Arts Council (CHAC) and the Colorado Folk Arts Council.

Fajardo was born to John and Barbara Fajardo in Denver, Colorado. She spent her formative years growing up in Curtis Park and the West Side of Denver, surrounded by her paternal grandparents and extended family before her family moved north into Adams County. She has Chicana/Native American, Filipino, and Jewish heritage.

Fajardo attended Peru State College in Nebraska and then University of Nebraska College of Law. She became a lawyer in order to "be a champion for other people."

After graduating from law school, she returned home to Denver. After passing the Colorado Bar Exam, her passion for youth, art education, and preserving traditional knowledge presented her with a unique opportunity. Instead of practicing law, she began utilizing her talents to support community endeavors that honored the importance of culture and art.

She found her passion in working with cultural performers and artists. As the director for the Crossover Project, she instituted the state's first free multicultural concert series for schoolchildren, the Cultural Concerts on Colfax Series at the Aurora Fox Arts Center, "to ensure all inner-city schoolchildren could experience their heritage firsthand on a fine arts stage."

Over the years, Fajardo instituted numerous projects that supported the expansion of cultural programming in the schools, including Dia de Los Muertos. She worked tirelessly to connect traditional knowledge bearers such as Raul Chavez of Azteca Huitzilopochtli and Mexican folklorist Rita Flores de Wallace to the larger community statewide.

Fajardo, Jeffco librarian Carl Ruby, and editor Ed Winograd co-created Tummy Tales, a series of nine children's books that preserves the legacy of Colorado's rich multicultural food traditions.

She and photographer Todd Pierson are cofounders of the Corn Mothers project. The multicultural award-winning exhibition and book project highlights the stories and portraits of more than seventy women from the Southwest who embody the Corn Mother spirit. The project was in response to a book gifted to Dr. Fajardo by her husband, Glen Anstine: *When Jesus Came, the Corn Mothers Went Away*. Fajardo's deep familial connection to the Pueblo story of Corn Mother, the life-giving force that sustains Mother Earth, inspired her to ask, "Where are the Corn Mothers and how do we find them?" Since its inception, the project has endeavored to answer that question by trekking throughout the region documenting and celebrating the contributions of women who nurture their communities. The project has been on display at dozens of venues including History Colorado in Denver from 2022 to 2023.

A Woven Tapestry

My concept of what America is has changed radically from when I was young to where we are now. I was mesmerized as a child by the many different ways a family could be. My mother was a Jewish kid raised in an orphanage. My dad's family took her in; they knew nothing about being Jewish, but they shared their culture with her and made her one of their own. I never thought about how she was a different color than me or my dad's family. I knew my grandpa was "Oriental" and that my grandma's people were called Mexican sometimes.

Folks were different colors, different in who they loved—gay or straight—different in how they prayed—Catholic, Jewish, or whatever Presbyterians were. This difference was a safe, magical space where I felt protected. Even as a kid, I embraced the many ethnicities that made me who I was. I did not realize then that I was raised by a Manito familia that was culturally accustomed to the concept of woven identities. To me then, America was a multitude of many beautiful cultures that were respected and embraced. I of course had no idea of the pain and suffering my own family had endured.

My first rude awakening came at eight years old, when my mother moved me to all-white neighborhoods. I was all of a sudden called Spic and Gook, and terrorized for being different and told to go back to Mexico or Japan. My perception that I lived in a place where my grandma's people had been for hundreds upon hundreds of years, a place I belonged to no matter where my mother or grandpa came from or whether my tíos and tías were gay, was shattered.

My next rude awakening came well into my adulthood, when I was told I was not a real Chicana, as I was part white. I am a woven person; I was raised in a very specific culture where I was made to feel part of a family and valued. Today, what happens is that kids like me are made to feel we are not enough—not white enough for some people and not brown enough for other people. I see that everywhere.

I want all of America to remember that America is not a single culture. America is a multitude. We are a political, geographical entity called America, where we belong to a nation. This is what I tell *mis hitos*, my children. America is a land that has constitutional rights and laws. Here, all cultures, all people, and all religions need to be respected, protected, and able to coexist.

What I want America to really understand, from my perspective, is that we are all Americans. Embrace everything that we are: the people who immigrate here, the multitudes of people who are here, the different cultures. Our current concept is our borders did not exist for hundreds of years before there was a place called America. If we want America to be good, we have to start thinking about the legacy we leave to our kids. We need to reflect and teach the whole history of all the people who call America home. We need to stop separating ourselves based on who we think is more entitled to be here. We need to stop being ableist and champion our most vulnerable.

At the university, I take on those populations of students who are at the highest risk of dropping out, students labeled as "neurodivergent." They don't get hired for jobs. People think they are unable to perform and don't give them a chance. We have to get unlocked from this mindset. If people are different and we can't understand them, we have to get to the point where we do understand them.

We need to work to make the world a better place. We can do great things with each other when we start treating each other like brothers and sisters. What we really need to do is look where we are and say, "What do I do to make where I live now better?" Respect everyone that's here and really pull together. Ask, "What do we do to treat each other with respect?"

I don't have any problem with anybody choosing whatever they want to be or how they want to identify or what they think. What I do want us to know is that you can't just keep dividing our country into these segments that are always fighting with each other, because the reality is that the world isn't an island.

We have bigger problems. We're going to have massive environmental problems. I thought that COVID would have taught the world that we are vulnerable. We all live on one earth spaceship. That's it. We've got this one ship. And we have to look at ourselves also as global citizens and people who are part of this big, breathing planet, and that really what we do to the least of us is actually how we affect all of us on some level.

If you have each other and you have your community, which are your neighbors and your people who are also your family, what else do you need to be happy? That's all you need. You just keep pushing on and surviving, because eventually you will get to the place with this beautiful tapestry where, by living that way, you will produce people who go out into the world and are not selfish people. They are people who look around and say, "I am going to do what I can all the time to help you and love you because we are here together."

I'm going to talk about my most important cultural values. My husband and I have seven children, six girls and one boy, and I think the biggest thing about my cultural value that I learned from my auntie is that the most important thing you can ever have is your family. And it does not matter whom they love or what kind of people they love.

It doesn't matter what color they are. All we care about is whether we have another person in our family who is going to carry on our ways, our kindness, our love, our traditions, and really make the world a better place. And that is the only way you have to grow them from the time they're little.

There are three ways we make family. You get born to us, you marry into us, or we choose you. The most important thing is to treat people like your family wherever you are. You have to focus on where you are with the people you are with now. The most important thing you can do is love the people that you're with and do the best that you can to put people in the world who are decent, giving, loving human beings.

I have two kids who are lawyers. One does immigration law, and the other one is a public defender. My daughter who's a public defender uses a quote that asks how do we gauge who we are as a people? It's how we treat the condemned, the poor, and our most vulnerable.

I remember my family making food and taking it to people they called hobos. We have a big house. I can't tell you how many people have lived in my house, like hundreds of people. We take people in. That's one of our values. This is our richness.

Racism is real. We need to understand what it is and how it affects us all. Start at home to combat it. Do not do it to our own people. I have a beef with this mentality dividing us on what color we are. We need to realize that Manitos, Latinos, Chicanos, or however we identify, we are all different colors. We can be white or dark and everything in between. Do not give in to dividing our own. That is one of the most important cultural values for me.

When you talk about cultural values, it's really about understanding that we're all connected. Address what it means to have "privilege" and how systemic and structural racism, sexism, adoptism, homophobia, ableism, and economic bias affect us all. I was not prepared to deal with these realities when I was taken from my home neighborhood as a child. I had no coping tools to deal with the harsh reality I was exposed to. But to have to bear the same treatment from my own people whom I identified with was isolating.

I do want to tell you some of my favorite memories. One of my very favorite memories is down on Fifth and Galapago for Thanksgiving or Christmas dinner. We've got the whole menagerie of everybody. The kitchen tables are are lined up. They are all kinds of smorgasbord tables. They don't even match each other. They line up the tables starting from the kitchen, and they line them up, and they go all the way into the living room. So basically, when you walk into the house, you walk in and you just see this row of tables that goes from the living room into the kitchen area. You're all sitting down, and all the food is being passed down. There's this great big, beautiful turkey and enchiladas and beans. It's just like every kind of food you can think of. The Italians brought over food, because we've got this whole thing going on with all the people who were working-poor people.

And the music was old music. My uncle would take out his mandolin or his violins, and the house was filled with laughter and the smells and just everything. Then there would be somebody who would get in a fight and one of the kids would run through the house, and they'd be screaming at each other outside, and nobody blinked an eye. Like, so what? Our dinners were definitely family dinners.

Another thing is that at Christmas Eve we'd make tamales in Auntie's house. All the windows would steam up with the steam from the tamales.

The other thing I really want to talk about is fishing. My mom, the Jewish orphan kid, didn't have anything growing up. McDonald's didn't exist. Not even pizzerias. But my Filipino grandpa would go fishing. That was the big thing. He'd go up to Red Rock Lakes, and they'd have their little baskets filled with their trout, and they would just take sandwiches and hard-boiled eggs. Everybody went fishing. That was our thing. We could all do it because it was inexpensive.

Back in the day, everybody, especially in New Mexico and southern Colorado, also went hunting. Somebody would get a deer, and then they would come home, and there'd be blood and stuff all over the garage and all this meat chopped up. I wasn't horrified. I was just like, "Wow, this is so great, because we're going to have meat." There are all these memories of these things that were just so simple. We maybe take those things for granted now, but it was almost like I stood still in time. My life was just filled with all these beautiful stories and richness and laughter.

I was born in 1958, and my mom moved us back and forth between Colorado and Nebraska a lot. I was always longing, longing, longing to come home. I went to Nebraska for law school. When I got home from law school, after I'd been gone for seven years, what happened is this: I came back with my husband to take care of my grandma and my aunties and to be in my land, with my people. So, I grew up all over, in what we now call the West Side, and the North Side, and the Points.

I did not know that our neighborhoods were redlined. I thought every person in the world was brown. We didn't use that word *Chicano* when I was little. I don't know if it existed yet. The people who were not brown like us, we never called them white, either. We'd say we were going to go over and see the Greeks, or we were going to go visit the Italians. We were going to go visit the Poles. So I had, in a way, this secluded life, where I just had this multicultural neighborhood.

But this is what was interesting at the time. I didn't know that there was some other world out there, but there was something. I just didn't know what it was. I knew that we weren't Greeks. We weren't Italians. I guess we weren't Americans, and we sort of fell into this category of . . . are we Spanish or Mexican?

I do not identify as a Chicana. When you say *Hispanic*, a lot of people get crazy and say, "Don't you ever use that word, 'cause that's a colonizer word." I want to say that what I have witnessed lately is that people on all sides of all cultural and religious backgrounds have gotten to the point where they think it's okay to treat each other with disrespect and hatred.

I am now at the point where I'm going to start standing up and saying it's not okay, because what I am and what I identify as is a *Manita*. And what does that mean to me? When I say *Manita*, it means that we are from a specific cultural area, from southern Colorado, northern New Mexico. For hundreds of years, we were secluded from everybody else in Mexico.

We actually are a very complex people that has been woven through the centuries into this beautiful tapestry, and it has different pieces that weave through it. When I say I'm a Manita, it means that I am a woven tapestry of a people who understood that the way that we're going to survive with each other is to treat each other like we are little brothers and sisters. I don't want to hear people telling me, I've got more Indigenous blood than you, I've got more Spanish blood, or I've got more blah, blah, blah. That is not what I'm talking about when I self-identify. I'm talking about who am I culturally, spiritually, and emotionally, and how am I tied historically to this land. I only feel at my very best when I'm here, because this is my land, and the blood of my people runs through it.

Nita Gonzales, MEd

Nita Gonzales, of Denver, Colorado, is a noted community activist, educator, and nationally recognized leader in the struggle for social justice and equality. Gonzales was the president and CEO of Escuela Tlatelolco Centro de Estudios, a nationally recognized model for Chicano/Mexicano and Indigenous education located in Denver. Escuela Tlatelolco was originally founded more than forty-one years ago to provide culturally competent and socially conscious education to predominantly Chicano youth. Gonzales also has a long record of supporting causes and activities that promote the economic, political, social, and educational strength of La Raza and underserved populations. She is a founder of the Chicano/Mexicano Education Coalition, founder of the Denver Youth Employment and Education Task Force, and cofounder of the Colorado Latino Forum. She also was a board member for numerous organizations working to promote the welfare of the Latino community, including Clinica Tepayac, the Denver City and County Community Oversight Board, and the President's Cabinet for

Metropolitan State College. Currently she is a Trustee of Regis University and board member of Four Winds American Indian Council, River Sisters Circle, and the Greenway Foundation.

As the oldest daughter of civil rights icons Corky and Geraldine Gonzales, Nita Gonzales was destined to become an activist. She began her activism career as a young adult during the Chicano Movement of the 1970s, which challenged the social injustices generations of Chicanos endured. She told *I Am Denver* how her parents' work inspired her to become a proud daughter of the movement.

Rooted in Ancestors, Rising in Love

When I think about being a citizen of this country, I think not just of the history that shaped this country, but of the histories we carry in our bodies, in our bloodlines, and in the songs of our elders. These aren't stories you find in textbooks. These are stories you inherit. Stories that live in kitchens and marches, in laughter and land, in struggle and ceremony.

When people ask what it means to be American, I hesitate. Not because I don't know—but because the word has never felt whole to me. Not as it's been defined. The term *American* is often used to describe someone from the United States, as if one country could own a name that belongs to an entire continent. I don't carry that identity in the narrow way this country often asks us to. I carry it with depth, with grief, with pride, with a clear-eyed understanding that I am part of something much older, much deeper, much more sacred.

I am American in the way that a mountain is American. In the way that an adobe wall holds generations of warmth. In the way that my grandmother's hands were American before she never spoke English or saw a map that drew arbitrary borders across our lands.

Being from this land means holding the deep tension between the promise and the reality of this country. It means knowing that the ideals written into founding documents were never meant to include us—and yet believing with every breath that we have the power to transform this nation into something more true, more whole. It's not about blind patriotism. It's about radical action. Action motivated by a love of this land that is willing to confront. Action that is willing to heal. Love that is willing to act.

My identity as a Chicana is rooted in this understanding. It is a declaration of memory, of resistance, and of belonging. It is political, spiritual, cultural. It tells the world: I know where I come from. I know the sacred ground I walk on. I know the responsibility I carry forward. That word—*Chicana*—holds both the wound and the wisdom. It holds the fire and the prayer. And I say it with pride.

My culture has always been my compass. It grounds me when the world feels unsteady. It reminds me of what matters when systems and headlines try to erase our truth. Our culture makes this country better—not because we assimilated, but because we remembered who we are.

Our traditions hold beauty and defiance. I remember the smell of chile bubbling on the stove, the sound of tortillas puffing up over the *comal*, the laughter of my tías as they gathered around the table with steaming mugs of café and stories that held lifetimes. Their voices carried memory. Their words carried medicine. This was our council. Our healing circle. Our form of news. But unlike the newspapers, what they shared was rooted in care: "*Mija está* struggling." "We should visit." "Let's make something to drop off." "Say a prayer."

I remember that no one ever left my grandparents' home hungry or empty-handed. The kitchen was sacred. The table was an altar. Food was love. And those values didn't stop at the front door. We lived in extended family, and that family stretched to include neighbors, organizers, elders, dancers, children. Our home became a refuge. A gathering place. A seedbed for resistance.

That's how I grew up—with the smell of fresh tortillas in the air and political strategy being whispered in the living room. With *corridos* playing from the radio and books stacked on every surface. With *danzas* in the park and poetry on the walls. And at the center of it all was my father—Rodolfo "Corky" Gonzales.

To many, he was the voice of a movement. To us, he was Dad. His fists once fought in the boxing ring, but his most powerful blows were his words. His poem "I Am Joaquín" shook awake a generation searching for identity, dignity, and voice. But it was how he lived that taught me the most. His life was his greatest poem.

He believed that the struggle for liberation had to start at home. So he raised us to think. To read. To speak truth. He challenged us to understand both sides of an issue—even when it was uncomfortable. Especially when it was uncomfortable. He told us, "You don't get to go along just to get along. You stand on truth. Even if you stand alone."

And when I questioned him—when I asked why women were treated as less in our tradition—he didn't dismiss me. He didn't scold me. He said, "You're right. That's something we must answer." That moment taught me more about leadership than any classroom ever could.

He taught us that education was not a path to approval—but to freedom. He didn't care if we got degrees—he cared that we could read deeply, think critically, and act justly. He passed down the teachings of great thinkers and revolutionary voices because he knew that if we didn't shape our minds, someone else would.

He was a warrior—but also soft in the ways that mattered. I still remember his hug. That bear hug that wrapped around you and let you know you were safe, no matter what the world threw at you. When he passed, that's what I missed most—that embrace. That sense that everything could still be okay.

And still, I dream. I dream of a country where every child knows they are sacred. Where the land and water are honored as relatives, not resources. Where Black, Indigenous, Brown, immigrant, and queer lives are not in danger, but celebrated. I dream of an America that walks at the pace of prayer, that pauses to reflect, that doesn't rush past its truth but reckons with it—honestly, humbly, and wholeheartedly.

I dream of a justice system rooted not in punishment but in healing. Where our people aren't locked away but lifted up. Where policies are made not for profit, but for people. I dream of a nation where the wisdom of ancestors is listened to, where culture isn't sold but held with reverence. Where everyone—not just the privileged—has the power to help shape the table and decide what's served on it.

We've walked this path for generations. And through it all—through the pain, through the joy, through the struggle—we've never let go of our stories. Our culture. Our spirit.

We are still here. And we are still becoming. So I will keep walking this path—with *corazón*, with *orgullo*, and with a love so radical it refuses to give up. Because this land remembers. And so do I.

Tony Ortega, MFA

Tony Ortega is a Denver-based visual artist, curator, and educator. His work has been exhibited in more than thirty solo shows and featured in collections at the Museum of Contemporary Art in Denver; the Boulder Museum of Contemporary Art; the Colorado Springs Fine Arts Center; the Harwood Museum of Art in Taos, New Mexico; the National Hispanic Cultural Center in Albuquerque, New Mexico; the Denver Art Museum; the Los Angeles County Museum of Art; the Blanton Art Museum in Austin, Texas; and the Museo Estudio Diego Rivera y Frida Kahlo in Mexico City, Mexico.

He holds an MFA in drawing and painting from the University of Colorado Boulder and is currently a professor at Regis University.

In 2018, Ortega was the Regis College Faculty Lecturer of the Year. He was the recipient of the Governor's Award for Excellence in the Arts (1999) and the Mayor's Award for Excellence in the Arts (1998).

Memories of Identity, Culture, and Family: Who Am I? A Reflection on Identity and Being American

The big questions are Who am I? Where do I come from? What is my context in the world? What is my identity?

Since childhood, family, society, and outsiders have tried to define me. But I've come to realize that identity isn't given—it's discovered through living. To answer this complex question, I need to look through the lenses of family, culture, ethnicity, politics, history, and even biology.

So, when someone asks, "What does it mean to be American?" I first think politically—about this nation-state made up of people from all walks of life, including those whose ancestors were here long before the United States existed. To me, being American comes with a kind of patriotic tribalism—a collective identity. We share rituals that link us: standing in school with hand over heart to recite the Pledge of Allegiance, rising for the national anthem at baseball games, cheering for US athletes at the Olympics, or casting our votes on Election Day. Interestingly, when we travel abroad, our passports don't say "Citizen of America"—they say "Citizen of the United States of America." Even the name is political. That distinction matters.

Yet the identity label of "American" can also erase nuance. I'll never forget when the Denver Art Museum acquired one of my large paintings. Curious about how they formatted the nationality portion of the label—Chicano? Mexican American?—I stepped closer. The label simply read: "American."

I also remember seeing my birth certificate for the first time in the late 1960s. Under race, it was marked "White." That's how things were categorized in New Mexico back then—no nuance, no recognition of cultural complexity. Yes, I am American, but that label alone cannot tell the full story.

My life and artwork revolve around identity. I've lived through many labels—Spanish American, Hispanic, Mexican American, Chicano, Manito, Indo-Hispano. Some were given to me by family, teachers, artists, and peers; others I chose myself. Each one touches on colonization, color, heritage, history, and place.

Labeling oneself as Spanish or Hispanic can signal European lineage—closer to whiteness, and therefore more acceptable in mainstream America. But it also risks denying the Indigenous side of our heritage. How can I honor my Indigenous ancestors if I choose to identify solely as Spanish or Hispanic? How do I show respect to my darker-skinned family members whose features reflect that ancestry?

My ancestors were here before the United States existed. They didn't cross the border—the border crossed them. From the Indigenous side came language, food, architecture, and deep knowledge of the land—the *adobes*, *vigas*, *latillas*, and *hornos* of New Mexico. From the Spanish side came religion, language, and cultural traditions. That blend is Indigenous, Mexican, and American histories. It's not a footnote—it's a multidimensional story.

If I could tell America one thing about me, it would be this: My identity is rooted in family. Since my parents never married, I was raised by my maternal grandmother, Trinnie Ortega; her sister, Pauline Segura (my great-aunt); and my mother, Mary Martinez. I also had the rare gift of knowing four generations of my family. In Pecos, New Mexico, I spent summers surrounded by extended relatives—talking, playing, learning.

The elders in my family spoke only Spanish. As a child, I made it a point to learn the language so I could communicate with them. I wanted to speak with my great-great-uncle Gavino and my great-great-aunt Clotilde—and Spanish was the key. Later, in college, I continued my studies of language, culture, and Mexican history at the Universidad de Veracruz in Jalapa. I learned that the Spanish spoken in New Mexico was archaic, influenced by Nahuatl, English, and local dialects—a kind of Spanglish. Being bilingual and bicultural has deeply shaped who I am as both a person and an artist.

Religion was also a cornerstone in the formation of my identity. I remember wondering why so many relatives were named Antonio—until I realized the name of the church in Pecos was San Antonio, the patron saint of the village. I was even named after him. Our holidays followed the rhythms of the church: Christmas, Easter, First Communion. I was baptized at the cathedral in Santa Fe, confirmed at the Santuario de Guadalupe, and received my First Communion at Our Lady of Guadalupe in Denver. I was even an altar boy. My mother, grandmother, and great-aunt were proud.

My memories are vivid, rooted in land, food, and tradition. I remember cleaning the *acequia* that irrigated the crops and helping my grandmother in the garden. One of my fondest memories was searching for the kitchen drawers at Tío Gavino and Tía Clotilde's home for fresh *pan de horno*, then spreading chokecherry jelly on it.

We ate *chicos*, *calabacitas* (squash with corn), beans, and for dessert: *capirotada* or *arroz con leche*. At Christmas, my grandmother and great-aunt made *tamales*—though like many families now, we often buy them. I went fishing for *trucha* (trout) with my uncle and gathered piñon nuts on blankets spread beneath the trees.

My dream for America is simple: I want our history, culture, and arts to be more inclusive. At Regis University—now a Hispanic-Serving Institution—I teach two courses on diversity and cultural traditions. One focuses on New Mexico's *santo* tradition, the other on Chicano art. Students often say, "I never learned about this history" or "I've never heard that story." These stories have been overlooked or erased—but they are part of America's story.

We need broader narratives—ones that reflect cultural identity, regional stories, and historical truths. I wish more people knew about us—not just our struggles, but our celebrations, our contributions, our richness.

My relatives are all Mexican American—*Manitos* from New Mexico. Even if some of the younger ones don't speak fluent Spanish, it is always there in the background. Our traditions—food, religion, language, music, and family—are the threads of who we are.

Once, a curator at RedLine Contemporary Art Center in Denver asked about my artwork. I used the word *Chicano* to describe it, and she asked, "Isn't that word archaic?" I thought to myself: *You're an art historian from San Francisco, and you're not aware of the deep roots of Chicano art in the Bay Area?* But I stayed verbally quiet—she was curating the show. My Chicano voice was in my artwork, and she included it in the exhibition.

That moment stuck with me. People think *Chicano* is outdated. But to me, it's alive—especially in the arts. It still means something. It still defines us. For me, it is a more inclusive word for my identity.

Yolanda Ortega, MPA

Yolanda Ortega is an accomplished educator, leader, and community advocate. Ortega spent more than thirty-five years as an administrator in higher education, retiring from Metropolitan State University of Denver as the Vice President of Student Affairs, and retains the honor of Emerita Vice President of Student Affairs.

Over her thirty-five years with the university, Ortega took on several leadership positions, rising to Vice President of Student Affairs. In this role, she supported fiscal strategies to keep higher education attainable; collaborated with faculty and staff to develop high-quality, inclusive programs and research opportunities; and spearheaded partnerships with businesses and industry to expand work-based learning for students.

An active member of the community, Ortega has served with several groups, including Clínica Tepeyac, the Art Students League of Denver, and the MSU Denver President's Community Cabinet. She currently serves on the boards of Firefly Autism and the Denver Civic Arts Foundation and has been an actor, director, and musician with Su Teatro Cultural and Performing Arts Center in Denver. She's also a cohost on the weekly KUVO Jazz radio show *Canción Mexicana*. She previously served as the governor's appointee to the Auraria

Higher Education Center Board of Directors, Escuela Tlatelolco, the Denver Mayor's Commission on Cultural Affairs, and the Denver Latino Commission.

Ortega graduated from Jonesboro State University with a bachelor's degree in history and German, spending a year studying at the Universidad de Madrid in Spain. She holds a master's degree in public administration from CU Denver.

Latina and Chicana—I Am Both

I call myself *Latina* and *Chicana*. However, being Latina in America has been very challenging for me. I'll tell you why. I did not grow up in the United States. I grew up for most of my young life in Panama because my dad was stationed there. My mother—she was Mexicana—did not speak English very well. When my dad was at work, we spoke to each other in Spanish. Spanish was essentially my first language, because I was with her. I lost a lot of it when I started going to school and because my father—he's Mexican American—forced us to speak English because he wanted us to speak English.

My dad was in the military. He joined the military when I was first born. My dad was stationed to Panama twice. When we moved to the United States, we lived in Washington State, Montana, Texas, Arkansas, Delaware. I was always the new kid. Always the only Brown kid in the school.

Living as a Latina in the United States was very strange for me for a couple of reasons. One is because many times I was the only Brown person in school. I always felt intimidated by that, wondering what everybody else thought of me, and kind of demeaning myself in a way, which was not good.

Part of that was because my mother was uncomfortable in the United States when she moved here, because she couldn't speak the language. While we were in Kansas, my mother, who was a newlywed, hated it. It was very hard for her. People would laugh at her because of her Spanish and English. She couldn't speak English.

It was very intimidating for her. I could see her cower with other people, not wanting to talk, because her English was not good. That also made me feel different, having a mother who could not speak English.

So, I would ask myself, how do I protect my mother? But also, in a very conflicting way, why was I ashamed of that?

When we moved to Montana, I remember knowing that there were Indigenous groups that lived in the area. One day my mom and dad took us shopping for jackets so that we could be warmer. I remember they picked a jacket that the Indigenous groups wore, kind of a furry thing. I did not want it because I did not want to be regarded as one of those Indigenous groups. I was like, "No, no, let's get another coat." And that's what I got.

Can you imagine? I wanted to be seen as everybody else; I didn't want to be seen as different. Now, thinking back at that, I think, *Oh, my gosh. Here I was being a racist. Here I was discriminating because I didn't want that jacket.* I remember that because the Indigenous groups would all wear those jackets, and I did not want to be seen as one of them.

That's how it got to be that for most of my middle school and high school, I was the only Brown face in the school. When I went to the university in Delaware, I was the only Brown person at this school. It was a very prestigious school. I don't know how I got in, but I did get scholarships. My dad helped me with that. I was the only Brown person there. All the others were family members of the DuPonts and the rich oil people and the industry people. I just remember feeling so out of it. I felt that I just wasn't good enough.

A really interesting and funny thing that happened was that the football players took me in. They protected me, and they brought me around with them. It was interesting because a lot of the other women who were the White women from the DuPonts and all of that, they envied me. I started becoming the envy of this group that I felt so demeaned by.

Years later and moving forward, I moved to Denver from Washington, DC, where I taught. I moved here not knowing anyone, not having a job. I just moved here. There was no reason at all. I just wanted to get out of DC. I didn't have a job for about a month, and then I found one at Metro State College. And that's when I started to experience what it was like being a Latina in a world that had conflicts with Latinas, or with Hispanos, or with Chicanos. My life kind of evolved from being a person who never knew what it was like to be Chicana, didn't know about the

Movement, was raised basically in a White world, to being someone who learned about the Chicano Movement, started to know people in the Chicano Movement, and started considering myself Chicana.

It was both very interesting and very stressful for me as well, because then I started to see how people really looked at me, instead of imagining how they looked at me. I started working at the university. I pushed myself out there as someone who was a Latina, but more as an educator and as an administrator. That's what I pushed. You may see me as Brown, but I would make you see me as an administrator, a person who was an educator. I think that's why I was given so many promotions, and eventually given the promotion to vice president, because I wanted them to see me as more than just a Brown person. I wanted them to see what I was good at, what I, as a Latina, could do.

Most Important Is to Serve Your Community

The fact that I knew the Latino communities was important to the university. My being in Su Teatro, and being part of so many organizations, was important to them. That was part of the reason, I think, that got me promoted to vice president.

I think being Latina in the United States presented a lot of conflicting experiences to me, but it also allowed me to flourish in my own community and to become part of a movement. I was able to flourish.

I would like America to know that service, serving others, is critical. Because I served in the community, I helped make many things flourish. Access to health, the arts, and education are my priorities. If America knew that's what I did, and that's what happened as a consequence of my service to my community, then maybe America would see service as a critical experience, as a critical part of life in America.

I want America to know that immigrants are a critical part of our community. My mother was an immigrant. A lot of my family were immigrants, and they have helped this country flourish. I want America to know that immigrants, and immigration, were part of my history, but also that it is an essential part of America's history and where we are now.

My dream for America would be that we appreciate the collective, that we bring democracy back to our way of living. That we encourage diversity.

That we encourage our children to grow up as they are. Children are very diverse. Children know how to play with each other if we allow them to do that. They don't have the ability to say, "Oh, you're Black, or you're Brown, and I need to stay away from you." They don't do that. We grown-ups have made them do that. I would like us to be like the children in our community, accepting all groups, and that we find ways to appreciate the work that many of us do.

Being in higher ed, I've seen so many students who have started at the university. Many of them were born here of parents who were not documented. It was very difficult for them to continue in the university. But we were able to provide resources for them. But again, now it is sad. Because in many ways, these students are having to Zoom in to classes because they don't want to leave their home. They're afraid to be on the road to the university. I would like to see that changed, where we are totally accepting of all of us and totally accepting of our community.

I have so many memories of my childhood. First of all, I have memories of being in Panama, living in Panama, going to school, having to wait by the canal locks as the ships go through, and we were singing on the bus, "Oh, the big ship goes through the Panama Canal," things like that. I have memories of Chinese markets along the sides of the roads, which were actually just open markets where they'd have fresh fruits and vegetables.

I used to own a monkey named Jackie. He was my best friend. Once my dad went to Colombia, and Jackie's mother was shot. My dad got the monkey, and he sent it to us in Panama. When I first opened the cage and saw Jackie, I knew he was mine. Every time I came home from school, he knew that it was me, and he would cry out, "Woo, woo!" He was a howler monkey, so he would be yelling. I remember my little Jackie.

I remember when we would come back to the United States and stay with my aunt in Nebraska. It was always in the summer, and it was so hot, and the women would be making tortillas in the kitchen. I hated it because I didn't like the heat, and it was humid. So, I would go out on the porch with the men who were drinking beer and talking. I would just sit there and listen to them, and my aunts would get back into the kitchen and start making tortillas, and I would never want to do that, and I would just say no. My uncles would say, "Leave her alone, leave her alone. She's just sitting here." So, I never learned how to make tortillas because of that.

Another memory was going to school and my lunches with little tacos my mother would make. I told her to stop doing that. So, she would make peanut butter and jelly sandwiches for lunch. She would cut them in half, and some of my friends wanted my sandwich, so I would trade them for their ham and cheese sandwiches or whatever.

Another of my memories are of my five sisters. We were far enough apart that I had to babysit them, and I hated that. I just remember in Panama I had to sit with my little sister, who never liked wearing clothes. She hated wearing clothes. All of a sudden, my younger sister started going out the door, and we were like, "What's going on?" I looked out the door, and there she was running down the street with no clothes on. We had to run after her, and I was so embarrassed that I had to run after my naked sister.

I remember my mom cooking her rice and her *fideo*. I remember every Saturday morning the smell of bread baking. She loved making bread real early in the morning.

I remember the feeling of missing my dad because he went on temporary duty for a month at a time, sometimes two months at a time, and I missed him a lot. So, I grew up missing my dad, never really having a whole lot of time with him, more with my mother. And that was very strange for me, because that was pretty much my whole childhood.

My dad and I were not in conflict, but we didn't know each other as much, I think, as I wanted him to know me. I think that's why when I became a Chicana, he just didn't like that. We couldn't talk about it because we really didn't have those experiences of talking a lot. My mother and I could sit outside and just chat about everything, and she would know exactly what was going on with me and everything, but I couldn't do that with my father. And that's a memory that haunts me to this day, you know, that I was never as close to my dad as I wished I could have been. I spent most of my young life missing him.

For a time, my dad worked for the School of Latin America in Panama, and a lot of his students were from different parts of Latin America, Chile, Argentina, and Brazil, He would bring them to the house, and we would have parties. I remember hearing Chilean music, hearing the music of Brazil, and I grew up with that as a young person.

One night, I went to spend the night with a girlfriend, and we were down the street, and all of a sudden, I heard all this noise and music, and I'm saying, "Oh, my gosh, who's making all that noise?" Her mother said, "Well, that's your family. You guys have these parties every week." I thought, *Oh, that's my house. Oh, wow, we are loud.*

That time was an important experience because that is when I got to know Latin Americans. I appreciated that when I came here and experienced so many different Latinos. A lot of people would say, "Well, they're not us." But to me, they were us because I grew up with them.

Another very important memory that I think changed my life is when I lived in Spain. I went to school my junior year abroad, and I didn't get much money from home because my parents never really had much money. I was there on scholarship. So I saved my little *pesetas*, you know, just for Christmas. Two friends of mine and I decided that we didn't have a whole lot of money. I think for the whole Christmas vacation between the three of us, we maybe had $200 or $300. But we decided to hitchhike throughout Europe. We hitchhiked. We got on a train, not buying a ticket. We just got on one, and people there on the train, they had baskets of food. They fed us. We crossed the Pyrenees and the Alps. Truck drivers would stop and pick us up, and they would offer us their wine or bread or whatever.

We hitchhiked a boat to Greece. We went all over Europe just hitchhiking. That was an incredible experience for me because it was exciting. It also was very, very, very difficult because there were days when we had no food. We didn't know where to go. We had no place to live. We had to kind of live in the park. So I was essentially homeless in many ways. But it taught us resilience. It taught me not only the experience of being resilient, but also the experience of knowing that I can overcome obstacles if I really put my mind to it and look to other people to help me do that. So that one experience, that one memory of going to all these places, truly shaped me for the rest of my life.

As for what I call myself now, I have settled on *Latina* because I serve a community that is a mixture of people, and it allows me to be accepted because the identity of being Latina is widely accepted in my community. I also call myself *Chicana*, which is part of my history in the Chicana Movement and because I was very active in the Chicana Movement.

I call myself *Chicana* because I am someone who was born here, but of an immigrant mother. I recognize her experiences and her past, and it is part of who I am. *Chicana* is political for me, but it's also part of my roots, part of what feeds me. It's more than just how I want other people to see me. It's how I see myself. Someone who is part of a movement to promote myself as a Brown person, as someone who is bilingual, as someone who has experienced an immigrant experience. That's why I call myself *Chicana*.

Dr. Lorenzo Trujillo, EdD, JD

Dr. Lorenzo Trujillo is a highly respected figure in the world of Southwestern music and culture, known for his lifelong dedication to preserving and promoting the rich traditions of folk music, dance, and arts. As the director of the Southwest Musicians and the artistic director of the MSU Denver Mariachi program, Trujillo has shaped the cultural landscape of the region for more than six decades.

A folk violinist, guitarist, vocalist, and accomplished ethnic dancer, Trujillo's contributions to the arts have earned him recognition on both national and international stages. In 1996, he was honored with the Governor's Award for Excellence in the Arts, a testament to his exceptional talent and tireless work in cultural preservation. His career has spanned a variety of roles, from arts administrator to folklorist and culture bearer, and he has had a profound impact on the traditional music and dance of southern Colorado and New Mexico.

Trujillo's achievements include working with the National Endowment for the Arts as a performing artist in 1976 and receiving the Hilos Culturales Distinguished Traditional Folk Artist Premio in 2004 for his lifetime of service to Hispanic traditions. His extensive body of work includes thousands of concerts, lecture demonstrations, and publications that document and celebrate the cultural heritage of the Southwest United States.

In recognition of his contributions to the arts, Trujillo has received several prestigious awards, including induction into the Colorado Chicano Music Hall of Fame in 2009 and the Tesoro Cultural Center Tesoro de Oro Award in 2011. His work continues to inspire new generations of artists and musicians, and his dedication to cultural heritage remains a cornerstone of his legacy.

Trujillo received his doctorate in education from the University of San Francisco in 1979 and his juris doctorate from the University of Colorado Law School in 1993. Trujillo was the Assistant Dean of Students and Professional Programs at the University of Colorado Law School from 2004 to 2010.

The Mosaic of America: A Reflection on Identity, Culture, and Hope

As we celebrate America's 250th and Colorado's 150th, I reflect on what it means to be American—not just in name or nationality, but in spirit, in contribution, and in legacy. For me, being American means being part of a living, evolving mosaic. A tapestry woven from many peoples, many histories, many cultures.

Some arrived by ship, others by foot. My people were already here before America bore its name. We have Native roots, we have Spanish roots, and we are part of the living story of this land. To reduce America to Plymouth Rock and a narrow colonial narrative is to miss the richness of what truly makes us whole. You can't bake a cake with flour alone—you need eggs, sugar, flavor. That's what we bring. We are the spice, the color, the melody. We are the mariachi that makes your soul dance. That's America.

Our culture—Latinos, Chicanos, Mexicanos, Indos—we make America better. We built the country and continue to build it, from the fields and kitchens to the classrooms and concert halls. We are laborers and leaders, creators and thinkers. We are asked to be twice as good to earn half the recognition, and yet, we rise—with excellence. I play classical music not to prove I can, but to remind others that genius and discipline live in all of us. We belong in every realm, not by permission but by birthright.

And yet, we are often seen as "other" in the country we helped build. There are those who try to box us in, assign labels that limit us: Chicano,

Hispano, Spanish, Indo. But I reject those boxes. I am all of them—and more. If you must name me, call me part of the *Raza Cósmica*, the cosmic race. I am past and present, reaching toward the future. I am not just one thing—I am a convergence of many. A brown man, a red man, a white man. I am Bach and I am rancheras. I am tortillas on the *comal* and the echo of Beethoven in the strings of my violin.

What I wish America knew is that our traditions are not relics—they are vessels of meaning, power, and memory. They are how we pass wisdom through generations. Through music, dance, food, and storytelling, we make the past live again. When I play a varsouviana or pass on the sound of my ancestors' violins, I am not preserving history—I am animating it, breathing life into the timeless. Our culture transcends prejudice because art goes where words cannot. It moves the heart.

My dream for America is that we rise, like a phoenix from the ashes, out of the darkness of division and fear into the light of understanding and unity. That we recognize nationalism and colonialism as outdated ghosts. That we embrace the full tapestry of who we are—not just the threads we prefer. There is no "pure" American, only Americans. Take a DNA test, and you will find you are many peoples. We all are.

As a culture bearer, I know my time is short in the arc of history. But my calling is clear: to share, to teach, to pass on. The violins I play today will sing in the hands of others tomorrow. We are caretakers, stewards of light. Each of us has a gift to offer. Mine is music, tradition, and love for the generations to come.

In this 250th year of America, and 150th of Colorado, I invite you to look deeper—not just at who we are, but at who we could become. Let us be a country that sees with many eyes, listens with many ears, and sings with many voices.

CHAPTER 6

GREAT READS

Books to Better Understand Hispanic Culture

There are many, many books addressing the lives of Hispanics living in the United States and navigating a life between two worlds. They cover a spectrum of genres including nonfiction, fiction, poetry, graphic novels, politics, biographies, education, plays, and more. The scope is so large and so significant it is literally an impossible task to compile a list of recommended readings. Any Google search of books about Hispanic culture in the United States will immediately produce a towering list of readings.

However, just as a journey of one thousand miles begins with a single step, a curious reader has to start with a first book. The following list is a recommended set of books whose subject matter reflects the themes of this book. Each book gives a deep and challenging insight reflecting the delicate path of being Hispanic in a dominantly Anglo country and constantly searching for the balance as both Hispanic and American.

The books cover the range of Hispanic experience in America, from its rural roots to its urban experiences. The books tell the stories from the traditional lives of the elder population to the hyper-modern concerns of its youthful populations. The books are also a mix of what are considered the classics of Latino literature as well as recent books addressing Latino issues.

An internet search for the book titles will present the book's publisher sites and promotional materials for a more detailed description of the book's contents. The books are available from the usual sites: publishers, libraries, and the internet, of course.

Barrio Boy—Ernesto Galarza

Autobiography of a young boy's youth in Mexico and his family's move to the United States. A true account of Galarza's acculturation into American life. Galarza grew up to be an important Chicano labor organizer, scholar, and activist.

Bless Me, Ultima—Rudolfo Anaya

Bless Me, Ultima is a coming-of-age novel by Rudolfo Anaya centering on Antonio Márez y Luna and his mentorship under his curandera and protector, Ultima. It has become the most widely read and critically acclaimed novel in the New Mexican literature canon since its first publication in 1972. A wonderful place to begin your understanding of Hispanic spiritualism.

Borderlands/La Frontera: The New Mestiza—Gloria Anzaldúa

This memoir and political work focuses specifically on Anzaldúa's own experiences growing up along the Texas-US Southwest/Mexican border. It presents her views on the issues of gender, identity, race, and colonialism.

Brown: The Last Discovery of America—Richard Rodriguez

The title of the book presents its central argument that America has Brown people as part of its core identity. In this powerful memoir, Richard Rodriguez describes Hispanic life in America and what that means for America going forward.

Citizens but Not Americans—Nilda Flores-Gonzales

Flores-Gonzales explores notions of national belonging, citizenship, and cultural identity.

This book is the result of her research and interviews with Latinos about their views being Hispanic in America.

Drink Cultura: Chicanismo—José Burciaga

A collection of essays about Chicanismo: the life and culture of Chicanos in the United States.

Finding Latinx—Paola Ramos

Journalist and activist Paola Ramos traveled the country conducting research on the meaning of *Latinx* in today's America. Through extensive interviews, as well as her own personal story, she reveals the challenges of being both Latino/a/x and American.

Hilos Culturales: Cultural Threads of the San Luis Valley—History Colorado

Founded in 2000, Hilos Culturales presents the traditional arts of the Indio-Hispano communities of southern Colorado and northern New Mexico. This book profiles forty honorees of the Premio Hilos Culturales Award—the musicians, dancers, and other living treasures who embody and preserve the continued vitality of the folklore of the Upper Rio Grande Valley.

How Did You Get to Be Mexican? A White/Brown Man's Search for Identity—Kevin Johnson

This book directly addresses the question "Who is a Latino?" The son of a Mexican American mother and an Anglo father, Kevin Johnson has lived in the psychological borderlands between racial identities. In his book, he examines issues of diversity, assimilation, race relations, and affirmative action in contemporary America.

In the Country of Empty Crosses—Arturo Madrid

Arturo Madrid's homeland is in the Rocky Mountains of northern New Mexico. This memoir, complemented with amazing images by acclaimed photographer Miguel Gandert, describes the truths of Madrid's life in northern New Mexico. A beautiful book with a poetic title.

Mexicans in the Making of America—Neil Foley

According to census projections, by 2050 nearly one in three US residents will be Latino, and the overwhelming majority of these will be of Mexican descent. This book examines what this demographic shift means for America and its politics, culture, and identity.

Once I Was You: A Memoir—Maria Hinojosa

Hinojosa, the Emmy Award-winning journalist, tells the story of immigration in American life. Her memoir is a description of her life and what it means to be an immigrant, a survivor, a feminist, and a citizen in America. This book is her call for America to recognize and understand its immigrant crisis.

Our Migrant Souls: A Meditation on Race and the Meaning and Myths of "Latino"—Héctor Tobar

In *Our Migrant Souls*, the Pulitzer Prize–winning writer Héctor Tobar delivers a personal exploration of what it means to be Latino in the United States. The book explores the challenges of a racially conflicted America in the twenty-first century.

Pocho—José Antonio Villarreal

The first significant Chicano novel. A dramatic presentation of what it means to be an immigrant in America negotiating two lives: traditional Mexican life and a new life in America.

Rain of Gold—Victor Villaseñor

The story of the Villaseñor family, from Mexico to Prohibition-era United States. A love story as well as a family odyssey, this book has been called a Chicano *Roots*.

So Far from God—Ana Castillo

A story of a New Mexican family of women, four exceptional sisters. The title comes from a quote of Porfirio Diaz, the Mexican dictator during the Mexican Civil War. He stated, "Poor Mexico. So far from God, so close to the United States."

The Death of the Brown Americano—Jose Uranga

The Death of the Brown Americano examines the experiences of one Hispanic family living in the territory of New Mexico from 1850 through 1913. *The Death of the Brown Americano* is the second book of the Buenavida trilogy—the first is *The Buenavida Dilemma* and the last is *The Buenavida America*. The trilogy describes the challenges Hispanics have concerning the dilemma of assimilation verses cultural heritage and tradition.

Tomás Rivera: The Complete Works—Tomás Rivera

Rivera is the acknowledged father of the Chicano literary movement. His masterpiece is *Y no se lo tragó la tierra/And the Earth Did Not Devour Him*. In twelve thematically linked stories, Rivera tells the story of the plight of migrant farmworkers as seen through the eyes of a child.

Yo Soy Joaquin/I Am Joaquin—Rodolfo "Corky" Gonzales

A heroic, epic poem tracing the roots of Chicano heritage and politics. The poem covers Aztec mythology, Mexican history, and contemporary Chicano sentiment. Joaquin represents all Chicano people and their struggles. The poem was immensely influential in the Chicano Movement and helped define Chicano political and cultural identity. A must-read to understand the Chicano Movement.

CHAPTER 7

GREAT MOVIES

Movies to Better Understand Hispanic Culture

It has often been said that cinema is the art form of our times. Indeed, movies dominate the cultural landscape, whether they be popular culture superhero stories, documentaries, international films, independent films, and others. The lives of movie stars entertain us through their constant presence on tabloids, television specials, podcasts, and celebrity talk shows. The modern media and movie celebrity landscape is a dominating presence.

The lives and stories of Hispanics in America, however, are a largely ignored story in movies and television. When they are told, the stories are rife with stereotypes that project limited views of the beauty, power, and diversity of Hispanic lives. Also, leading and protagonist roles for Hispanic actors are extremely limited.

Acclaimed actor, writer, and producer John Leguizamo has spoken forcefully and eloquently about the dearth of roles for Hispanic actors and Hollywood's historically inadequate efforts to tell Hispanic stories. Almost singlehandedly he has directly addressed the movie and television industries about these issues and challenged them to expand their hiring and producing practices.

Developing a list of recommended movies, therefore, is a challenge because of the relative lack of movies about the lives of Hispanics in America. In spite of this limited experience, the following movies and television shows give a solid foundation for understanding Hispanic culture. The movies range from depictions of the rural roots of Hispanic culture to the hectic urban experience.

As well as being a cinematic introduction to Hispanic culture, each of these films is a fascinating and entertaining glimpse into the inner lives of Hispanic families and people. They are colorful, engaging, and emotionally rewarding, as only movies can be. These movies prove John Leguizamo's premise that the lives of Hispanic families and people are an endless source of incredible stories and deserve a higher profile. They also display the incredibly wide-ranging talents of Latino actors and filmmakers.

Additional information on the movies is available from various movie and television publicity websites. The shows are available from the usual sources: DVD publishers, various streaming sites, and YouTube. Also, most libraries have extensive DVD collections and are another possible place to find these shows. The Internet Movie Data Base, IMDb, is a fantastic site for further information about the shows, and it also lists places to access the shows.

¡Alambrista!

The deeply moving story of a Mexican youth who illegally immigrates to the United States. A painful but truthful look at what life is like for immigrants. Life at the bottom of America is daunting, challenging, and dangerous.

And Now Miguel (1953 black and white version)

Here is a film that never got a physical release. The film is only available on YouTube. Written and produced for the US Government by Joseph Krumgold, this simple but profound documentary depicts the Chavez family, whose members herd sheep in and around Las Cordovas, New Mexico. This film is a wonderful companion piece to *Bless Me, Ultima,* for it depicts the probable life of the young boy in *Bless Me, Ultima*. This is a very quiet and sweet story with a depiction of a family life long eclipsed by the coming of modern life. Worth the search. I felt I was watching a part of my own childhood.

The Ballad of Gregorio Cortez

The true story of the most famous manhunt in Texas history. The subject of one of the most well-known *corridos* in *Tejano* music.

In 2022, the film was selected for preservation in the United States National Film Registry by the Library of Congress as being "culturally, historically, or aesthetically significant."

Bless Me, Ultima

Based on acclaimed author Rudolfo Anaya's novel, *Bless Me, Ultima* is semi-autobiographical, drawing on the author's own experiences and New Mexican folktales. The book holds the position as the first and most important book about Chicano culture in rural America.

The book is also listed in the chapter Great Reads: Books to Better Understand Hispanic Culture. As is often the case with movie adaptations from novels, there is internet conversation as to whether the book or the movie was better. Read the book and watch the movie and decide for yourself.

Cesar Chavez: History Is Made One Step at a Time

Chronicling the birth of a modern American movement, *Cesar Chavez* tells the story of the famed civil rights leader and labor organizer. Chavez inspired millions of Americans from all walks of life to fight for social justice. His journey is a remarkable testament to the power of one individual's ability to change the world.

Chulas Fronteras

Chulas Fronteras is a documentary film by Les Blank about the *Norteño* or *Conjunto* music played on both sides of the Texas-Mexican border. *Chulas Fronteras* translates into "Beautiful Borderlands." Fantastic music!

It is an insightful look at the Chicano experience as mirrored in the lives and music of the most acclaimed Norteño musicians. It features legendary accordion player Flaco Jiménez.

In 1993, the film was selected for preservation in the United States National Film Registry by the Library of Congress as being "culturally, historically, or aesthetically significant."

Coco

A wonderful movie for the whole family. A must-see. It tells the heartwarming story of Miguel as he travels through the Land of the Dead to discover truths of his family history.

El Norte

Reviewers have described the film as surreal, lyrically beautiful, and frightening. *El Norte* is the story of two teenage Guatemalan refugees, a brother and sister, who dream of going to El Norte, the land to the north—America. The movie tells of their doomed efforts to have part of the American dream.

El Norte received an Academy Award nomination for Best Original Screenplay in 1985. In 1995, the film was selected for preservation in the United States National Film Registry by the Library of Congress as being "culturally, historically, or aesthetically significant."

Encanto

An animated film in the style of *Coco,* telling another tale of a search for family history and meaning, this is a wonderfully entertaining movie for the whole family. It has an enormously catchy musical score, and it won the Oscar for Best Animated Feature Film.

John Leguizamo's Latin History for Morons

Actor and producer John Leguizamo examines the history of Hispanic culture throughout American history in *Latin History for Morons.* In this one-man Broadway show, John Leguizamo traces three thousand years of Latin history in an effort to help his bullied son with a school project.

Dramatists Play Service describes the play as follows: "When John takes a peek at his son's history textbooks, he is shocked to find . . . well nothing, at least when it comes to the impact of Latin culture over thousands of years. Excited to share his heritage with his son, John dives deep, exploring everything from the Mayans to modern-day heroes. This zippy, irreverent and laugh-out-loud investigation of the past will make you take a second look at the present."

This movie is a presentation of John Leguizamo's hit Broadway play.

La Bamba

La Bamba is the biography of the first Chicano rock star. Los Angeles teenager Ritchie Valens becomes an overnight rock 'n' roll success in 1958, thanks to a love ballad called "Donna" that he wrote for his girlfriend, whose parents didn't want her to date a Latino boy. The movie features a fantastic song list, and Valens is best remembered for his classic hit "La Bamba." The movie also features music by the great Chicano band Los Lobos.

In 2017, the film was selected for preservation in the United States National Film Registry by the Library of Congress as being "culturally, historically, or aesthetically significant."

Mi Familia

Mi Familia, by the director of *El Norte*, is the three-generation story about the Sanchez family from the 1920s to the 1980s. The movie covers the familiar territory of a Mexican family that comes to America and its struggle to make a successful life.

In 2024, the film was selected for preservation in the United States National Film Registry by the Library of Congress as being "culturally, historically, or aesthetically significant."

The Milagro Beanfield War

The movie is a film adaptation of John Nichols's novel *The Milagro Beanfield War*. For a time, the book was among the most widely read novels about Latinos.

Filmed in Truchas, New Mexico, the high country of northern New Mexico, the film accurately captures the lives of people whose lives are intricately tied to the land and water.

Our Quinceañera

An uplifting, award-winning documentary. A high school principal in a Texas town hosts a yearly quinceañera for underprivileged students. The entire border town gets together to teach these girls that with the power of community, any dream can come true. A film for the whole family.

This deeply heartwarming film might be tricky to find, but it is worth the effort.

Real Women Have Curves

The 2002 award-winning film adaptation of the play *Real Women Have Curves* was an important moment in cinema for Latina representation since roles for Latinas are so limited in media. Its portrayal of Latinas was a cinematic breakthrough.

It gained fame after winning the Audience Award for best dramatic film and the Special Jury Prize for acting in the 2002 Sundance Film Festival.

In 2019, the film was selected for preservation in the United States National Film Registry by the Library of Congress as being "culturally, historically, or aesthetically significant." It is the first Latina-directed film to be inducted into the Registry.

The Salt of the Earth

This is a film history classic. The 1954 semi-documentary tells the true events of a strike of Chicano workers in zinc mines in New Mexico. One of the first films to feature Chicano actors playing Chicanos, the movie was a rallying point for the 1960s Chicano movement. The movie was also one of the first major American films to present minority workers and their causes with dignity and understanding. The film was blacklisted in the McCarthy era.

In 1992, the film was selected for preservation in the United States National Film Registry by the Library of Congress as being "culturally, historically, or aesthetically significant."

Selena

The films tells the story of Selena's rise to musical fame before she was tragically murdered at the age of twenty-three by the president of her fan club. While the film ends on a tragic note, its basic message is uplifting, and it features a beautiful soundtrack of Selena's music.

In 2021, the film was selected for preservation in the United States National Film Registry by the Library of Congress as being "culturally, historically, or aesthetically significant."

Stand and Deliver

The film is based on the real-life story of a group of Latino students at an East Los Angeles high school who, under the tough love guidance of their math teacher, Jaime Escalante, take an Advanced Placement calculus exam. To the amazement of everyone except their dedicated teacher they pass the test only to be accused of cheating by school authorities.

In 2011, the film was selected for preservation in the United States National Film Registry by the Library of Congress as being "culturally, historically, or aesthetically significant."

This movie is as uplifting as it gets!

Tortilla Soup

This film is similar to *Real Women Have Curves* in that it provided many powerful and significant roles for Latinas. Labeled as a comedy-drama, it tells the story of the tumultuous but loving relationships inside generational Hispanic families. Is there any story more filled with comic drama than one telling the story of an old-fashioned father and his modern daughters?

Zoot Suit

A zoot suit is a men's suit with high-waisted, wide-legged, tight-cuffed, pegged trousers, and a long coat with wide lapels and wide padded shoulders. It is most notable for its use as a cultural symbol among the Hepcat and Pachuco subcultures.

The movie is based on the play *Zoot Suit*, the 1978 Luis Valdez musical staged at the Mark Taper Forum. The play and the movie were based on the real story of the Sleepy Lagoon case, the Zoot Suit riots, and the anti-Chicano hysteria of the 1940s.

The movie is a powerful depiction of the struggles of Chicano youth to find their identity in America. Living between two cultures and generations, their story is one of youthful rebellion and tragic racial discrimination.

In 2019, the film was selected for preservation in the United States National Film Registry by the Library of Congress as being "culturally, historically, or aesthetically significant."

BIBLIOGRAPHY

Chapter 6 of this book lists books not included in this bibliography. It recommends more recent books of a wide-ranging nature on the topics of Hispanic culture and life in modern America. These books, along with the movies recommended in chapter 7, are wonderful places to start with for a better understanding of Hispano life in America.

This bibliography is for the reader seeking more detailed reference material on many of the subjects discussed in the book. Many of the references are considered classics of the genre: books on the history, culture, and traditional arts of the Hispanic Southwest and Mexico. I myself have used these reference books for my own research.

In our modern days, Google and Wikipedia have become first stops for information and a wealth of excellent material is available at these two internet resources. Also, the advent of artificial intelligence, A.I., is beginning to be a common presence in research. Frequently, Google searches for historical research begin with an A.I. synopsis of the subject searched. However, even with the increasing dominance of the internet for research, nothing beats a great book for immersive study.

Of course, there are many more books on these subjects than listed here, but these are recommended as good starting places for the general reader. This bibliography contains commentary for each entry on its merits as a reference. They are to help the reader in making decisions on which reference to utilize for further and more in-depth research. They are also meant as guides for the reader interested in selecting references for more casual reading.

Acordándose del Pasado, Extenderse al Futuro. Remembering the Past, Reaching for the Future. El Escritorio, 1995. A varied and interesting small collection of folklore. The booklet presents a folklore research model and publication example that is perfect for schools and communities.

Alvarez, Luis. *The Power of the Zoot: Youth Culture and Resistance during World War II.* University of California Press, 2009. Considered the best and most comprehensive book on zoot suit culture, society, and race conflict in World War II.

Aranda, Charles. *Dichos: Proverbs and Sayings from the Spanish.* Sunstone Press, 2014. A small collection of folk proverbs. Contains all the common and well-known dichos. A good beginner's collection.

Awalt, Barb, and Paul Rhetts. *Charlie Carrillo: Tradition and Soul.* LPD Press, 1995. Without a doubt, one of the best and most beautiful books on the *santero* tradition, featuring the work of Charlie Carrillo, arguably the best of the modern santeros. The book not only discusses in detail the history and identifying characteristics of the santos in devotional art but also presents explanations of how the santos are part of Hispanic life and religious faith. The photos of the santos are beautiful!

Boss, Gayle, and Cheryl Hellner. *Santo Making in New Mexico: Way of Sorrow, Way of Light.* Potter's House Press, Inc., 1991. A beautiful presentation of the art, craft, and spirituality of santeros.

Boyd, E., *New Mexico Santos: Religious Images in the Spanish New World.* Museum of New Mexico Press, 1995. A beautiful, small book with illustrations and short descriptions of forty-one santos. An excellent reference book. Also, a really cool cover!

______. *Popular Arts of Spanish New Mexico.* Museum of New Mexico Press, 1974. Extensive presentation of Hispanic traditional arts and crafts. Scholarly discussion of origins, history, and artistic practice. Excellent color plates of traditional arts. The first large comprehensive ethnographic study of the material folk culture of New Mexico Hispanic culture.

Bright, Brenda Jo, and Liza Bakewell, eds. *Looking High and Low: Art and Cultural Identity.* University of Arizona Press, 1995. An extremely interesting collection of essays examining the expressions of ethnic art, especially in Hispanic and Native American communities. Read it to be challenged with new, intellectually stimulating ideas about the relationships between high art, popular arts, and ethnic culture. Bright's PhD dissertation was on lowriders!

Cabello-Argandoña, Roberto. *Cinco de Mayo: A Symbol of Mexican National Resistance.* Floricanto Press, 1993. A small, easy-reading presentation of the historical events of Cinco de Mayo. The book also contains Mexican poetry about Cinco de Mayo.

Campa, Arthur L. *Hispanic Culture in the Southwest.* University of Oklahoma Press, 1979. A classic scholarly book. A must for every collection on the Southwest. Especially thorough presentation of the historical development of the area. A good book to begin your collection.

Campbell, Richard C. *Two Eagles in the Sun: A Guide to U.S. Hispanic Culture.* Two Eagles Press, 2003. Extensive information about the Hispanic Southwest presented in an engaging and accessible question-and-answer format. Covers culture, history, and politics. A good book for the generalist and casually interested person.

Caso, Alfonso. *The Aztecs: People of the Sun.* University of Oklahoma Press, 1988. An excellent history of the Aztec culture and society. One of the classic texts on Aztec culture. Detailed, colorful illustrations of Aztec gods. Especially good discussion of the Aztec gods and cosmology.

Champe, Flavia Waters. *The Matachines Dance of the Upper Rio Grande: History, Music, and Choreography.* University of Nebraska Press, 1983. An excellent reference book on the *Matachine* dance. Scholarly analysis of history and development. Detailed diagrams of dance steps and formations. Historical documentary photographs.

Chavez, Fray Angélico. *My Penitente Land: Reflections of Spanish New Mexico.* Sunstone Press, 2012. A deep, heartfelt presentation about the spirit of the Hispanic Southwest.

Cobos, Rubén. *Refranés: Southwestern Spanish Proverbs.* Museum of New Mexico Press, 1985. Very complete, collection of more than 1,600 folk proverbs. Very helpfully indexed by subject.

Cockcroft, Eva, John Weber, and James Cockcroft. *Toward a People's Art: The Contemporary Mural Movement.* University of New Mexico Press, 1998. A very informative book written at the height of the mural movement. Written from the perspective of both the scholar and the active mural artist. Covers the complete mural movement in the United States, not just the Chicano mural movement. Interesting section on children's mural art.

Coles, Robert. *The Old Ones of New Mexico.* University of New Mexico Press, 1973. Very highly recommended. Essays and wonderful photography of the Hispanic elderly.

Coulter, Lane, and Maurice Dixon Jr. *New Mexican Tinwork 1840–1940.* University of New Mexico Press, 1990. A magnificent book on a little-explored traditional art. Exhaustive research. Insightful historical analysis. Beautiful photography.

de Baca, Vincent C., ed. *La Gente: Hispano History and Life in Colorado*. Colorado Historical Society, 1998. Excellent collection of essays on the history, culture, and lives of Hispanos in Colorado.

Díaz del Castillo, Bernal. *The History of the Conquest of New Spain*. University of New Mexico Press, 2009. A vivid eyewitness account of the conquest of Mexico by one of Cortés's soldiers writing fifty years after the historic events. Detailed, in-depth, astounding recollection. This is as good as a personal account of history gets. Several translations exist; the more recent, the easier to read.

Dickey, Roland F. *New Mexico Village Arts*. University of New Mexico Press, 1990. Very enjoyable and easy-reading essays on traditional Southwestern Hispanic culture. Good coverage of traditional arts in daily village life.

Duggan, Anne Schley, Jeanette Schlottman, and Abbie Rutledge. *Folk Dances of the United States and Mexico*. The Ronald Press Company, 1948. Presents historical and background information on traditional Mexican dances. Includes music notation and illustrated diagrams of steps for dances. Costume color plates also.

Espinosa, Aurelio. *The Folklore of Spain in the American Southwest: Traditional Spanish Folk Literature in Northern New Mexico and Southern Colorado*. University of Oklahoma Press, 1985. A detailed collection of information on all aspects of Hispanic culture. Another must-have book for your collection.

Flores, Richard R. *Los Pastores: History and Performance in the Mexican Shepherd's Play of South Texas*. Smithsonian Institute Press, 1995. A scholarly examination of the Los Pastores play. The author spent two years performing the play with a South Texas community. Excellent personal observations as well as academic analysis of the meaning of the play in Hispanic culture.

Frank, Larry. *New Kingdom of the Saints: Religious Art of Northern New Mexico 1780–1907*. Red Crane Books, 2004. A coffee table–type book on the santo tradition of the Spanish colonial era. Extraordinarily beautiful photography. Scholarly informative essays on classic santos through the early twentieth century.

Garcia, Nasario. *Chistes: Hispanic Humor of Northern New Mexico and Southern Colorado*. Museum of New Mexico Press, 2004. Classic collection of the short, anecdotal humorous tales of the Hispanic people. Have a lot of fun reading them.

Gates, Zethyl. *Mariano Medina: Colorado Mountain Man*. Loveland Museum and Gallery, 1992. This book is the definitive book on the life of one of the most fascinating characters in the history of the American West.

Glazer, Mark. ed. *A Dictionary of Mexican American Proverbs*. Green Wood Press, 1987. An immense and scholarly collection of folk proverbs.

Gonzales, Rodolfo "Corky." *Message to Aztlan*. Arte Publico Press, 2001. The only collection of writings by this major figure of the Chicano Movement. Includes the renowned epic poem "I Am Joaquín." Any examination of the Chicano movement is incomplete without this volume.

Hoobler, Dorothy and Thomas, *The Mexican American Family Album*. Oxford University Press, 1994. A thorough presentation of the history of Mexican Americans in the United States. Contains many period photographs and personal narratives and does read like a family album. A very interesting way to present history.

Huerta, Jorge. *Chicano Theater: Themes and Forms*. Bilingual Press, 1982. A detailed, scholarly presentation on the history and practice of Chicano theater. Provocative discussion of the cultural importance of Chicano theater.

Kalb, Laurie Beth. *Crafting Devotions: Tradition in Contemporary New Mexico Santos*. University of New Mexico Press, 1994. A beautiful book. Discusses the history, development, tradition, and craft of santos. Special profiles on santeros. Excellent photography.

Kanellos, Nicolás. ed. *Mexican American Theatre: Then and Now*. Arte Publico Press, 1983. A small, academic discussion of Mexican American theater. Good discussion of little-known theater groups.

______. *Mexican American Theater: Legacy and Reality*. Latin American Literary Review Press. 1987. A fascinating collection of "you must read" essays on Mexican American theater. Covers theater as a cultural, historical, and political force. Even includes an essay on the Mexican American circus in the Southwest.

Lankford, Mary D. *Quinceañera, A Latina's Journey to Womanhood*. The Millbrook Press, 1994. A children's picture book about the quinceañera. Many excellent photographs giving the reader a clear idea about the preparation and ceremony of the quinceañera.

Martinez, Patricia, and Herman Martinez, *Hilos Culturales: Cultural Threads of the San Luis Valley*. History Colorado, 2023. A wonderful book presenting the modern musicians who have received the Premio Hilos Culturales Awards for preserving traditional musical arts. Excellent introductory essay by Enrique R. Lamadrid on the San Luis Valley and its musical traditions.

Miller, Robert R. *Mexico: A History*. University of Oklahoma Press, 1989. There are many books about the history of Mexico. This is one of the most thorough and easiest to read. Covers all the ground from the ancient Indigenous cultures to the turmoil of the modern area in historically detailed text. But the writing style is a great improvement over the usual dry and dense academic treatment of history. Enjoyable reading for history buffs and the layperson alike.

Moore, Michael. *Los Remedios: Traditional Herbal Remedies of the Southwest.* Museum of New Mexico Press, 2008. A very thorough presentation of traditional herbal remedies. Describes the uses and preparations for a wide variety of medicinal plants used in the Southwest. Covers both traditional and recently recognized medicinal herbs. One of the few books to address the issue of toxicity in herbal remedies. An excellent resource.

Mora, Jo. *Californios: The Saga of the Hard-Riding Vaqueros, America's First Cowboys.* Dober Hill, Ltd., 1994. An easy-to-read and informative book about the origins of the Vaquero. Wonderful illustrations by the author.

Museum of International Folk Art. *Spanish Textile Tradition of New Mexico and Colorado.* Series in Southwestern Culture. Museum of New Mexico Press, 1979. A deeply informative collection of essays about the history, textiles, and techniques of Hispanic weaving. Many quality photographs of representative textiles.

Myres, Sandra L. *Westering Women and the Frontier Experience, 1800–1915.* University of New Mexico Press, 1982. A unique, in-depth, and scholarly examination of Western history during the frontier days, with an emphasis on women's experiences.

National Textbook Company. Roberto A. Galván, ed. *The Dictionary of Chicano Spanish.* McGraw-Hill, 1995. A dictionary of the Spanish spoken in the Southwest United States. Includes words, slang, and expressions not found in standard references. Also includes a section on *dichos*, folk proverbs.

Newall, Venetia. *An Egg at Easter: A Folklore Study.* Indiana University Press, 1989. A fascinating book about the egg and the symbolic and ritualistic role it has played in world cultures. Discusses in great detail world history, myth and legends, cultural rites, and traditional practices of decorating eggs for cultural practices throughout the world. Beautiful color plates also included.

Novas, Himilce. *Everything You Need to Know About Latino History.* Plume, 2008. Really, it is everything you need to know about Latino history. Written in a fun question-and-answer format.

Oglesby, Richard E. *Manuel Lisa and the Opening of the Missouri Fur Trade.* University of Oklahoma Press, 1963. The best book on one of the most interesting unsung heroes of the American West.

Paxson, Frederic L. *History of the American Frontier, 1763–1893.* Simon Publications, 1925, most recent reprint 2022. This is an amazing history book.

Extremely detailed in its accounting of the events and people who explored and settled the American frontier. Especially strong in its presentation of how the states of the frontier became admitted to the Union. Winner of the Pulitzer Prize in 1925 and regularly reprinted since, it is somewhat dated in some of its language descriptions, but it is a strong addition to a history collection.

Pearlman, Steven R. *Mariachi Music in Los Angeles*. PhD dissertation, University of California, Los Angeles, 1988. A doctoral dissertation on mariachi music in Los Angeles. Emphasis on the origins and development of mariachi music, musical analysis of mariachi music, and the culture and social structure of mariachi groups in the Los Angeles area.

Peña, Manuel. *The Texas-Mexican Conjunto: History of a Working-Class Music*. University of Texas Press, 1985. A fascinating, scholarly, in-depth study of *conjunto* music. Covers the origins and development of the music, as well as its founding and most influential musicians. Also examines the cultural and social interaction of conjunto music and Mexican Texas culture.

Philippus, M. J., and John F. Garcia. *The Two Battles of Cinco de Mayo*. The Education Foundation, 1990. Another small and easy-reading text on the history of Cinco de Mayo.

Rael, Juan B. *Cuentos Españoles de Colorado y Nuevo México*, Arno Press, 1977. The classic and definitive collection of Hispanic folktales. Hundreds of complete tales in original Spanish, with accompanying story synopsis in English.

Rietstap, Johannes Baptista. *V. & H. V. Rolland's Illustrations to the Armorial Général*. Naval and Military Press, 2014. A multivolume reference of family name crests. Thousands of entries, very complete. Illustrations of each crest entry. The best reference for looking up your family crest.

Rivera, José A. *Acequia Culture: Water, Land, and Community in the Southwest*. University of New Mexico Press, 1998. Excellent research book on the history, legal aspects, community traditions, and water and land management issues of the acequia water systems in the river valleys of southern Colorado and northern New Mexico.

Robb, John Donald. *Hispanic Folk Music of New Mexico and the Southwest: A Self-Portrait of a People*. University of New Mexico Press, 2014. Very detailed and scholarly presentation of traditional music forms. Extensive verse and music notation. In-depth essays on origins and development of music and traditions. A true reference book on the subject.

Robe, Stanley L., ed. *Hispanic Folktales from New Mexico: Narratives from the R. D. Jameson Collection*. University of California Press, 1977. A good collection of folktales. Tales in English, mostly in synopsis form. Easy reading.

______. *Hispanic Legends from New Mexico: Narratives from the R. D. Jameson Collection.* University of California Press, 1980. Another good collection of folk legends and lore. More easy reading.

Rodríguez, Antonio. *A History of Mexican Mural Painting.* G.P. Putnam's Sons, 1969. A magnificent, coffee table–type book. A complete work of in-depth scholarship. Extensive analysis and discussion of the history, development, and leading painters of the Mexican mural movement. Hundreds of photographs.

Salinas, Bobbi. *Indo-Hispanic Folk Art Traditions I & II.* Piñata Publications, 1987. Informative and good presentation of Hispanic Day of the Dead and Christmas traditions. Excellent activity guides.

Schwendener, Norma, and Averil Tibbels. *Legends and Dances of Old Mexico.* A.S. Barnes and Company, 1933. An old book you'll only find in your public library. Worth the search, however. Legends about the musical accompaniments to and origins of Mexican dances. Costume illustrations and step diagrams included.

Sedillo, Mela. *Mexican and New Mexican Folkdances.* University of New Mexico Press, 1935. Another small, old, and hard-to-find book, but also worth the search. History of the dances. Costume illustrations. Music notation. Step diagrams. Simple but more than sufficient.

Thompson, Stith. *The Folktale.* University of California Press, 1978. The classic academic book on folktales. Also good for its discussion of folk culture.

Toor, Francis. *A Treasury of Mexican Folkways.* Crown, 1973. A true classic. An immensely detailed presentation of Mexican society, life, and culture. An extraordinarily valuable and complete resource. Photographs, color plates, musical scores.

Townsend, Richard. *The Aztecs.* Thames and Hudson, 2000 (revised). An excellent scholarly study of Aztec history, society, and culture. Comprehensive, well researched, enjoyable reading.

Trotter II, Robert T., and Juan Antonio Chavira. *Curanderismo: Mexican American Folk Healing.* University of Georgia Press, 1997. Good reading for someone interested in a more in-depth, reflective discussion. Emphasis on the examination of the spiritual, psychological, and cultural meaning of folk healing, not just information on the actual practices of curanderismo.

Trujillo, Lorenzo. "Hispanic Tradition, Folkloric Music and Dance." *Ayer Y Hoy* 13. Taos County Historical Society, 1992. Scholarly article on Hispanic dance traditions. Detailed dance descriptions of two traditional dances with musical arrangements.

Trujillo, Lorenzo, and Marie Oralia Trujillo. "La Entriega de Los Novios." *Ayer Y Hoy* 19. Taos County Historical Society, 1995. An easily readable scholarly article on La Entriega.

Trulillo, Marie Oralia Durán, *Autumn Memories, My New Mexican Roots & Traditions.* El Escritorio, 1999. A deeply personal memoir of the author's life in New Mexico. Contains historical and family recollections. Highly recommended.

Tushar, Olibama López. *The People of El Valle, A History of the Spanish Colonials in the San Luis Valley.* El Escritorio, 1997. Wonderful and personal book with an interesting history of publication. Insightful chapters on the historical settling of the Southwest.

Vigil, Angel. *The Corn Woman: Stories and Legends of the Hispanic Southwest.* Libraries Unlimited, 1994. An award-winning collection of folktales from the Aztecs to modern times. Includes discussion of origins and development of oral traditions. Beautiful photographs of Latino art commissioned for the stories.

Vigil, Ernesto. *The Crusade for Justice: Chicano Militancy and the Government's War on Dissent.* University of Wisconsin Press, 1999. An important and highly detailed book on the Crusade for Justice and its work for the betterment of Chicano communities. Recommended reading to learn more about not only the Crusade but the tenor of the times against ethnic liberation movements.

Weigle, Marta, and Peter White. *The Lore of New Mexico.* University of New Mexico Press, 2003. Very detailed scholarly presentation of Hispanic culture. Many interesting photographs. Another good addition to your collection.

West, John O., ed. *Mexican-American Folklore: Legends, Songs, Festivals, Proverbs, Crafts, Tales of Saints, of Revolutionaries, and More.* August House, 2005. Excellent presentation of Hispanic culture. Easy reading, detailed, scholarly. Another good addition to your collection.

Wroth, William, ed. *Hispanic Crafts of the Southwest.* Taylor Museum of the Colorado Springs Fine Arts Center, 1977. A museum exhibition catalog. Extensive and thorough discussion of traditional arts and crafts. Good historical essays. Many illustrations and photographs of both art and artists. Puts the traditional arts in the context of practicing artists.

______. *Weaving and Colcha from the Hispanic Southwest.* Ancient City Press, 1985. A good, hands-on, how-to presentation of two traditional arts. Emphasis is on the practice of the art. Many line art illustrations of traditional patterns.

PERMISSIONS

Illustration and Photography Credits

The graphic symbols displayed throughout this book are ancient symbols from Indigenous pre-Hispanic Mexico and the Spanish Colonial era of New Spain. Artisans used these symbols to adorn their decorative arts in painting, furniture, and metalwork.

Figures:

1 America 250 logo, Chermayeff & Geismar & Haviv (per source), public domain, via Wikimedia Commons.
2 Colorado 150 logo graphic, History Colorado Center, Denver, Colorado.
3 The map of the Class of 1848, the states and territories formed from the Mexican Cession and Gasden Purchase, map by Fulcrum Publishing.
4 Spanish Flag, Wikimedia Commons, public domain.
5 Mexican Flag, Wikimedia commons, public domain.
6 United States 30-Star Flag, Wikimedia Commons, public domain.
7 *American Progress*, John Gast, Wikimedia Commons, public domain, Library of Congress Prints and Photographs division, digital ID ppmsca.09855.
8 *Cortés Meets Moctezuma*, Wikimedia Commons, Bibliothèque Nationale de France, département Bibliothèque-musée de l'opéra, ESTAMPES SCENES FernandCortez, public domain.
9 Spanish Missionary, Wikimedia Commons, California Missions, The Diary and Itinerary of Francisco Garces, a Spanish Pioneer and Missionary Priest, 1775, public domain.
10 Saca Y Pon Dreidel, Angel Vigil photograph.
11 Map of Mexican Land Grants in Colorado, History Colorado Center, SER 2553.60, used by permission.

12 Tierra Amarilla Land Grant in New Mexico and Colorado, Wikimedia Commons, U.S. House, 58th Congress, 2nd Session, H.doc.5/30 (Serial Set 4649), 1903, public domain.

13 Acequia System of El Rancho de las Golondrinas. Archinia, CC BY-SA 3.0 <https://creativecommons.org/licenses/by-sa/3.0>, via Wikimedia Commons.

14 Statue of Father Miguel Hidalgo y Costilla, Wikimedia Commons, Dolores Hidalgo, Mexico, Adam Jones, Creative Commons Attribution Share-Alike 2.0.

15 Mexican agricultural workers topping beets. Stockton, California, 1943, Marjory Collins, Library of Congress, Prints and Photographs Division, public domain.

16 Cesar Chavez, Wikimedia Commons, Joel Levine, Creative Commons Attributes 3.0.

17 United Farm Workers Flag, Manuel ChavezVectorization: Aztecas Califas, Thespoondragon, public domain. Via Wikimedia commons. Reprinted by permission of the United Farm Workers of America. The UFW Eagle is the property of the United Farm Workers and is used with permission. For more information about the United Farm workers, please visit www.ufw.org.

18 Dolores Huerta, Wikimedia Commons, El Malcriado, The Voice of the Farmworker, No. 21, "HUELGA", public domain.

19 West Side Dreams, National Chicano Dance Theater, 1979, photograph used by permission of Daniel Salazar.

20 Zoot Suit Mexican Drape Style, Probation 22, no. 3. 1944: 83, public domain, via Wikimedia Commons.

21 Somos Aztlan graphic used by permission of Emanuel Martinez.

22 Mestizo Face graphic used by permission of Alfredo Cárdenas.

23 Rugolfo "Corky" Gonzales addressing demonstrators at State Capitol, Denver, Colorado, History Colorado Center, 2019.41.1, photograph used by permission of Juan Espinosa.

24 Chicano Youth Liberation Conference Announcement, Published *EL Gallo Newspaper*, January, 1969, public domain.

25 Lalo Delgado mural by Carlos Frésquez and his 2008 University of Denver class members. Permission granted in personal correspondence.

26 Brown Beret women marching, 1970 by Patricia Borjon-Lopez. Wikimedia Commons, public domain.

27 Cesar Chavez flanked by two Brown Berets, Wikimedia Commons, *Los Angeles Times*, Creative Commons Attributes 4.0 International.

28 The Vaquero, James Walker, Wikimedia Commons, public domain.

29 Manuel Lisa, Wikimedia Commons, Unknown, public domain.

30 Mariano Medina, Wikimedia Commons, Unknown, public domain.

31 Olibama Lopez Tushar, used by permission of Charlene Garcia Simms.

32 Teresita Sandoval, Wikimedia Commons, sketched by Alexander Barclay in 1853, photo courtesy of Colorado Historical Society, public domain.

33 The Matanza, photograph by Angel Vigil.

34 Se Habla Español, Joshua Tree National Park, public domain, via Wikimedia Commons, photograph by Robert Zuniga, NPS.

35 Vigil Crest, carved by Santero Pat Vigil, photograph by Angel Vigil.

36 Wedding March graphic used by permission of Carol Kimball.

37 Day of the Dead—La Calavera Catrina, Wikimedia Commons, M.I. King, Creative Commons Attribues-Share Alike 4.0.

38 Ofrenda graphic used by permission of Carol Kimball.

39 The Virgin of Guadalupe and Juan Diego graphic used by permission of Carol Kimball.

40 Farolitos/Luminarias graphic used by permission of Carol Kimball.

41 Poinsettia graphic used by permission of Carol Kimball.

42 El Santuario de Chimayó, photo by William Aranda, CC BY-SA 3.0 creative commons via Wikimedia Commons.

43 Manzanilla graphic used by permission of Carol Kimball.

44 Zabila graphic used by permission of Carol Kimball.

45 Chimayo Weaver at His Loom, Wikimedia Commons, Post Card, Published by Southwestern Arts & Crafts, Santa Fe, New Mexico, Tichnor Bros. Inc, Boston, Mass, Boston Public Library Print Department, The Tichnor Brothers Collection, no known restrictions.

46 Jerga weaving design, Albuquerque Museum, PC1998.25.23, used by permission.

47 Saltillo weaving design, Wikimedia Commons, Cleveland Museum of Art, 1921.558, Creative Commons CC0 1.0 Universal Public Domain Dedication.

48 Rio Grande weaving, used by permission of Denver Art Museum, 1860, Neusteter Textile Collection at the Denver Art Museum: Gift of Charles Winfred Douglas, Accession Number 1934.11.

49 Chimayó vest, photograph by Angel Vigil.

50 Santo carving used by permission of Judy Miranda.

51 Piñata graphic used by permission of Carol Kimball.

52 Papel Picado, Wikimedia Commons, timlewisnm, Creative Commons Attributes- Share Alike 2.0.

53 Ojos de Dios, God's Eye graphic used by permission of Carol Kimball.

54 Cascarones graphic used by permission of Carol Kimball.

55 Doña Sebastina, used by permission of Denver Art Museum, José Inéz Herrera, *Death Cart*, 1890–1910, Accession Number 1948.22A-C.

56 Mexican Mariachi, Wikimedia Commons, Dorotea Kraatz, Creative Commons Attribution-Share Alike 4.0 International.

57 Aztec Dancer, Wikimedia Commons, Alejandro Linares Garcia, Creative Commons Attribution-Share 3.0.

58 *Danza del Venado*, Deer Dancer graphic used by permission of Carol Kimball.

59 *Los Viejitos* Dancers graphic used by permission of Carol Kimball.

60 *El Jarabe Tapatio* Dancers graphic used by permission of Carol Kimball.

61 *Los Matachine* Dancers, Wikimedia Commons, Larry Lamsa, creative Commons Attributes-share Alike 2.0.

62 *Valse de la Escoba*, Waltz of the Broom graphic used by permission of Carol Kimball.

63 *Valse de los Paños*, Waltz of the Scarves graphic used by permission of Carol Kimball.

64 Historical Mural in Delta, Colorado, used by permission of Emanuel Martinez.

65 Low Rider Car Hopping, Wikimedia Commons, Jarek Tuszyúski, creative Commons Attributes-Share Alike 3.

66 Lowrider Bicycle, Wikimedia Commons, Thelmadatter, Creative Commons Attributes-Share Alike 4.0.

Writings:

1,2 Bernal Diaz quotes (pages 38 and 39) reprinted by permission of the University of New Mexico Press.

3 The Dr. Devon Peña water rights quote (page 65-66) reprinted by permission of *La Jicarita* Online Magazine.

4 *La Entriega* verses and translation (page 138) are reprinted with the permission of Olibama Tushar and Charlene Garcia Simms, El Escritorio Publishing, Pueblo, Colorado.

5 Lorenzo Trujillo *Valse de los Paños* quote reprinted by permission of Lorenzo Trujillo.

GLOSSARY OF SPANISH WORDS

A

Abuelita: grandmother
Acequia: traditional Spanish communal water sharing system
Actos: one-act Chicano plays with political or social statements
Adios: goodbye
Adivinanzas: riddles
Adobe: mud and straw brick used in Southwest construction
Agua: water
Aguinaldos: little gifts
Ajenjibre: ginger
Ajo: garlic
Alabados: religious songs, mournful hymns, often associated with members of the fraternity of Penitentes
Álamo asuco: poplar
Albácar: basil
Alfalfa: alfalfa
Alhucema: lavender
Amigo: friend
Amole: yucca root
Ancianos: the old ones, the elderly
Ante pasados: ancestors
Arbolario: a healer who specializes in casting out evil spells
Arriba: up, get up
Arroz: rice

Artes: arts
Atole: a blue corn drink
Atolli: the Aztec word for a cornmeal drink
Aztlán: the mythical homeland of the Aztecs, the American Southwest

B

Baile: a social dance, also the dance and reception of the courtship and wedding ceremony
Bajo sexto: a twelve-string guitar
Barba de maíz: corn silk
Barrio: Chicano neighborhood
Batalla: Battle
Belén: Bethlehem
Biscochitos: anise cookies
Blanco: white
Boda: wedding
Bolero: a musical form with romantic lyric content common to mariachi music, "slow couples dance" music
Brujas: witches. The belief in witches is part of a complex supernatural legend system in Spanish culture.
Bueno: good, well
Bulto: image of a saint carved in wood

C

Cacahuates: peanuts
Calabacitas: summer squash
Calabazas: squash, pumpkins
Caliente: hot
Caló: A Spanish-English urban street dialect particular to Pachuco culture
Cancioneros: Spanish *romance* songs
Canela: cinnamon
Capirotoda: bread pudding
Capulín: wild cherry
Caravelas: Spanish galleons, a large Spanish ship of the fifteenth and sixteenth centuries

Carpa: Mexican tent play
Carreta de la muerte: a hand-carved wooden cart, the death cart of Doña Sebastiana
Cascabeles: sleigh (jingle) bells
Casorio: the actual wedding of the courtship and wedding ceremony
Cebolla: onion
Cempasúchil: Aztec Nahuatl name for marigold, the "flower of the dead," used in celebrations of Día de los Muertos
Chambelán de honor: the young man who escorts the honoree at the quinceañera
Chambelánes: young men who are escorts at the quinceañera
Champurrado: a chocolate-flavored cornmeal drink
Charro: a rural horseman from Jalisco, a traditional Mexican horseman
Chicos: dried corn kernels cooked in beans
Chile colorado: red chile
Chile con carne: chile with meat
Chile rellenos: cheese-stuffed green chile, fried in an egg batter
Chile verde: green chile sauce
Chistes: short anecdotal stories, usually with a comic twist at the end
Cholo/a: street name for Mexican American youth with their own well-defined urban style
Cilantro: coriander
Cocina: kitchen
Comal: a flat cast-iron skillet used for cooking or reheating tortillas
Comida: meal
Commedia dell'arte: an Italian theater form from the Renaissance, characterized by masks, zany energy, traveling troupes, and improvisational comical and satirical plots
Compradrazco: the system of naming a child's godparents
Compadre: the godparent of one's child, more commonly, a very close friend
Con: with
Conchero: dancers who perform the traditional and sacred Aztec dances
Conjunto: a musical ensemble featuring accordion and polka music

Conquistadores: Spanish soldiers and explorers
Copal: a resin incense
Copla: the most common verse structure of Hispanic music: four lines to a verse, eight syllables to a line
Corazón: heart
Corridos: a narrative song
Criados: Native American servants of the Spanish
Criollos: pure Spaniard, born in the New World
Cuentista: a storyteller
Cuento: a story
Cuetlaxochitl: the Aztec name of the poinsettia plant
Cuialli: Aztec school of song and dance
Cupil: the headdress of the dancers in *Los Matachines*
Curandero: a healer, a person who has the knowledge of the healing powers of plants and natural substances.
Curanderismo: the practice of Hispanic folk medicine
Curar: to heal

D

Damas: young women who are escorts at the quinceañera
Danzas: dances
Despedida: the final, farewell verse of a corrido
Diablo: devil
Dichos: proverbs

E

El Diablo: the devil
Elote: corn
Empanaditas: mincemeat fried turnovers
Encomienda: a Spanish land grant system
Entriega de Novios: the delivery of the newlyweds. A part of the Hispanic wedding ceremony in which the newly wedded couple is presented to their families and they receive the blessing and advice of their families. Also consists of verses sung and accompanied by violin and guitar.

Entregador: the singer who sings the verses of the Entriega de Novios
Es: is, it is

F

Familia: the family
Farolitos: candle-lit paper bags
Fiesta: celebration
Flor: flower
Flor de Santa Rita: Indian paintbrush
Folklórico: Mexican traditional dance
Frijoles: beans

G

Gato: cat
Genízaro: Native servants of Hispanic families
Gorra: cap
Gracias: thank you
Grito: yell or cry
Guaje: a gourd rattle used in the dance of *Los Matachines*
Guitarrón: a six-string bass guitar

H

Hacienda: an estate
Hermana: sister
Hermano: brother
Hijos: children, sons
Hojalateros: Mexican Indian tin artists
Horno: a traditional outdoor oven, made with adobe bricks

I

Iglesia: church
Incensario: the incense burner
Independencia: independence
Indio-Hispano: Indian-Hispanic, a term recognizing the mixed nature of a culture containing both Indian and Hispanic influences

Indio: Indian
Indita: a Spanish narrative song influenced by Indian rhythms
Inmortal: antelope horns

J

Jarabe: Mexican dance style
Jarana: a guitar-like stringed instrument
Jerga: a rough wool woven rug
Jita: a diminutive form of *hija*, daughter, a term of endearment

L

La Gloria: heaven
La Llorona: the Weeping Woman
Latillas: sticks or small branches, usually of stripped pine, cedar or aspen, laid across the main beams, vigas, to form a ceiling
Lazo: rope or lasso
Lecheros: milkweed
Leña: firewood
Leñero: firewood seller
Lengua del toro: bull's tongue
Linda: beautiful, pretty
Listones: ribbon and material hanging from the back of the headdress in the costumes of the dancers in *Los Matachines*
Loco: crazy
Los Ancianos: the old ones, the elderly
Lucha: the fight, the struggle
Luminarias: small bonfires, also refers to candle-lit paper bags

M

Madrina: the maid of honor at a wedding
Maíz: corn
Mal de Ojo: a curse caused by a harmful look
Mamacita: a term of endearment for mother
Mande: command me, order me to do a task, at your command

Manito: the dimunitive form of *hermano*. A term describing the descendants of Spanish colonialists in southern Colorado and northern New Mexico.
Mano: a stone held by hand used for grinding corn
Mantas: the Spanish term for Native American woven cotton cloth
Manzanilla: chamomile
Matanza: a centuries-old tradition by which families and communities prepare and store meat for the long winter
Matraca: the rattle used to accompany an *alabado*
Masa: corn dough
Mayordomo: ditch boss of acequia water system
Médico: a healer who combines the knowledge of natural remedies with religious practices
Mestizos: a person of mixed Indian and Spanish heritage
Metate: a concave stone used for grinding corn
M'hijos: my children
Milagro: miracle
Mis: my
Monte: mountain
Movimento: movement
Mucho: very
Muerte: death
Mulato: a person of mixed Black and Spanish heritage
Mundo: world
Muralistas: muralists

N

Nahuatl: the Aztec language
Nichos: a niche or holder for a *santo* or other religious object, often made of tinwork
Natillas: milk pudding
Nopal: cactus
Nuestras raíces: our roots

O

Ofrenda: an altar decorated for the Day of the Dead celebration
Ojo de Dios: god's eye, a folk craft of yarn wrapped around a cross
Oregano: oregano
Orgullo: pride
Oshá: root of wild celery

P

Padre: father, a priest
Padrino: a child's godparents, the best man at the wedding
Padrino de arras: the attendant who gives the bride and groom a box with gold or silver coins in it in a traditional wedding
Padrino de lazo: the attendant who wraps an ornamental rope around the bride and groom in a traditional wedding
Palito: little stick
Palma: a three-pronged fan representing the Holy Trinity used in the dance of *Los Matachines*
Pan de muertos: a special bread baked for the Día de los Muertos celebrations
Papel picado: cut paper, a decoration
Para: for
Partera: a midwife
Pastores: shepherds
Patron: land owner of a hacienda
Pedimiento: the proposal part of the courtship and wedding ceremony
Peninsulares: pure Spaniards born in Spain
Pelado: Mexican theater comic character
Peones: native slave workers on haciendas
Peso: the basic Mexican monetary unit
Piñon: a pine tree, which provides piñon nut, a favorite eating nut of the region
Pito: a reed flute used to accompany *alabados*
Placa: nickname
Plaza: a central square typical of Spanish cities
Poeta: poet

Poncho: a woolen blanket with a hole in the middle, to be worn pulled over the head

Posada: an inn

Posole: hominy stew

Prendorio: the engagement party of the courtship and wedding ceremony

Puro: purely, totally, completely

Q

Que delicioso: how delicious

Que no: idiomatic phrase for "don't you think so?" or "isn't it?"

Querencia: homeland

Quinceañera: a girl's fifteenth birthday celebration

Que viva: hurrah

R

Raíces: roots

Rancheras: Mexican rural "ranch" folk music

Ratoncitos: little mice

Raza: the people, race

Rebozo: a Mexican shawl

Rellenos: cheese-stuffed green chile, fried in an egg batter

Remedios: remedies

Retablo: devotional painting

Rio: river

Rito: archaic Spanish for river

Ristra: a string of red chile, usually hung outside the home

Romances: the oldest style of Southwestern Hispanic music, a narrative ballad of Spanish origin

Rosa de castilla: rose

S

Sabanilla: a light, plain, white wool woven cloth, the backing for *colcha* embroidery

Sabor: flavor

Santero: a sculptor who carves small wooden religious statues called *santos*
Santos: small wooden carvings of Catholic saints and religious figures
Sarape: a Mexican blanket worn as a poncho
Savana: sheet or plains
Señor: mister, sir
Señora: a married woman or an elder woman
Señorita: an unmarried woman or a young woman
Sí: yes
Sigue: continues
Sin fronteras: without borders
Sin verguenza: without shame, shameless, scoundrel, rascal
Sobadora: a healer specializing in bodily manipulations
Sones: the most typical style of mariachi music
Sopa: soup
Suave: slang for "cool"

T

Tamales: chile and meat wrapped in a steamed cornmeal dough
Teatro: theater
Tejano: the Spanish name for Mexican-Texas culture
Tía: aunt
Tierra: land
Tío: uncle
Tilma: a poncho or sarape
Tololoche: a stand-up string bass
Toloache: jimson weed
Trucha: trout
Tsihuri: Mexican Huichol god's eyes

U

Un: a, one

V

Valses: waltzes
Vato, vato loco: street dude
Vayanse: go
Veintenas: Aztec calendar festival days
Vengan: come
Velorio: the wake at a funeral
Vibora: snake
Vieja: old woman
Viejo: old man
Vigas: wooden beams used in the traditional adobe architecture of the American Southwest
Vihuela: a small, round-back, five-string guitar
Virgen: the Virgin of Guadalupe

Y

Yerba buena: mint
Yerba: herbs

Z

Zambos: a person of Black and Indian heritage
Zapateado: the characteristic heel-toe Mexican dance step common to *sones* and *jarabes*
Zarzuelas: Spanish operetta

INDEX

Z

ABOUT THE AUTHOR

www.angelvigil.com

Angel Vigil by C. Chase

Angel Vigil is an award-winning author, performer, stage director, and teacher. His awards include the Heritage Artist Award and the Master Artist Award from the Colorado Council on the Arts. He has also received the Governor's Award for Excellence in Education and the Mayor's Individual Artist Fellowship Award. He also was awarded the Colorado State Theatre Educator of the Year Award.

He is retired Chairman of the Visual and Performing Arts Department and Director of Drama at Colorado Academy in Denver. He also is an educator for the History Colorado Center.

Angel is the author of seven award-winning books on Hispanic and Western culture and arts. His book *The Corn Woman, and Other Stories and Legends from the Hispanic Southwest* won the prestigious New York Public Library Book for the Teen Age National Award. His book *Una Linda Raza, Cultural and Artistic Traditions of the Hispanic Southwest* won the Border Library Association Southwest Book of the Year Award and the Colorado Book of the Year Special Recognition Award.

His other books are *Borderlands—Living in Two Worlds, The Story of Hispanics in the American Southwest*; *Teatro—Plays for Young Audiences*; *Riding Tall in the Saddle—The Cowboy Fact Book*; *The Eagle and the Cactus—Stories and Legends from Mexico*; and *Papi, How Many Stars Are in the Sky? —A Children's Fable.*

Angel is a Colorado Heritage Artist storyteller who has performed throughout the nation at festivals, universities, schools and art centers. He has been featured storyteller at the National Storytelling Festival in Jonesborough, Tennessee, Keepers of the Word Festival at Amherst College, the Rocky Mountain Storytelling Festival, the International Reading Association, the National Independent School Library Association, the Four Corners Storytelling Festival, the Mesa Storytelling Festival, the Greenville Chautauqua Festival and the Nebraska Storytelling Festival. His specialty is the oral traditions of the Hispanic Southwest.

Angel is also a member of the Colorado Endowment for the Humanities Chautauqua program for his historical presentation. Angel has created six historical characters: El Vaquero, America's First Cowboy; El Conquistador, The Explorer of New Worlds; Tezcatlipoca, The Supreme God of the Aztec Emperors; Manuel de Lisa, Northwest Trapper and Explorer; Mariano Medina, Colorado Pioneer; and Casimiro Barela, Colorado politican and legislative legend.